Nonmonotonic Reasoning:
Logical Foundations of Commonsense

Cambridge Tracts in Theoretical
Computer Science

Managing Editor
Professor C.J. van Rijsbergen, Department of Computing
Science, University of Glasgow

Editorial Board

Titles in the series

Nonmonotonic Reasoning: Logical Foundations of Commonsense

Gerhard Brewka
GMD,
Sankt Augustin, Germany

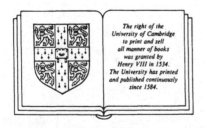

The right of the
University of Cambridge
to print and sell
all manner of books
was granted by
Henry VIII in 1534.
The University has printed
and published continuously
since 1584.

CAMBRIDGE UNIVERSITY PRESS

Cambridge

New York Port Chester Melbourne Sydney

CAMBRIDGE UNIVERSITY PRESS
Cambridge, New York, Melbourne, Madrid, Cape Town, Singapore,
São Paulo, Delhi, Dubai, Tokyo, Mexico City

Cambridge University Press
The Edinburgh Building, Cambridge CB2 8RU, UK

Published in the United States of America by Cambridge University Press, New York

www.cambridge.org
Information on this title: www.cambridge.org/9780521383943

First published 1991

A catalogue record for this publication is available from the British Library

ISBN 978-0-521-38394-3 Hardback

CONTENTS

FOREWORD

Systems of whatever kind are becoming increasingly complex. This is certainly true for technical systems. Just think of the unimaginable complexity of the entire 'Space Shuttle' system (including all the computing machinery involved). But it is true of non-technical systems as well, such as social systems (eg. social insurance). Evidence can be encountered every day that this complexity surpasses man's capabilities.

It is unlikely that there is an easy way of solving the resulting problems by attempting to reduce the complexity. So it seems that the only viable alternative consists in providing man with facilities that support his dealing with systems of such complexity. Such an 'interface' system will itself have to become quite complex indeed. Its complexity might be concealed from the user, however, provided its behavior simulates that of a human assistant or expert; for humans have no difficulty in communicating with human 'interfaces'.

In order to approximate the behavior of a human knowledgeable in some special area of expertise, such as providing knowledge about other complex systems, it seems to be necessary to get the system to reason the way human beings do. This is the ultimate goal motivating the material presented in this book.

This goal is far easier stated than achieved. What exactly is the way human beings use reasoning, in the first place? Even if there was some uniform way and we had found it, there would still remain the task of casting it into a formalism suitable for computers. The combination of both these tasks leaves us with what seems the only way of approaching the goal: start with some conjecture about the human way of reasoning; cast it into a formalism; test the formalism's behavior in applications, in comparison with human reasoning; if necessary revise the conjecture and start over again; and so forth.

Research in many places all over the world has already undergone a number of cycles in this procedure already with no end in sight. This situation is well reflected in the present book which introduces as possible candidates, several different formalisms that have been developed by different authors during the last decade. Most of these are extensions of logic, a formalism that evolved in earlier cycles over the past two thous-

and years. One of the book's virtues is its contribution to the clarification of the relationships between those different formalisms. Obviously any future cycle is the more promising the more insight we use in the revision on which it will be based.

The book also offers interesting new ideas towards such a revision. The author's interesting proposal of preferred subtheories is a good example. The book should therefore be valuable for the specialist interested in such new proposals and in the clarified relationships, as well as for the novice in the field who wants to learn about the present state in this area, and hence also for anyone in between these two extremes. I am confident that such readers will find studying this text as rewarding as it has been for me.

W. Bibel,
Lindenau

PREFACE

You can't always get what you want,
but if you try some time you get what you need.
Mick Jagger, Rolling Stones

Yes, you are right. It is probably not the best idea to write a book in a field which is developing as rapidly as nonmonotonic reasoning and where everything is still in a state of flux. Whenever a chapter is finished someone writes another important paper which raises new ideas on that very topic. Not so long ago only a small circle of a few people interested in Artificial Intelligence thought about the problems discussed in this book - and their results were presented at conferences under the heading 'exotic logics'. Now those times are over; there is an explosion of interest. More and more scientists from various areas - philosophers, logicians, linguists, and of course those interested in Artificial Intelligence - detect the importance of nonmonotonic reasoning and contribute their ideas to the field.

So, due to such broad interest, along with the difficulties comes the justification for a book like this. There is no chance to be complete in any sense. I have tried to include in my presentation those approaches which promise to have a bearing on future developments. Of course, there are no clear criteria for selecting the material to be included, and some readers may find their favourite nonmonotonic system is missing. One indicator of quality I used was the appearance of an approach in one of the important Artificial Intelligence journals. And in fact all of the approaches in this book - or at least particular instances of the approaches - have been published in one of them. I hope that this gives my selection at least some objectivity and guarantees that the approaches presented have a certain degree of stability and persistence.

The main goal of this book is to give a broad overview on the state of the art in different fields of research in the area of nonmonotonic reasoning. The book should be understood as a providing a first orientation in a rapidly emerging field. I seek to make it easier to read the original papers, but not superfluous.

After discussing in Chapter 1 various types of nonmonotonic reasoning and their possible applications I present the major logics for nonmonotonic reasoning:

- modal approaches, in particular McDermott and Doyle's nonmonotonic logic and autoepistemic logic (Chapter 2);

- default logics based on nonmonotonic inference rules (Chapter 3);

- various forms of circumscription (Chapter 4);

- the preferred subtheory approach, a generalization of Poole's logical framework for default reasoning (Chapter 5); and

- Delgrande's conditional logic for default reasoning (Chapter 6).

Theorem proving techniques for these logics are described in Chapter 7. Chapter 8 contains a discussion of a number of formalizations of nonmonotonic inheritance. A pragmatic approach to nonmonotonic reasoning based on nonmonotonic rules is analyzed in Chapter 9. Chapter 10 discusses the achievements in the field in the light of the famous Yale shooting example.

A more detailed overview of the book can be found in Section 1.4.

Two leitmotifs guide the presentation:

- I try to clarify the relation between different research activities in the field which often have been performed independently of each other, and provide some of the missing links; and

- I see many of the different activities as alternative ways of achieving a common goal, the combination of a sound theoretical foundation and efficient computation.

In nonmonotonic reasoning this combination is much harder to achieve than in classical monotonic reasoning. The computational properties of the nonmonotonic logics are awkward, at least if they are general enough to subsume classical first order logic as a special case, because it can be proved that no correct and complete proof procedures exist. But this does not mean that there is no chance at all of doing theoretically sound nonmonotonic reasoning efficiently. In fact it is one of the objectives of this book to present different ways of achieving or, probably better, approximating this goal.

This book does not just give an overview: new results and proposals are presented in some of the chapters. Trying to produce such a combination of a general overview and new material carries some danger: readers interested in an overview may be unhappy about the author's emphasis on his own ideas; readers familiar with the literature and interested in new results may be bored by the many parts they already know. My hope is - on one hand - that the contributions are of enough interest to be contained in an overview, and - on the other hand - that specialists in nonmonotonic reasoning will not find it too difficult to skip the sections they know all about. The readers of this last type are referred particularly to the following sections.

In Chapter 3 we define a new version of default logic which avoids some counter-intuitive inferences and, most importantly, is cumulative, i.e. the addition of theorems to the premises does not change the derivable formulae.

In Chapter 5 we develop an approach to default reasoning - the preferred subtheory approach - which is based on the notion of preferred maximal consistent subsets of the premises. I define a general framework, show that Poole's system is a particular instance of this framework and describe two generalizations which allow priorities between defaults to be represented. An advantage of this approach is that no non-classical operators or rules have to be introduced. Thus default reasoning can be integrated more easily with other types of commonsense reasoning.

Chapter 7 describes nonmonotonic theorem proving techniques. Our contribution in this chapter is presented in Section 7.4: a modal default proof procedure for a common subset of McDermott and Doyle's nonmonotonic logic and autoepistemic logic. The procedure has been described in earlier papers (Brewka, Wittur 84) (Brewka 86).

Chapter 8 on inheritance systems contains the author's formalization of frame systems, a very popular form of inheritance systems. This formalization is based on circumscription and an earlier version has been published (Brewka 87).

In Chapter 9 we discuss nonmonotonic process systems which are based on the notion of 'current unprovenness' (as distinct from unprovability). I show that the Doyle-style truth maintenance systems commonly used in nonmonotonic process systems can be seen as propositional default logic provers (Brewka 89) (Reinfrank *et al.* 89), which provides this type of truth maintenance systems with a model theoretical semantics. I further present a critique of dependency-directed backtracking, a common consistency maintenance technique, showing that sometimes unwanted results are obtained. Intermediate inconsistencies may lead to the generation of justifications which produce results having nothing to do with the problem solver's knowledge base. Modifications of the algorithms which avoid these problems turn out to be intolerably inefficient.

The book is based on the author's thesis (Brewka 89), but large parts have been re-written to increase readability and completeness. To keep the length of the text reasonable (and to avoid much repetition) proofs have been omitted but can be found in the original references. Readers should be familiar with classical first order logic. The book uses standard set-theoretical and logical notation with the usual binding rules, i.e. $\forall x.P(x) \land Q(x) \lor R(x) \supset S(x)$ reads as $\forall x.([(P(x) \land Q(x)) \lor R(x)] \supset S(x))$. The syntax of first order logic and other logics examined is defined in the Appendix.

ACKNOWLEDGEMENTS

Many people have contributed to this book. Only few of them can be named explicitly here. First of all I'd like to thank my thesis supervisors Prof. Dr. B. Neumann, Universität Hamburg, and Prof. Dr. W. Bibel, Technische Hochschule Darmstadt, for many helpful comments and suggestions. GMD, the German National Research Center for Computer Science, provided me with a stimulating environment, a powerful text processing system, and many interesting colleagues. My colleague Ulrich Junker spent many hours discussing all parts of the book with me. I also thank the other members of GMD's Hybrid Inference Systems group, Franco Di Primio, Peter Henne, Gerd Paaß, and Karl Wittur for many interesting discussions. Many members of GMD's Expert Systems group also helped to improve the book, in particular Tom Gordon, Joachim Hertzberg, and Hans Voss.

Thanks also to many participants of the Second International Workshop on Nonmonotonic Reasoning, Grassau, 1988. I benefitted a lot from discussions with Jon Doyle, Oskar Dressler, Vladimir Lifschitz, Paul Morris, David Poole, Michael Reinfrank and many others. The anonymous referees contributed a lot to the final form of the book. I am particularly indebted to David Makinson who always helped to clarify my ideas.

Needless to say that this book would not have been possible without private support of various kinds, most of which was due to three very young ladies named Kristina, Janna and Alena - and their mother.

CHAPTER 1: INTRODUCTION

1.1: What is Nonmonotonic Reasoning?

The goal of Artificial Intelligence (AI) is to improve our understanding of intelligent behavior through the use of computational models. One of the few things researchers in this young science commonly agree upon is the importance of knowledge for intelligence. Thus the study of techniques for representing knowledge in computers has become one of the central issues in AI.

Of course, it would be convenient if we could tell our computers what we want them to know in natural language. But so far this is just a dream. We thus need artificial, formal languages for representing knowledge which can be handled more easily by computers. Formal languages have the advantage of allowing for a much higher degree of precision and clarity than any natural language - admittedly at the cost of flexibility and adaptability.

If our formal knowledge representation languages are to be more than collections of meaningless strings, if they are to represent anything at all, we have to show how expressions and symbols are related to the (part of the) world we want to represent, that is we have to define a semantics for these languages. At this point formal logic plays an important role.

Logic is, first of all, the study of inference. But the perspective of the logician is normative, not empirical or descriptive. The separation between knowledge given in an explicit, declarative form and knowledge which is implicit, that is can be inferred from the given premises, makes it necessary to come up with a criterion for the validity of inferences. This criterion itself must be based in some way on the meaning of the formulae used for expressing the knowledge.

The discussion about the role of logic in AI is as old as AI itself. The relation between human reasoning and the theoretically sound reasoning formalized in logic has always been a matter of debate, particularly in the light of Gödel's famous impossibility theorems. We share the views expressed by Pat Hayes (Hayes 77), Robert Moore (Moore 82) and Wolfgang Bibel (Bibel 84). Logic - and logic here does not necessarily mean classical first order logic - is of fundamental importance to AI since, besides providing a proof theory, it gives us a clear and precise way of assigning meaning to symbols and of judging the validity of inferences based on this meaning.

We do not claim that logic is the only possible way of doing this, nor do we claim that logic by itself solves the problems of AI. Logic separates valid from invalid conclusions, but it says nothing about what beliefs to adopt in specific situations where limited resources may be available and the cost of computation has to be taken into account. Moreover, logic is based on ontological assumptions (the existence of a domain of identifiable nonchanging objects, the existence of nonchanging relations between these objects) which may not be adequate for some purposes. But it should be clear that whoever proposes a 'nonlogical' representation formalism has to find other, hopefully equally clear and intuitive, ways of assigning meaning to his language and hence providing a criterion for distinguishing between semantically justified and unjustified inferences.

The motivation behind the development of classical logic at the end of the last century was to put mathematical reasoning on a precise formal foundation. Of course, the reasoning of a mathematician trying to establish a mathematical result differs from everyday reasoning. The knowledge we base our decisions on in real life is never as precise and complete as in the ideal setting of this analytical science. We should, therefore, not be astonished that classical logic does not model all forms of everyday reasoning adequately. The main topic of this book is to show how some of the less than ideal forms of human reasoning can be formalized. What we are looking for is a precise mathematical theory of commonsense reasoning.

Classical logic has the following property: if a formula p is derivable from a set of premises Q then p is also derivable from each superset of Q. The reason should be clear: every proof of p from Q is, by the definition of proof in classical logic, also a proof of p from each superset of Q. This property is called the *monotonicity* of classical logic.

To formalize human commonsense reasoning something different is needed. Commonsense reasoning is frequently not monotonic. In many situations we draw conclusions which are given up in the light of further information. The 'canonical' example is the flying ability of birds. If we know that Tweety (one of the most famous animals in AI circles) is a bird, we tend to draw the conclusion that it flies since birds typically fly. Given the information that it is a penguin we certainly withdraw our former conclusion but - and this is important - without withdrawing any of our former premises. We still believe Tweety is a bird and still believe that birds, typically, fly. Such forms of reasoning which allow additional information to invalidate old conclusions are called *nonmonotonic*.

If the notion of nonmonotonic reasoning is understood in a broad sense, then probabilistic reasoning can also be subsumed: additional evidence, obviously, can decrease the conditional probability of a statement in a probabilistic setting. However, probabilistic reasoning - as possibilistic or fuzzy reasoning - has usually been treated numerically. Numbers are used to represent the degree of plausibility, certainty, confirmation or whatever. The standard use of the term nonmonotonic reasoning is more restricted, being confined to nonnumerical, logic based approaches.

I shall not discuss any of the numerical approaches in this book. This does not mean, however, that I think they are unimportant. Numbers certainly have their advantages. But one of the common views underlying the research in this area is that we should try to find out how far we can get without them. Some interesting recent results, for example in (Geffner, Pearl 88), indicate a close relation between nonmonotonicity and infinitesimal probability. The theory of infinitesimal probabilities might turn out to be one way of providing nonmonotonic formalisms with a semantics. I shall not, however, investigate further this possibility in this book. For a survey of results about the relationship between nonmonotonicity and probability see (Pearl 89) which also contains references to further relevant literature.

Some readers may wonder whether it really is impossible to handle the Tweety example in classical logic. How about the following representation?

(1) $\forall x.\ \text{BIRD}(x) \land \neg\text{EXCEPTIONAL-BIRD}(x) \supset \text{FLIES}(x)$

(2) $\forall x.\ \text{EXCEPTIONAL-BIRD}(x) \equiv \text{PENGUIN}(x) \lor \text{DEAD}(x) \lor \ \dots.$

(3)   BIRD(TWEETY)

However, this makes it necessary to list all possible exceptions explicitly. There are so many unforeseeable circumstances in which something potentially can go wrong with a bird's flying ability that this in itself is an impossible task. And even if we were able to come up with a complete list of exceptional birds the above representation still· would be unsatisfactory: we have to show that TWEETY is not a penguin, not dead, etc. in order to derive from these formulae that TWEETY flies.

We would like to be able to derive that TWEETY flies when there is no information that TWEETY is exceptional without having to prove that TWEETY is not exceptional. This is beyond the power of classical logic.

It is interesting to compare this first order representation with a corresponding representation in the programming language Prolog. One feature that distinguishes Prolog from first order logic is the treatment of negation. NOT P is true in Prolog whenever P cannot be derived (negation as failure). This makes the following representation of the Tweety example possible:

    FLIES(_x) :- BIRD(_x), not EXCEPTIONAL-BIRD(_x).

    EXCEPTIONAL-BIRD(_x) :- PENGUIN(_x).

    BIRD(TWEETY).

Since EXCEPTIONAL-BIRD(TWEETY) cannot be proven Prolog derives NOT EXCEPTIONAL-BIRD(TWEETY). Note that this derivation is not possible in first order logic from the corresponding set of implications. This together with BIRD(TWEETY) allows us to derive FLIES(TWEETY) via the first rule. If we add

PENGUIN(TWEETY).

then FLIES(TWEETY) can no longer be derived since now EXCEPTIONAL-BIRD(TWEETY) is provable. Prolog, hence, is nonmonotonic.

There have always been AI systems which, like Prolog, were able to draw some sort of nonmonotonic conclusions. An early example was the planning system PLANNER (Hewitt 72) with its nonmonotonic THNOT-operator. This operator, applied to a proposition, failed when the proposition could be proven and succeeded otherwise.

Another type of nonmonotonic system in common use for many years, particular in expert system tools, is the frame system. Frames are representations of object classes consisting of a collection of slot-value pairs. These pairs describe typical values of certain attributes (slots) of members of the particular class. Moreover, the frames form a sub/superclass hierarchy. In case of a conflict the most specific information wins. For example, using the frame language of the expert system tool BABYLON (di Primio, Brewka 85) one might define two frames as follows:

(defframe CAR

    (slots (WHEELS 4) (SEATS 5) (CYLINDERS 4)))

(defframe SPORTSCAR

    (supers CAR)

    (slots (CYLINDERS 6)))

The supers-specification in the second definition states that SPORTSCAR is a subclass of CAR. Given a particular instance of SPORTSCAR, say SPEEDY, we derive that it has 6 cylinders, 5 seats and 4 wheels. If we add information that sportscars typically have 2 seats, i.e. if we change the second frame definition to

(defframe SPORTSCAR

    (supers CAR)

    (slots (SEATS 2) (CYLINDERS 6)))

then it is concluded that SPEEDY has 2 seats and not 5, an example of the nonmonotonic behaviour of frame systems based on the principle that more specific information is to be preferred. The following diagram shows from where SPEEDY inherits information in each case:

original knowledge base   augmented knowledge base

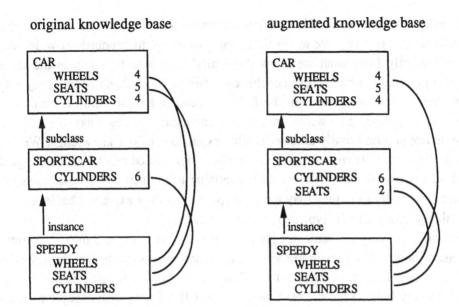

But if such systems and programming tools have been in use already, why was it nec-essary to think about such complicated things as nonmonotonic logics at all? The answer is that the existing tools have either been too restrictive and could not be gen-eralized without a formal theory, or, when they were more general, they produced results which were not understood well enough. This was, for instance, the case with PLANNER where the user was responsible for avoiding circular dependencies. Such dependencies could lead to groundless belief or non-terminating programs (McDermott, Doyle 80).

We do not want to depend only on the system developer's intuitions. They may be commonly agreed in simple, restricted examples, but in more complicated cases intui-tion is no longer a sufficient guide. Moreover, the logics will enable us to prove theo-rems about the behaviour of various systems and tell us how far we can go with ex-tending them. There seems to be no alternative: we have to give our intuitions a formal grounding. We need precise mathematical definitions of nonmonotonic infer-ence which can be given a semantic justification.

1.2: Types of Nonmonotonicity

Nonmonotonic reasoning is not a single phenomenon. Various different types can be distinguished. Let us first have a somewhat closer look at four of them:

1. Default Reasoning
The need for nonmonotonic reasoning arises whenever our knowledge is incomplete and does not allow for the sound derivation of the conclusions necessary to base our decisions, plans and actions on. Of course, in less ideal settings than mathematics this

is the rule, not an exception. Very often we are forced to act in spite of such gaps in our knowledge, i.e. we have to fill those gaps, to 'jump' to conclusions which do not follow logically from what we know ('logically' here is to be taken in the sense of classical logic, of course). These conclusions, then, are less than certain. They may be called beliefs or assumptions. In the light of additional information it may turn out that we have 'jumped' to a wrong conclusion. The conclusion then has to be retracted.

We do not choose blindly among possible extensions of our knowledge. We do not simply flip a coin. There are many cases where our choice can be rationally guided. Much of our experience of the world is available in the form of general rules which are not universally true; they may have exceptions but they express what is true under normal conditions. 'Birds (typically) fly' is one example.

Such rules are very convenient, easy to learn and remember, and they can guide our choices of how to fill gaps in our knowledge when necessary. In the absence of conflicting information, the rule about the flying ability of birds justifies preferring the belief 'Tweety flies' to the belief 'Tweety doesn't fly'. Rules with exceptions are also called defaults and reasoning based on them default reasoning. The conclusions obtained from defaults are less than certain, i.e. default reasoning is a form of plausible reasoning.

Some researchers additionally distinguish between

(1)   rules of the form 'An A is typically B' or 'a normal A is B' and

(2)   rules expressing statistical facts like 'most A are B'.

They claim that prototypical reasoning based on the first type of rules has nothing at all to do with statistical reasoning (Reiter, Criscuolo 82), (Nutter 87).

This claim seems somewhat overstated. In psychology the term 'prototype' is used to denote an instance, possibly imaginary, of a class of objects with the characteristic properties of the class members. Prototypes can be used for two purposes: we match objects against them in order to decide class membership, and if we know that an object is a member of a certain class we tend to ascribe to it the properties of the prototype.

But what makes properties characteristic? How do we create our prototypes? We still do not understand these phenomena very well. However, the role of prototypes is to enable reasonable guesses to be made. They would certainly not be very useful if they did not lead to good decisions in most cases. This indicates that there must be at least some intricate, possibly very indirect, connection between the notions 'typically' and 'most'. Admittedly, 'most' here has to be understood as relative to a certain context, as 'most amongst those objects we will possibly encounter in every day life'. This excludes all the dead birds that ever lived on earth from consideration: most of these certainly do not fly. We can possibly see a prototype as a compilation of (nonnumerical) probabilistic knowledge into a form which allows for efficient use.

I shall not pursue these issues further here. I use the term 'default' in the sense of a rule with possible exceptions, be the reasons for adopting the rule of a statistical, prototypical, methodological ('working hypotheses'), or decision-theoretic nature (taking the costs of possible errors into account as in the case of the presumption of innocence in law).

As we shall see, the standard formalizations of default reasoning do not syntactically distinguish between safe, irrefutable knowledge and plausible or tentative knowledge. The only way to distinguish between the certain and the defeasible parts of a knowledge base is to inspect the proofs. Consequently, these logics do not model any loss of plausibility when, for instance, long chains of defaults are needed to derive a conclusion. The logics are based on the view that jumping to a conclusion means assuming that the conclusion is true and has the same impact on further derivations as any other premise. In this sense the handling of defaults differs from any probabilistic treatment - unless infinitesimal probabilities are used (Pearl 89).

2. Autoepistemic Reasoning

Assume one of your colleagues asks you whether John McCarthy is going to give a talk at your department next week. You probably say no (unless your department is at Stanford). But nobody told you that there will be no such talk. How did you know the answer? You probably have reasoned along the following lines: if there were a talk there would have been an announcement, or I would have received an electronic mail, or one of my colleagues would have told me about it, or I would have heard about it from somewhere else. Anyway, if there were such a talk I would know about it. But I do not. Hence, there (unfortunately) is no talk given by John McCarthy next week in our department.

Moore (Moore 85) has called this form of reasoning *autoepistemic*, since it involves reasoning about one's own knowledge. Autoepistemic reasoning follows the pattern

I.   *If statement x were true I would know it.*

II.   *I don't know whether x is true.*

III. *Therefore x is not true.*

It is important that the second antecedent in this pattern is not a premise but can be derived from the knowledge at hand. Otherwise we would not have nonmonotonicity.

Here is the standard example. Let us assume the knowledge base of an agent contains

(1)   *If someone is my brother I know it.*

(2)   *John is my brother.*

and there is no information in the knowledge base which allows to conclude that Peter is my brother. Then we conclude

   Peter is not my brother.

since

I don't know that Peter is my brother.

can, in an intuitive sense to be made precise later, be derived from the premises. However, adding the information

(3)   *Peter is my brother.*

to the premises makes, obviously, the previous conclusion impossible.

Autoepistemic reasoning is a form of sound reasoning: after the addition of (3) we know that (1) must have been wrong when we used it to derive *Peter is not my brother*. The wrong conclusion was possible only because the premise was wrong.

What, then, has this to do with nonmonotonic reasoning? Look at (1) again. We are in a position to say that this proposition was wrong with respect to the former knowledge base. But this does not mean that we have to throw (1) away for that reason. It is quite possible (and reasonable to assume) that (1) is absolutely right now, in the new state of knowledge. The meaning of the proposition has simply changed. It refers to our knowledge, and if the knowledge changes, its meaning changes correspondingly.

The nonmonotonicity of autoepistemic reasoning is thus a consequence of the fact that the meaning of statements about one's knowledge is context-sensitive, or - in other words - these statements are indexical. For a more detailed analysis of this type of nonmonotonic reasoning we refer to (Moore 85).

Since plausible default reasoning and autoepistemic reasoning are so very different one would not necessarily expect that a common formalization is possible. Konolige, however, - as we shall see in Section 3.3 - came up with a quite surprising result: default logic, one of the most important formalizations of default reasoning, and the logic developed by Moore for autoepistemic reasoning are equivalent, in a sense to be made precise later. This seems to suggest that different types of reasoning do not necessarily imply different formalizations.

3. Representation Conventions

Assume you want to know whether there is a train from Bonn to Munich at 10.00 a.m. At the station you find a timetable. Let us assume that the timetable mentions no train to Munich leaving at 10.00 a.m. You will conclude that there is no train to Munich at that time. This conclusion is probably not based on a default like 'There is typically no train at 10.00 to Munich'.

You know that railroad officials follow a certain implicit convention: the convention that information about train connections missing from the timetables is simply false, i.e. if there is no train connection mentioned then there is none.[1]

Such conventions are economical and convenient because they make the exchange of information very efficient. The conventions are usually left implicit: there is no extra

---

[1] Of course, combinations of conventions and defaults are possible and frequent. Our focus here, however, is the *distinction* between different types of commonsense reasoning.

note on the timetable that connections missing from the timetable don't exist. It is assumed that everybody has learned how to use such timetables in the right way.

If, on the other hand, the convention were made explicit, then sound logical reasoning would lead to our conclusion: if there were a 10.00 train to Munich then our 'all trains are there' convention would have been violated, i.e. the premise that connections missing from the timetable do not exist would be false.

Assume that, later, an additional connection between Bonn and Munich at 10.00 is established. The timetable has to be augmented accordingly. This makes our earlier conclusion underivable, but the convention is still the same: this timetable is complete. As in the case of autoepistemic reasoning nonmonotonicity is an effect of the indexical meaning of our convention: 'this timetable' refers to another timetable after the addition of an entry.

Such communication and information storing conventions are very common in the theory of databases and have also been studied formally there. In many cases the *closed-world assumption* (CWA) captures the effects of these conventions:

Definition 1.1: *Let T be a set of formulae. We say that p is derivable from T under the closed-world assumption iff*

$$T \cup ASS(T) \vdash p$$

where ASS(T) := {¬q| q is atomic and not T ⊢ q}.

The time table from our train example, for instance, can be represented as a set of atomic formulae of the form CONNECTION(x,y,t) stating that there is a train connection from x to y starting in x at time t. Assume CONNECTION(BONN, MUNICH, 10.00) is not contained in this set. Then this formula is underivable from T, the description of the time table. Hence ¬CONNECTION(BONN, MUNICH, 10.00) is in ASS(T) which implies that this formula is derivable from T under the CWA.

Unfortunately, the CWA can lead to inconsistency. If, for instance, T={a ∨ b}, then ¬a as well as ¬b are in ASS(T) which - together with a ∨ b - is inconsistent. This shows that the CWA is not general enough to capture all the interesting cases of nonmonotonic reasoning. See (Genesereth, Nilsson 87) for an overview of various subcases where there is no danger of becoming inconsistent.

Conventions and autoepistemic reasoning certainly are closely related. Knowledge about our own knowledge is often based on knowledge about communication conventions. We know that we would know about a talk of John McCarthy since we know how people communicate. However, the fact that we would know about such a talk itself is not a convention (it may be a consequence of conventions) as it is no convention that we know all our brothers. And there are clearly cases of autoepistemic reasoning having nothing at all to do with conventions (for instance if you believe that your car did not explode since otherwise you would have heard it). It therefore seems justified to treat the two as different types of nonmonotonic reasoning.

4. Reasoning in the Presence of Inconsistent Information

Nonmonotonic reasoning, interestingly, not only arises when the knowledge is incomplete, but also when the knowledge is too complete, i.e. inconsistent. Assume you come home in the evening and find the following short note on the table: *Hi, I went to the cinema with John, the children are visiting Grandma, Peter will visit us on Monday 17th. See you later.* You immediately realize that Monday is not the 17th, i.e. the information at hand is inconsistent. But does that mean that you do not know where the children are?

You probably isolate the inconsistent subpart of the information and remain agnostic with respect to Peter's visit. But you do not throw away the rest. You believe that the children are visiting Grandma and that your husband is in the cinema.

However, if you suddenly remember that Grandma is on holiday in Paris, then this additional information will certainly cause you to withdraw the belief about where the children are. The additional information made other parts of your knowledge inconsistent and conclusions based on these parts are withdrawn.

The example shows that every agent who is able to draw reasonable conclusions based on possibly inconsistent information must reason nonmonotonically.

Another form of reasoning in which some parts of the knowledge have to be disregarded in certain cases is counterfactual reasoning (Lewis 73; Ginsberg 86). A counterfactual is a statement of the form 'if p then q' (denoted p > q) where p is known or expected to be false. Typical examples are 'If the electricity hadn't failed, dinner would have been ready on time' or 'If you had thought a little bit harder you wouldn't have made this mistake' or 'If you were not writing this book you could go to the beach with us'. If we were to interpret conditionals as material implications then they would be always true, because their preconditions are false.

We distinguish, however, between true and false counterfactuals. Roughly, the truth of a counterfactual p > q can be determined as follows: add p to your world description. This renders the description inconsistent. Try to find consistent world descriptions which are as similar as possible to this inconsistent description and which contain p. If q holds in all of them, then p > q is true, else it is false.

It often happens that a true counterfactual becomes invalid when additional information is obtained. 'If the electricity hadn't failed, dinner would have been ready on time', for instance, becomes false when we get the additional information that Peter forgot to go shopping.

I shall not give a precise formal account of these intuitive ideas here, especially of the notion of similarity. The reader is referred to (Ginsberg 87) for a discussion of various formalizations and an investigation of computational aspects of counterfactual reasoning.

In this section we have tried to isolate different types of reasoning. In real life they very often appear in combination. For instance, it may be the case that we believe that certain conventions are not necessarily, but typically followed, or it may be the case that I would presumably know about a talk of John McCarthy since my colleagues typically tell me about such things. The types of reasoning I have discussed should be seen as some of the ingredients which together form human commonsense reasoning. It may well be the case that other forms of nonmonotonic reasoning exist. I do not claim that my list is complete.

The main focus of this book is on default reasoning. I am mainly interested in the use of the nonmonotonic logics for expressing rules with exceptions.

1.3: Applications of Nonmonotonic Reasoning

Historically one of the research topics which led to the development of the whole area of nonmonotonic reasoning was *reasoning about action and time*. Hayes and McCarthy proposed a situation calculus to reason in logic about the effects of events in time (Hayes, McCarthy 69). The basic idea is that facts are indexed by the situation in which they hold, for instance:

HOLDS(IN(FRED,KITCHEN), SITUATION105)

HOLDS(COLOR(KITCHEN,RED), SITUATION105)

Events transform a situation into another one:

SITUATION106= RESULT(GO(FRED,BATHROOM),SITUATION105)

Additional axioms specify how events change the world:

∀x,y,s. HOLDS(IN(x,y),RESULT(GO(x,y),s))

The problem is: how can we derive that the kitchen is still red after Fred went to the bathroom? We have a new situation and know nothing about it unless we have additional axioms such as

∀x,y,v,w,s. HOLDS(COLOR(x,y),s) ⊃ HOLDS(COLOR(x,y),RESULT(GO(v,w),s))

Such *frame axioms* are needed for every possible event and every property which is not affected by the event. This is very impractical, unnatural, and computationally demanding. Most facts are not affected by an event. We do not want to have to list all of them explicitly. Are there better ways of specifying what doesn't change when an event occurs?

This problem has been called the *frame problem*. A natural solution seems to be the replacement of the huge number of frame axioms by one single axiom, an axiom which, roughly, says: typically an event does not change the truth of a fact. With this 'persistence default' it is sufficient to specify the changes caused by each modelled event. The inclusion of such a default, obviously, introduces nonmonotonicity. If it is not specified, for instance, that switching on the light changes the temperature, then the default can be used to conclude that the temperature remains the same. Adding information that the burning light increases the temperature makes the former conclusion impossible.

As we shall see later it turned out that a simple straightforward representation of this axiom in a nonmonotonic logic does not produce the expected derivations. This result was surprising. Even more surprising was that it took so many years after the development of the first nonmonotonic logics before anybody became aware of this fact. I discuss the frame problem and its nonmonotonic solutions again in Chapter 10.[2]

Another problem that becomes apparent when modelling the effects of actions is that something always can go wrong. If you sit in the car and turn the key the car will start - unless the battery is flat, or there is no more fuel, or someone has stolen the engine, or the key breaks off, or ... . The list of possible exceptional circumstances is open-ended. As in the exceptional birds example in Section 1.1 it is not possible to give a complete list of possible exceptions.

We certainly assume that the car will start if we do not know that the circumstances are exceptional. We do not try to prove the absence of an exception explicitly. If further information is obtained indicating that something goes wrong we withdraw the conclusion. Thus reasoning about the effects of actions in a real world where exceptional circumstances may change these effects is nonmonotonic. The problem of specifying the effects of an event in the light of an open-ended list of possible exceptions is known as the *qualification problem*.

The relevance of nonmonotonic reasoning for *diagnosis* has been thoroughly investigated (Reiter 87a), (Poole 89b). Two different diagnostic paradigms can be distinguished:

(1) Diagnosis from first principles (Reiter 87a) assumes a given functional description of a device which specifies the *normal* behavior of each component. This allows us to predict the behavior of the device under normal circumstances. We assume, by default, that each component works correctly. If we obtain information that the actual behavior differs from the predicted behavior, then we conclude that there must be some component(s) for which the normality assumption canot be made. These are the component(s) we are looking for when trying to diagnose the source of the fault.

(2) Abductive diagnosis on the other hand, is based on information about faults and how they typically manifest themselves. In this case the diagnosis we are looking for consists of a minimal set of assumptions which together with the background knowledge entail the observations.

Both types of diagnosis, and the continuum between the two, have been analyzed in (Poole 89b).

---

[2] A logical approach which handles the frame problem without explicit persistence defaults is presented in (Bibel 86). In this approach the frame axioms are handled implicitly in the deductive machinery.

Another important application of nonmonotonic reasoning is *natural language understanding*. Many communication conventions rule the ways we talk to each other, and we base our conclusions on the assumption that these conventions are not violated unless explicitly mentioned. Contrastives like 'but' or 'however' are used to indicate explicitly cases where such expectations are violated. Perrault has investigated the relationship between speech acts and nonmonotonic reasoning (Perrault 87). Asher presents the following example for anaphora resolution to illustrate the close relation between nonmonotonic reasoning and natural language understanding (Asher 84):

The Vice-President entered the President's office.

He was nervous and clutching his briefcase.

Most of us will interpret the pronoun 'he' in the second sentence as referring to the Vice-President. It is part of our commonsense knowledge that people lower in a hierarchy have more reason to be nervous. But what if the story continues as follows:

After all, he couldn't fire the Vice-President without making trouble for himself with the chairman of the board.

Now there is a possible explanation for the President's being nervous, and the pronoun's interpretation will shift after this additional information has been obtained.

In *vision* similar things happen frequently. We see part of a scene and make default conclusions about the complete scene, e.g. object boundaries, interpretation of edges etc. This completion is, of course, subject to later revision. More information can show that the scene is less regular and more complicated than expected.

As a last example for possible applications of nonmonotonic reasoning we mention the representation of law (Gordon 87). A great part of law is written in the form of rules with exceptions. The law is, thus, nonmonotonic. Here is an example:

Contracts are valid.

Contracts with minors are not valid.

Contracts which have been ratified by a guardian of a minor are valid.

The list of possible applications mentioned in this section is far from being complete. Nonmonotonicity seems to be a fundamental aspect of human commonsense reasoning in all kinds of areas.

1.4: An Overview of this Book

Before describing the organization of the book in detail I would like to discuss a problem which is common to all approaches and so explains why defining a nonmonotonic logic turns out to be technically quite difficult. Any formalization of defaults must be able to handle conflicting defaults. Here is the standard example:

Quakers are typically pacifists.

Republicans are typically not pacifists.

Nixon is a Republican and a Quaker.

The question is: is Nixon a pacifist or not? Each of the possible answers can be just-ified by a default, but, of course, we cannot both believe that he is and is not a pacifist at the same time. We shall see that some of the approaches to be examined handle this kind of problem by generating different belief sets. These sets of formulae can be def-ined via a fixed point construction. The remaining question is: if we have multiple belief sets, what are the derivable formulae?

Two different answers can be given. We can define the theorems as the intersection of all belief sets. This corresponds to the view that we should remain agnostic in the case of conflicting information. This approach has been favoured by McDermott and Doyle (McDermott, Doyle 80). Reiter, on the other hand, interprets each of the generated fixed points - they are called extensions in his logic - as an acceptable set of beliefs (Reiter 80). This 'brave' or 'credulous' behaviour of a reasoner has advantages and disadvantages: on the one hand more conclusions are obtained and hence more of the missing parts in the incomplete knowledge are filled. On the other hand these conclusions depend on the choice of the extension, and as our example shows contradictory beliefs can be supported by different fixed points. (Tell me what you want to prove and I will tell you which extension to choose). Which is more appropriate, the agnostic or credulous view, depends on the kind of reasoning to be formalized and the intended application. There is, I hope, no-one who wants the decisions of an expert system supervising a nuclear reactor to be based on an uncontrolled choice of one of the fixed points.

The attitude towards conflicting defaults is just one of the distinguishing features of the logics. There are other interesting questions we will discuss. How expressive are the logics? Can priorities between defaults be expressed? How are the logics to be used? Is there a recommended default methodology? Which types of defaults lead to desired results? How can unwanted consequences of contraposition be handled?

The book is organized as follows. Chapters 2 - 6 give an overview of the most im-portant existing nonmonotonic logics. I also present some modifications or general-izations which produce better results or increase expressiveness, in particular in Chapters 3 and 5. I have included in these chapters only those approaches which are general enough to subsume full first order logic as a special case. There are five main approaches:

(1)   Modal approaches (Chapter 2): these extend the logical language and use a modal operator to represent that something is consistent or believed. Examples presented in this book are McDermott and Doyle's nonmonotonic logic NML (McDermott, Doyle 80) and Moore's autoepistemic logic (Moore 85). NML is

presented partly for historical reasons. Its prominent successor autoepistemic logic is certainly favored now. Many of the basic ideas of the modal approach were developed by McDermott and Doyle however, and can be suitably illustrated with their logic. Moreover, as we shall see in Chapter 7, for an interesting subset, NML and autoepistemic logic coincide.

(2) Approaches based on nonmonotonic inference rules (Chapter 3): these inference rules specify ways of extending the set of classical theorems of some premises to contain some additional, retractable beliefs. The most prominent example of this kind of approach is Reiter's default logic (Reiter 80). We propose certain modifications of his logic that in some cases produce more intuitive results or extend the expressiveness. In addition we give a methodology for using this logic which is based on a naming technique for defaults.

(3) Circumscription (Chapter 4): here the nonmonotonic theorems of a set of premises A are defined to be the monotonic theorems of a certain superset A∪X of A (McCarthy 80) (McCarthy 84). When A grows the additional X changes. This is what makes circumscription nonmonotonic. There exist various different versions of circumscription:

    predicate circumscription (McCarthy 80),
    domain circumscription (McCarthy 80),
    variable circumscription (McCarthy 84),
    formula circumscription (McCarthy 84),
    prioritized circumscription (McCarthy 84),
    protected circumscription (Minker, Perlis 84),
    pointwise circumscription (Lifschitz 86),
    set circumscription (Perlis 87),
    autocircumscription (Perlis 88),

and it seems that every major AI conference produces yet another variant. We present the two basic and most important versions, predicate and variable circumscription, in detail and sketch prioritized circumscription more briefly in Section 4.3.

(4) Preferred subtheories (Chapter 5): instead of starting from a consistent set of premises and extending the theorems to include some additional retractable formulae the starting point of this approach is a set of inconsistent formulae with different degrees of reliability. Theorems are defined in terms of preferred maximal consistent subsets. A simple instance of this approach is Poole's theory of default reasoning (Poole 88). Two generalizations of his approach are presented which allow for the representation of priorities between defaults.

(5) Approaches based on conditionals (Chapter 6): as in the modal approaches the logical language is extended, but instead of a modal operator a new binary connective is introduced to express default implication. We describe Delgrande's

system (Delgrande 88), currently the best developed conditional approach to
default reasoning.

In the appendix the reader will find a table showing some of the main features of the
examined logics.

Our classification of approaches to nonmonotonic logic is based on different ways of
defining nonmonotonic theoremhood. How about the semantics? It turns out that a
common and elegant way to give a model theoretic account of the meaning of formulae is based on standard, classical models. Entailment, however, is not defined in
terms of validity in all models. Instead, a relation is defined - either on the models
themselves (circumscription) or on sets of models (default logic). Only those (sets of)
models are considered, which are minimal (respectively maximal) with respect to this
relation.

Here I have to mention a problem shared by all the nonmonotonic logics presented
in this book. In their general form they are computationally intractable. In fact - with
the exception of the first order version of circumscription described in Section 4.1 -
they are all not even semi-decidable; that is there provably exists no algorithm which,
given a set of premises A and a formula q, returns 'derivable' iff q is a theorem of A
in the respective logic. This result stems from the fact that the logics refer either to
the notion of consistency[3] (modal, rule based, conditional and preferred subtheory
approaches) or they are based on higher order logic (circumscription).[4]

This result is unpleasant. It seems to be the price we have to pay for a general formal theory of nonmonotonic reasoning. It does not mean, however, that the logics are
useless for AI practice. In fact, a great part of this book tries to address the question
how we can combine theoretical foundation and computational tractability in nonmonotonic reasoning systems. What the negative result tells us is that all the nonmonotonic provers we try to build will either be incomplete or incorrect, or will be able to
deal only with a subset of one of the logics.

What can we do in such a situation? At least three ways of combining theoretical
foundedness and computational tractability are possible:

(1)   We can try to identify interesting subsets of the logics for which efficient proof
       procedures exist.

(2)   We can take existing implemented nonmonotonic systems and try to understand
       them in terms of the logics, in other words give them a logical semantics.

(3)   We can try to approximate the theoretically required results.

---

[3] In classical first order logic consistency of a formula, i.e. underivability of its negation, is not
semi-decidable. If it were then first order logic would be decidable.

[4] It should be mentioned that propositional versions of the logics are decidable. A tableau based
decision procedure for propositional NML, for instance, is described in (McDermott, Doyle 80).

All three approaches are discussed in detail in Chapters 7 - 9. The first is the subject of Chapter 7 on nonmonotonic theorem proving. We present a number of proof procedures for restricted versions of the logics, in particular for circumscription, default logic and for a common subset of NML and autoepistemic logic.

In Chapter 8 we will discuss inheritance systems as a good example of the second approach. In fact, the first two can be viewed as different sides of the same coin, the difference simply being whether one starts from the logic and looks for a procedure, or from a program and looks for its logic. However, the existence of efficient implementations of inheritance systems was only one of the reasons for our interest in them. The basic idea underlying inheritance, preferring the most specific information in case of a conflict, seems to be a general principle of commonsense reasoning which is important to formalize.

Unfortunately, the formalization of this principle turns out to be very difficult, even when the logical language is very restricted. It also emerges that some of the existent efficient programs, for instance shortest path inheritance reasoners, have to be thrown away since they may - except in the simplest cases - produce counterintuitive results (see Section 8.1). So research in this field has shown that existing inheritance systems could not in each case be interpreted as specialized provers. In this sense the second approach was not always successful. In Section 8.2 we discuss a simple positive exception, however, the so-called frame systems.

Nonmonotonic systems based on the notion of *current unprovenness* (rather than 'unprovability') can be viewed as an example for the third approach. We call such systems nonmonotonic process systems. Here a nonmonotonic rule can be applied if no exceptional condition has been proven in the current problem solving state. A truth maintenance system is used to establish the current set of beliefs and to keep track of dependencies between beliefs. An extension of a knowledge base is approximated by incrementally computing an extension of a finite but continually growing subset of the knowledge base. Such systems and their relation to nonmonotonic logics are the subject matter of Chapter 9.

The last chapter (Chapter 10) weighs up the achievements in the field. We discuss the famous Yale Shooting example, which has shown that a straightforward use of nonmonotonic logics does not by itself solve the frame problem. The conclusion we draw is that we should implement more and more real life applications based on the available formalizations. Our experience with these systems will help us to detect overlooked problems and to improve our formalizations still further.

One additional clarificatory remark might be useful. The term 'logic' is used by some authors in a more restricted sense than I use in this book. For instance, McCarthy wrote (McCarthy 80) that circumscription is *not* a nonmonotonic logic. His approach certainly shows how to reduce nonmonotonic reasoning to classical reasoning from an augmented premise set. On the other hand, however, circumscription defines a new inference relation, an inference relation that can be given an independent semantic justification which is more than the classical semantics of the augmented premises. If a logic is taken to mean the formalization of an intuitive notion of inference based on a model theoretical semantics then we see no problem in subsuming circumscription under this term.

A last word about the examples used in this book. Tweety has already been mentioned. From time to time people tend to get bored with him and they look for alternatives. That is why in the next few chapters I mainly use another simple example involving the organization of a party and in particular certain drinking preferences. But for some reason, after a while, people remember Tweety, and they begin to like him again. This must have happened to the author because Tweety reappears in later chapters.

CHAPTER 2: MODAL NONMONOTONIC LOGICS

2.1: McDermott and Doyle's Nonmonotonic Logic

NML (McDermott, Doyle 80) is a logic where inferences can be based not only on the (classical) derivability of some formulae but also on the consistency of formulae. In particular, defaults such as

Germans typically drink beer

are interpreted as

If x is a German

and there is no information that x does not drink beer

(i.e. it is consistent to assume that x drinks beer)

then x drinks beer.

In order to reason about consistency in the logic we introduce a modal operator M with the intuitive meaning 'is consistent', i.e. the logical language is extended so that Mq is a formula whenever q is. Our default can then be syntactically represented as

(1) $\forall$x.GERMAN(x) $\wedge$ M DRINKS-BEER(x) $\supset$ DRINKS-BEER(x)

In this way defaults can be represented but we are not yet done since this alone does not allow nonmonotonic conclusions to be drawn. If we have in addition

(2)   GERMAN(PETER)

then all we can derive is

(3)   M DRINKS-BEER(PETER) $\supset$ DRINKS-BEER(PETER)

What we need is the ability to obtain formulae of the form Mq in a way corresponding to the intuitive meaning of M.

How can this be achieved? As we mentioned, M is intended to mean 'is consistent'. q is consistent if $\neg$q is not derivable. So why not simply add to the logic the inference rule

If $\neg$q is not derivable then infer Mq

This may be simple but it is useless. The reason is that this inference rule is circular. It defines derivability in terms of derivability. To see how this leads to inconsistency consider the formula

$$Mq \supset \neg q$$

If we use this formula as single premise, then with the new 'inference rule' $\neg q$ is derivable iff $\neg q$ is not derivable (for the only-if-part consider that there is no way to derive $\neg q$ without Mq from the premise, and Mq can only be obtained from our new 'inference rule' when $\neg q$ is not derivable).

In fact it turns out that the definition of derivability in NML is inevitably quite tricky. McDermott and Doyle define an operator whose fixed points are used to define the derivable formulae. The fixed points, intuitively, correspond to belief sets which can be obtained by applying the standard inference rules of classical logic and throwing in as many formulae of the form Mp as possible. In Section 1.4 we discussed the problem of conflicting defaults. In the case of a conflict the operator produces multiple fixed points in each of which as many defaults as consistently possible have been applied.

After these intuitive remarks let's make the idea precise.

Definition 2.1: *Let A and S be sets of formulae where A is the set of premises. We define the set of assumptions of S with respect to A as*

$$Ass_A(S) = \{Mq | \neg q \notin S\} - Th(A)$$

$Th(A)$ here denotes the set of the classical theorems of A and the minus operator stands for set difference. The theorems of A are excluded from the assumptions for terminological reasons only.

Definition 2.2: *Let A and S be sets of formulae. The fixed point operator NM is given as*

$$NM_A(S) = Th(A \cup Ass_A(S))$$

This operator is interesting only for one reason: it has interesting fixed points. Assume that S is a fixed point of NM_A, i.e. we have

$$NM_A(S) = S$$

In this case S contains

(1)   all premises A

(2)   all monotonic theorems of A

(3)   as many formulae of the form Mq as can consistently be added, and

(4)   all theorems of (1) ... (3).

The fixed points of NM_A thus correspond to the sets of formulae intuitively 'sanctioned' by the premises contained in A under the intended interpretation of M.

The problem with this fixed point approach is, of course, that in general fixed points are hard to describe and difficult to find, since their definition is not constructive. Here are some simple examples:

$A_1 = \{ \}$

There is exactly one fixed point. It contains all tautologies as well as the formulae

$\{Mq \mid q$ is not a contradiction$\}$.

$A_2 = \{Mp \supset p\}$

There is exactly one fixed point containing both Mp and p.

$A_3 = \{Mp \supset p, \neg p\}$

There is exactly one fixed point. It contains neither Mp nor p. Since A_3 contains A_2 as a proper subset we have a first example of the nonmonotonicity of NML.

$A_4 = \{Mp \supset \neg r, Mr \supset \neg p\}$

There are two fixed points, one of them containing Mp and $\neg r$, but not Mr and $\neg p$, the other one containing Mr and $\neg p$ but not Mp and $\neg r$.

$A_5 = \{Mp \supset \neg p\}$

It is not difficult to see that there is no fixed point in this case. Let S be a set of formulae. Then either S contains $\neg p$ or not. If (1) it contains $\neg p$ then $Ass_A(S)$ does not contain Mp. But then $\neg p$ cannot be derived from the union of A and $Ass_A(S)$. Hence S is not a fixed point of NM_A. If (2) S does not contain $\neg p$ then $Ass_A(S)$ contains Mp, $NM_A(S)$ contains $\neg p$ and again S is not a fixed point of NM_A.

We have seen that there may be no, one or multiple fixed points of NM for specific sets of premises A. We shall simply call them fixed points of A from now on. Given these fixed points the derivable formulae still need to be defined. McDermott and Doyle choose the intersection of all fixed points. This corresponds to the view that in case of conflicting information (such as the Nixon example in Section 1.4) the logic should not prefer any of the conflicting conclusions.

Definition 2.3: *Let A be a set of premises, FP(A) the set of fixed points of A. TH(A), the set of nonmonotonic theorems of A, is the set of formulae*

$\{p \mid p \in S$ for all $S \in FP(A)\}$.

Note that this definition yields the set of all formulae if there is no fixed point at all, i.e. that case is treated as an inconsistency.

Consider our party example.

(1) $\forall x.\text{GERMAN}(x) \wedge M \text{ DRINKS-BEER}(x) \supset \text{DRINKS-BEER}(x)$

(2) GERMAN(PETER)

Since $\neg\text{DRINKS-BEER(PETER)}$ cannot be derived even with the addition of any assumption, i.e. a formula of the form Mq, M DRINKS-BEER(PETER) is contained in the only fixed point. Therefore DRINKS-BEER(PETER) is also contained in the fixed point and hence derivable. If we add

(3)   EATS -PIZZA(x) ⊃ ¬DRINKS-BEER(x)

(4)   EATS -PIZZA(PETER)

then ¬DRINKS-BEER(PETER) is monotonically derivable, M DRINKS-BEER(PETER) and DRINKS-BEER(PETER), therefore, are not contained in the single fixed point. If we replace (3) by

(3')   EATS -PIZZA(x) ∧ M ¬DRINKS-BEER(x) ⊃ ¬DRINKS-BEER(x)

we get two fixed points, one containing DRINKS-BEER(PETER), and the other one containing ¬DRINKS-BEER(PETER). According to Definition 2.3 none of the formulae is contained in the nonmonotonic theorems of the premises.

We now state some results about NML. All proofs are to be found in (McDermott, Doyle 80). If A is a set of classical formulae not containing M, then there is exactly one fixed point of A. This fixed point contains the monotonic theorems of A and no other formulae without modal operator (ordinary formulae). If A is monotonically inconsistent, then the set of all formulae is the only fixed point of A. All fixed points of a set A are minimal, i.e. if S1, S2 ∈ FP(A) and S1 is contained in S2, then S1=S2. Moreover, if S1, S2 ∈ FP(A) and S1≠S2, then S1 ∪ S2 is inconsistent.

McDermott and Doyle defined the semantics of NML as follows:

Definition 2.4: *Let A be a set of formulae. A nonmonotonic model of A is a pair (V,S) where V is a classical model of S and S a fixed point of A.*

This is not very helpful since the definition is based on just the fixed points that were used to define derivability. We trivially get completeness and soundness, but not much light is shed on the meaning of formulae. Our discussion of other approaches will show that better ways of defining a semantics for nonmonotonic logics have been found.

McDermott and Doyle themselves diagnosed a major problem with NML: the logic is too weak in that the modal operator does not fully capture the meaning of consistency. It can easily be verified that, for instance, A = {Mp, ¬p} is consistent in NML. A has a single fixed point containing Th({¬p}) as ordinary formulae. On the other hand, the set of premises {¬Mp} is inconsistent, since it has no fixed point: ¬p is not derivable with any additional assumptions besides Mp, but adding Mp to any set of formulae containing the premise makes this set inconsistent and prevents it from being a fixed point.

The source of this problem lies in the fact that there are some expected derivations involving the modal operator which cannot be performed. These derivations, however, do seem to be necessary under the intended interpretation of the modal operator. For instance, we expect ¬Mp to be derivable from ¬p since p is not consistent if ¬p can be derived.

Dependencies like the one just mentioned are formalized in modal logics. It is, therefore, a natural idea to base a nonmonotonic logic on a modal logic to overcome the weakness of NML.

Modal logics formalize the concepts of *possibility* and *necessity*. Mp stands for 'p is possible', Lp for 'p is necessary'. Lp can be expressed as ¬M¬p. *Possible* and *necessary* can also be interpreted - as has been done in the beginning of this section - as *consistent* and *provable*. In modal logics additional axioms and inference rules are added to the axioms and rules of classical logic, e.g.:

(1)   Lp ⊃ p

(2)   L(p⊃q)⊃(Lp⊃Lq)

(3)   Lp⊃LLp

(4)   Mp⊃LMp

(R1) if p is derivable, then Lp is derivable

The standard modal logics are called T (axioms 1,2), S4 (axioms 1,2,3) and S5 (axioms 1,2,4). S5 is stronger than S4, S4 stronger than T. For an excellent introduction to modal logic see (Hughes, Cresswell 68).

McDermott (McDermott 82) has defined nonmonotonic versions of the logics. This can be done by simply replacing Th in the definition of NM with Th$_T$, Th$_{S4}$, Th$_{S5}$, the set of theorems of T, S4, S5, respectively.

The most plausible candidate for formalizing consistency seems to be S5. Surprisingly it turns out that the nonmonotonic version of S5 is actually equivalent to monotonic S5 (McDermott 82). McDermott proposes to use nonmonotonic S4 instead, a proposal whose only motivation seems to be the collapse of nonmonotonic S5. Nonmonotonic S4 has never gained much popularity. The main reason for this is that autoepistemic logic is a better alternative.

2.2: Autoepistemic Logic

Moore's Autoepistemic Logic, AEL, (Moore 85) can be seen as another, more successful, proposal for overcoming the weaknesses of NML. AEL has become by far the most prominent nonmonotonic logic based on a modal extension of the logical language.

Moore starts from a very different viewpoint. Instead of formalizing the concept of consistency he aims at giving a formal account of an ideal agent reasoning about his own beliefs. Such an agent is assumed to have complete introspective capabilities in the sense that he knows that he knows p, whenever he knows p, and he knows that he does not know p, whenever he does not know p.

Because of this different goal of AEL the modal operator is given an epistemic interpretation. The basic operator L is read as 'it is believed that', the dual operator M,
correspondingly, as 'it is not believed that not'. The the modal operators in the language allow us to express a relationship between what is believed and what is true in
the world. For instance, we can express that if Peter is a German and we do not
believe that he does not drink beer, then he drinks beer:

(1)   GERMAN(PETER) ∧ ¬L¬ DRINKS-BEER(PETER) ⊃ DRINKS-BEER(PETER)

Syntactically, this representation is equivalent to the one used in NML.

For semantical reasons Moore does not allow quantification into the scope of the
modal operator. A formula such as

(2)   ∀x.GERMAN(x) ∧ ¬L¬ DRINKS-BEER(x) ⊃ DRINKS-BEER(x)

is not allowed. The corresponding default has to be represented as a schema

       GERMAN(x) ∧ ¬L¬ DRINKS-BEER(x) ⊃ DRINKS-BEER(x)

which stands for all its ground instances. x here is a parameter. This reduces the expressiveness but still seems adequate for default reasoning purposes. Moore describes
the difficulties of quantifying in as follows (Moore 88, p. 119f):

*It is far from clear how to characterize the stable expansions (the fixed points in his
logic) of a set of premises once we allow quantifying into the scope of B (Moore
writes B instead of L in this later paper). Suppose that our set of premises is*

        {P(A), P(B), ∀x(P(x) ⊃ B(P(x)))}

*and we are asked to decide whether ¬P(C) should follow from these premises. At
first, it might appear that it should, since the third premise says that every object
with property P is believed to have property P, and only A and B are believed to
have property P. But what if C=A or C=B is true? The quantifier ... ranges over
objects, not names of objects, so the possibility is open that P(C) is true, because C is
believed to have property P under a different name. Rather than ¬P(C), it seems
that what we want to be able to infer is P(C) ⊃ (C=A v C=B). It is not immediately
clear what is the most general pattern of reasoning of which this is an instance, or
how to describe it formally.*

Konolige recently suggested how to extend AEL to handle quantifying (Konolige
89). We shall not, however, discuss here his extension of AEL and assume that Lp is
allowed only if p has no free variables, in other words p is a sentence.

As mentioned before our goal is to model introspective knowledge. What should be
the beliefs of an ideal introspective agent given a set of premises A? A first natural requirement is that they should be deductively closed (logical omniscience). Moreover,
according to the intended interpretation of L, we expect Lp to be a belief if p is, and
¬Lp if p is not. This gives rise to the following definition:

Definition 2.5: *A set of sentences T is called stable iff the following properties hold*

(1)   If p1,...,pn ∈ T, and p1, ...,pn |- q, then q ∈ T (where '|-' stands for classical monotonic derivability).

(2)   If p ∈ T, then Lp ∈ T.

(3)   If p ∉ T, then ¬Lp ∈ T.

Stability makes no reference to the set of premises A the agent is given. We must also require that the beliefs should contain the premises A together with those formulae necessary to satisfy the stability conditions:

Definition 2.6: *A set of sentences T is grounded in a set of premises A iff every formula of T is included in the set of (classical) theorems of*

$$A \cup \{Lp \mid p \in T\} \cup \{\neg Lp \mid p \notin T\}$$

With these definitions we can characterize the belief sets of the ideal agent:

Definition 2.7: *T is an (AEL-) extension of A iff T is stable and grounded in A.*

In (Moore 85) extensions were called stable expansions but as the term extension which also is used in Reiter's logic has become more popular it is used here.

To see the important difference between NML and AEL it is useful to give an equivalent characterization of extensions in terms of a fixed point operator. S is an extension of A iff it is a fixed point of the operator NM' defined as follows:

$$\text{NM'}_A(S) = \text{Th}(A \cup \{Lp \mid p \in S\} \cup \{\neg Lp \mid p \notin S\})$$

Moore describes the difficulties of NML (Moore 85, p.86):

In nonmonotonic logic, {LP | P ∈ T} is missing from the base of the fixed points. This makes it possible for there to be nonmonotonic theories that contain P but not LP. So, under an autoepistemic interpretation of L, McDermott and Doyle's agents are omniscient as to what they do not believe, but they may know nothing as to what they do believe.

We now show that extensions have an exact semantical counterpart. We define the notions of autoepistemic interpretation and autoepistemic model. Formulae without the modal operator, the ordinary formulae, will be treated as usual, and sentences of the form Lp as propositional constants. Formulae of the latter type are interpreted relative to a certain belief set, that is an arbitrary set of formulae. Following (Konolige 88a) we call this belief set the modal index.

Definition 2.8: *Let T be a set of sentences. An interpretation I of T with modal index T' is a truth assignment to the sentences of the language of T such that*

(1)   I conforms to the usual truth recursion for classical logic

(2)   a formula Lp is true in I iff p ∈ T'.

Definition 2.9: *An autoepistemic interpretation of T is an interpretation of T with modal index T.*

Definition 2.10: *An autoepistemic model of T is an autoepistemic interpretation of T in which all the sentences of T are true.*

With these definitions we can introduce notions of completeness and soundness as follows:

Definition 2.11: *T is semantically complete iff T contains every formula that is true in every autoepistemic model of T.*

Soundness has to be defined relative to a set of premises A.

Definition 2.12: *T is sound with respect to a set of premises A iff every autoepistemic interpretation of T in which all the sentences of A are true is an autoepistemic model of T.*

Intuitively, T is sound with respect to A if all beliefs in T must be true, provided the premises in A are true and modal formulae are interpreted with respect to T, i.e. Lp is true iff $p \in T$.

Moore has shown (Moore 85) that a set of formulae T is stable iff T is semantically complete, and that T is grounded in A iff it is sound with respect to A, i.e. we have the following soundness and completeness result [1]:

Theorem 2.1: *A set of sentences T is semantically complete and sound with respect to a set of premises A iff T is an extension of A.*

In (Konolige 88a) an equivalent, somewhat more compact characterization of extensions has been given. We write $A \models_T p$ to express that p is true in all interpretations of A with modal index T which make all formulae in A true. Extensions of A now are exactly those sets T which satisfy the equation

$$T = \{p \mid A \models_T p\}.$$

Interestingly, it is also possible to describe extensions in a similar way using the ordinary entailment relation without modal index (Konolige 88a). For that purpose the modal part of the extension has to be made explicit on the left hand side of the $\models$ sign. Let LT denote the set of formulae $\{Lp \mid p \in T\}$, $\neg L\overline{T}$ the set $\{\neg Lp \mid p \in \overline{T}\}$ where $\overline{T}$ is the complement of T. We now can state the following

Proposition 2.2: *T is an extension of A iff it satisfies the equation*

$$T = \{p \mid A \cup LT \cup \neg L\overline{T} \models p\}.$$

There is a third equation for the set T which lies somewhere between the two. This equation will be useful for describing the exact relation between AEL and Reiter's default logic (Section 3.3). We restrict the modal indices to stable sets as just defined and note the corresponding entailment relation as $\models_{SS}$, i.e. $A \models_{SS} p$ means that p is true in

---

1 It should be mentioned that Moore also defined an alternative Kripke-style possible worlds semantics for AEL in (Moore 84).

all interpretations which make the premises A true and use a stable set as modal index. T_0 denotes the set of formulae in T without modal operator (ordinary formulae). As shown in (Konolige 88a) this gives an alternative definition of extension:

Proposition 2.3: *T is an extension of A iff it satisfies the equation*

$$T = \{p \mid A \cup LT_0 \cup \neg LT_0 \mid=_{SS} p\}.$$

Note that in this proposition the complement operator has a stronger binding than the 0-index, that is $\neg LT_0$ is to be read as $\{\neg Lp \mid p$ ordinary and $p \notin T\}$. The use of a stronger type of entailment allows us to eliminate from the definition all self-referential assumptions except those expressing belief or non-belief in ordinary formulae.

It should not be surprising that, as in NML, there are sets of premises giving rise to one, multiple, or zero extensions. An example of the last case is A = {Lp}. There can be no extension since there is no way of obtaining p from A whichever modal formulae are added. Therefore ¬Lp would have to be contained in every extension. But this is inconsistent with A.

Back to our party example. We had

(1)   GERMAN(x) ∧ ¬L¬ DRINKS-BEER(x) ⊃ DRINKS-BEER(x)

(2)   GERMAN(PETER()

Remember that (1) is a schema representing its ground instances. There is exactly one extension containing DRINKS-BEER(PETER): there is no way of deriving ¬ DRINKS-BEER(PETER) from the premises. Hence ¬L¬ DRINKS-BEER(PETER) is contained in the extension and from this together with (2) and the right instance of (1) we get DRINKS-BEER(PETER).

If we add

(3)   EATS-PIZZA(x) ∧ ¬L¬ DRINKS-BEER(x) ⊃ ¬DRINKS-BEER(x)

(4)   EATS-PIZZA(PETER)

we get two extensions, one of which contains the formula DRINKS-BEER(PETER), the other one its negation.

It was shown in (Moore 85) that extensions are completely characterized by their ordinary formulae. If two extensions agree on their basic beliefs they are equal. Moreover, if A is a set of ordinary premises, then it has exactly one extension whose ordinary formulae are exactly the classical theorems of A (Konolige 88a).

After our discussion of nonmonotonic T, S4 and S5 in Section 2.1 some readers may wonder whether the lack of additional modal axioms in AEL can cause any problems, as it did in NML. Moore has shown that in AEL no problems arise (Moore 85). In fact, every instance of an axiom schema of 'weak' S5, which is obtained from S5 by removing the axiom schema Lp ⊃ p, is true in every AEL extension. Therefore adding any of the axioms of weak S5 to a set of premises has no effect on the resulting extensions. All links between belief, non-belief and truth expressed in these axioms are implicit in AEL.

It is important to note that AEL extensions are not necessarily minimal with respect to their ordinary formulae, that is there may be two extensions E_1 and E_2 such that the ordinary formulae of E_1 are a strict subset of those of E_2. Consider the example

   $A = \{Lp \supset p\},$

a premise set which has two extensions. One of them contains p, the other one not. In the first extension belief in the formula p has been used to derive p. (Konolige 88, p. 352):

   This certainly seems to be an anomalous situation, since the agent can, simply by choosing to assume a belief or not, be justified in either believing or not believing a fact about the real world.

This led Konolige to introduce the notion of a moderately grounded extension.

Definition 2.13: *An extension T of A is moderately grounded in A if there is no stable set S containing A such that the ordinary formulae of S are a proper subset of the ordinary formulae of T.*

Konolige has shown that moderately grounded extensions of A can be characterized as those sets satisfying the equation

   $T = \{p \mid A \cup LA \cup \neg LT_0 \models_{SS} p\}$

It is not difficult to see that only one of the extensions of $A = \{Lp \supset p\}$ is moderately grounded, the extension which does not contain p. The other extension is not minimal with respect to its ordinary formulae.

As the example shows, introducing moderately grounded extensions eliminates some of the unwanted derivations of a formula from belief in that formula. There are, however, more complicated cases which cannot be captured by the notion of minimality. Consider the example $A' = \{Lp \supset p, \neg Lp \supset q\}$. We get two extensions. One extension, T, contains p but not q. There is again no way of deriving p without first assuming Lp, and hence this extension might be considered anomalous for the same reasons as the non-minimal extension of A. But in this case the minimality criterion is insufficient to eliminate this extension. The second extension, T', does not contain p, but it contains q and hence its ordinary formulae are not a proper subset of those in T. Hence both extensions are moderately grounded.

Konolige has shown that it is possible to strengthen the definition of extensions adequately in order to eliminate the remaining 'anomalous' extensions. We give the precise definition of his strongly grounded extensions in Section 3.3, where the exact relation between AEL and Reiter's default logic is described. It turns out that both logics are equivalent in the sense that the ordinary parts of strongly grounded AEL extensions correspond exactly to Reiter's extensions and vice versa (Konolige 88a).

This result is surprising. Moore understands his logic as a formalization of autoepistemic reasoning and explicitly not as a formalization of default reasoning. Default Logic, on the other hand, is one of the most prominent logics for default reasoning. The equivalence result suggests that forms of nonmonotonic reasoning as different as autoepistemic and default reasoning may not necessarily require different formalizations.

Based on this result many authors, for instance Konolige (see following section), simply speak of representing defaults in AEL. We follow them in this respect keeping in mind that Moore's original intention was not the formalization of defaults.

2.3: Hierarchic Autoepistemic Logic

Konolige (Konolige 88b) recently presented a modification of AEL, called hierarchic autoepistemic logic, HAEL. HAEL allows us to represent priorities between defaults and, moreover, has some nice computational properties: there always exists exactly one extension, and this extension has a constructive definition. To achieve all this a strict partial ordering $<$ on subtheories T_i is introduced. The basic idea is that the modal operator L in each subtheory is allowed to refer only to theories lower in the hierarchy. Technically this is achieved by indexing L. $L_i p$ means that p is believed in subtheory T_i.

Sets of subtheories with such an ordering are called HAEL structures. Konolige defines the notion of extension for a structure as follows:

Definition 2.14: *A complex stable set for a HAEL structure T is a sequence of sets of sentences $\Gamma_0, \Gamma_1,...,$ corresponding to the subtheories $T_0, T_1, ..., $ of T, that satisfies the following conditions:*

(1)   Every Γ_i contains T_i,

(2)   Every Γ_i is deductively closed,

(3)   If p is an ordinary sentence of Γ_j, and $T_j < T_i$, then $p \in \Gamma_i$,

(4)   If $p \in \Gamma_j$, and $T_j < T_i$, then $L_j p \in \Gamma_i$,

(5)   If $p \notin \Gamma_j$, and $T_j < T_i$, then $\neg L_j p \in \Gamma_i$.

Definition 2.16: *A complex stable set Γ for T is minimal iff for each subset Γ_i of Γ, there is no stable set Γ' for T that agrees with Γ on all $\Gamma_j < \Gamma_i$, and for which Γ'_i is a proper subset of Γ_i.*

Konolige has shown that every HAEL structure T has a unique minimal complex stable set; the extension of T.

Using the Nixon example discussed in Section 1.4 we can show how the structure of subtheories can be used to represent priorities. Assume the following representation:

$T_0 = \{QUAKER(NIXON), REPUBLICAN(NIXON)\}$

$T_1 = \{QUAKER(NIXON) \wedge \neg L_0 \neg PACIFIST(NIXON) \supset PACIFIST(NIXON)\}$

$T_2 = \{QUAKER(NIXON) \wedge \neg L_1 PACIFIST(NIXON) \supset \neg PACIFIST(NIXON)\}$

where $T_0 < T_1 < T_2$. Since $\neg PACIFIST(NIXON))$ is not believed in Γ_0, we get $\neg L_0 \neg PACIFIST(NIXON)$, and hence $PACIFIST(NIXON)$ in Γ_1. This blocks the default from T_2. This shows that the introduction of the different theory layers corresponds to the introduction of preferences between conflicting defaults.

Unfortunately, this approach not only gives us the possibility of expressing preferences between defaults, it also forces us to do so, since otherwise we get an inconsistency. If, for instance, we put the default from T_2 one level lower, with the corresponding replacement of the modal operator L_1 by L_0, then we immediately have an inconsistent extension. Both conflicting defaults are applicable since neither $PACIFIST(NIXON)$ nor its negation are believed in Γ_0.

This seems to be a very high price. There are many cases where no knowledge is available about priorities between conflicting defaults. Even worse, in the general case it is not even decidable whether two defaults are conflicting or not. It is questionable whether the computational advantages of HAEL outweigh this obvious drawback. Nevertheless, Konolige argues in his paper that there might be some interesting applications for the logic anyway. (Appelt, Konolige 89), for instance, describes an application of HAEL to formalizing speech acts.

CHAPTER 3: DEFAULT LOGIC

3.1: Defaults, Default Theories and Extensions

Reiter's default logic, DL, (Reiter 80) is in many respects similar to the logics described in the previous chapter. In particular, Reiter interprets defaults exactly as McDermott and Doyle do, i.e. 'As are typically Bs' is interpreted as 'if x is an A and it is consistent to assume that x is a B, then it is a B'. His logic, however, differs in one important aspect from the modal approaches: instead of extending the logical language and representing defaults *in* the language the defaults are used as additional inference rules inducing so-called *extensions* of classical logical theories. The defaults specify how a logical knowledge base can be extended to a belief set containing formulae not logically derivable (in the classical sense) from the knowledge base.

The defaults themselves are written

$$\backslash F(A(x): B_1(x), \dots , B_n(x); C(x))$$

where $A(x)$, $B_1(x)$, ..., $B_n(x)$, and $C(x)$ are classical formulae whose free variables are contained in $x = x_1, \dots, x_m$. The intended meaning of the default is as follows: if, for a specific x, $A(x)$ can be shown and $\neg B_1(x)$, ..., $\neg B_n(x)$ cannot be shown, then derive $C(x)$. $A(x)$ is called prerequisite, $C(x)$ consequent, and the $B_i(x)$ justifications of the default. We will very often also use the alternative, less space consuming notation $A(x) : B_1(x), \dots , B_n(x) / C(x)$ for a default.

For technical reasons we also admit the case where $n = 0$, i.e. defaults with no justifications. Such defaults behave like standard inference rules. Admitting them makes the analysis of the relation between DL and AEL (Section 3.3) as well as that between DL and truth maintenance systems (Chapter 9) somewhat easier.

A *default theory* is a pair (D,W), where D is a set of defaults and W a set of classical formulae. W describes what is known about the world. For closed default theories, which are theories where the prerequisite consequent and justifications of the defaults do not contain free variables, a fixed point operator Γ is defined as follows:

Definition 3.1: *Let S be a set of closed formulae, (D,W) a closed default theory. $\Gamma(S)$ is the smallest set such that:*

D1 $W \subseteq \Gamma(S),$

D2   Th(Γ(S)) = Γ(S),

D3   If A: B1, ... , Bn/C ∈ D, A∈Γ(S) and ¬Bi∉S (i∈{1,...,n}), then C∈Γ(S).

Reiter calls the fixed points of this operator *extensions* of (D,W). Condition D1
guarantees that what is known about the world is contained in each extension, D2 says
that beliefs have to be deductively closed, and D3 has the effect that as many defaults
as possible - with respect to the extension itself - actually are applied. Moreover, the
minimality condition makes it impossible to have 'ungrounded' beliefs, i.e. beliefs for
which no argument based on W and D can be constructed, in an extension.

Reiter presents an alternative, but equivalent definition of extensions. This definition
is interesting because it gives a quasi-inductive characterization of extensions. This
characterization makes precise in which sense beliefs have to be 'grounded' in W and
D and is particularly useful for proofs. The term 'quasi-inductive' is due to
D. Makinson and refers to the fact that the result of the 'induction', E, appears in the
inductive step:

Proposition 3.1: *Let E_0 = W, and for i≥1*

$$E_{i+1} = Th(E_i) \cup \{C \mid (A: B1, ... , Bn/C) \in D, A \in E_i, \neg Bj \notin E \ (j \in \{1,...,n\})\},$$

then E is an extension of (D,W) iff $E = \bigcup_{i=0}^{\infty} E_i$.

The definitions so far handle only closed default theories. Defaults containing free
variables are interpreted as schemata representing all ground instances of the default.
To be able to draw certain default conclusions about objects which are only implicitly
defined Reiter introduces Skolemized forms of default theories where existential
quantifiers are replaced by new constants and functions (Reiter 80, Section 7). For
our purposes it is sufficient to consider the free variables as ranging over ground
terms built from the available symbols.

Here is the representation of our party example in DL. Since it is clear from syntax
which formulae belong to D and which to W we leave the distinction between D and
W implicit in this and all following examples for DL:

(1)   GERMAN(x): DRINKS-BEER(x)/DRINKS-BEER(x)

(2)   GERMAN(PETER)

We get exactly one extension, namely

            Th({GERMAN(PETER), DRINKS-BEER(PETER)}).

That this actually is an extension can easily be checked with the quasi-inductive definition. If we add the formulae

(3)   ∀x.EATS-PIZZA(x) ⊃ ¬DRINKS-BEER(x)

(4)   EATS-PIZZA(PETER)

then the single extension contains ¬DRINKS-BEER(PETER). Replacing (3) by the default

(3')   Eats-Pizza(x): ¬DRINKS-BEER(x)/¬DRINKS-BEER(x)

produces two extensions, one containing ¬DRINKS-BEER(PETER), the other one DRINKS-BEER(PETER).

Many of the results described in Chapter 2 for NML have also been proven for DL (Reiter 80). Theories without defaults have exactly one extension, namely Th(W). If W is inconsistent then the set of all formulae is the only extension. Extensions are (set inclusion) minimal, that is if E_1 and E_2 are extensions and $E_1 \subseteq E_2$ then $E_1 = E_2$. There are default theories with no, exactly one or multiple extensions. To see that there may be no extension at all consider the default theory (D,W) where D = {:p/¬p} and W is empty. Let S be an arbitrary set of formulae. If S does not contain ¬p then the default is applicable and Γ(S) contains ¬p. If S contains ¬p then the default is inapplicable and Γ(S) = Th(W). Since W is empty ¬p $\notin$ Γ(S). Hence in both cases S is not an extension.

We have already mentioned in Section 1.4 that Reiter interprets each extension as an acceptable set of beliefs. This credulous view is not necessarily combined with DL. We could use the extensions and simply define the theorems to be those formulae contained in all of them. DL is open in this respect, in contrast to circumscription where as we shall see in Chapter 4, the skeptical view is built into the logic, at least in its syntactic form.

Reiter did not define a semantics for his logic. It took seven years after the publication of Reiter's paper in the Artificial Intelligence Journal before a semantics was finally produced by Etherington (Etherington 87a) (Etherington 87b)[1]. The basic idea of his semantics is that defaults are used to define a preference relation on sets of standard first order models. This preference relation is used to rule out sets of models not 'admitted' by the defaults. Formally:

Definition 3.2: *Let* $\delta = (\alpha{:}\beta 1,...,\beta n/\omega)$ *be a default,* Γ_1 *and* Γ_2 *sets of models.* δ *prefers* Γ_1 *to* Γ_2 *(*$\Gamma_1 \geq_\delta \Gamma_2$*) iff*

(1) $\forall \gamma \in \Gamma_2. \gamma \models \alpha$,

(2) $\exists \gamma 1,...,\gamma n \in \Gamma_2. \gamma i \models \beta \iota$, and

(3) $\Gamma_1 = \Gamma_2 - \{\gamma \mid \gamma \models \neg \omega\}$.

For sets of defaults D the preference relation $\geq_D$ *is defined such that* $\Gamma_1 \geq_D \Gamma_2$ *iff* $\exists \delta \in D$ *such that* $\Gamma_1 \geq_\delta \Gamma_2$.

It is not difficult to see that, due to property (3), both relations are antisymmetric, that is Γ_1 R Γ_2 and Γ_2 R Γ_1 implies $\Gamma_1 = \Gamma_2$ for R $\in$ {$\geq_\delta$, $\geq_D$}. It can be shown that

---

[1] His approach is based on Lukaszewicz's definition of a semantics for normal default theories (Lukaszewicz 84).

for a *normal* default theory (D,W), where each default is of the form A:B/B, each
$\geq_D$-maximal set of models preferred to MOD(W) the set of all models of W, is
exactly the set of all models of an extension of (D,W) and vice versa. An example.
We assume our language consists of two propositional constants A, B, and we have
the default theory

> $(\{:B/B, :A/A\}, \{\neg A \lor \neg B\})$

Using (x,y) to represent the model where x and y are both true we get as models of
W the set

> $\{(A,\neg B), (\neg A, B), (\neg A,\neg B)\}$

From our first default we get

> $\{(\neg A,B)\} \geq_D \{(A,\neg B), (\neg A, B), (\neg A,\neg B)\}$

The model set $\{(\neg A,B)\}$ is maximal and corresponds to one extension. From our second default we get

> $\{(A,\neg B)\} \geq_D \{(A,\neg B), (\neg A, B), (\neg A,\neg B)\}$

which corresponds to the second extension.

For non-normal defaults the situation is somewhat more complex. Assume we have

> $(\{:\neg B/\neg B, :B/A\}, \{ \ \})$

then since W is empty we start from the set of all models

> $\{(A,B), (A,\neg B), (\neg A, B), (\neg A,\neg B)\}$

If we use the default :B/A we get

> $\{(A,B), (A,\neg B)\} \geq_D \{(A,B), (A,\neg B), (\neg A, B), (\neg A,\neg B)\}$

From the other default we get

> $\{(A,\neg B)\} \geq_D \{(A,B), (A,\neg B)\}$

and this new set containing one model cannot be further reduced. There is however,
no extension of the default theory containing A. The reason for the difficulty is that
the justification of a default used to establish the maximality of a set of models (here
:B/A) can be refuted by another default (here :¬B/¬B) used for the same purpose.
Therefore, we need the following additional condition of stability:

Definition 3.3: *Let* $\Delta=(D,W)$ *be a default theory,* Γ *a* $\geq_D$-*maximal set of models
such that* $\Gamma \geq_D MOD(W)$. Γ *is stable for* Δ *iff there is a* $D' \subseteq D$ *such that*

(1) $\Gamma \geq_{D'} MOD(W)$ and

(2)   for each $(\alpha: \beta1, ..., \beta n / \omega) \in D'$ there exist $\gamma 1, ..., \gamma n \in \Gamma$ such that $\gamma i \models \beta i$.

Stability guarantees that there exists a set of defaults, D', which is sufficient to
reduce the set of models of W to a $\geq_D$-maximal one and whose default justifications
are consistent with the resulting set of models. It is not difficult to see that the set of

models $\{(A,\neg B)\}$ in the last example is not stable. The single stable model set is $\{(A,\neg B), (\neg A,\neg B)\}$.

Etherington has demonstrated the soundness and completeness of DL with respect to this semantics, i.e. that the following theorem holds:

Proposition 3.2: *Γ is the set of all models of an extension of a default theory Δ iff Γ is stable for Δ.*

3.2: Which Defaults are Needed?

In his original paper (Reiter 80) Reiter was convinced that the only interesting defaults are *normal* defaults, which are defaults of the form

$\qquad$ A(x): B(x)/B(x)

where the single justification is equivalent to the consequent. Theories consisting only of such defaults (normal default theories) have nice computational properties. They always have extensions and if a normal default theory has an extension E and other normal defaults are added to the theory, then the new theory has an extension E' such that E' contains E (*semi-monotonicity*); in other words, new defaults can augment but never destroy previous extensions.

There are cases, however, where the use of normal defaults gives rise to unwanted extensions. Consider the following slight modification of an example from (Reiter, Criscuolo 81):

(1)   STUDENT(x):¬MARRIED(x)/¬MARRIED(x)   (3)   STUDENT(PETER)

(2)   ADULT(x):MARRIED(x)/MARRIED(x)   (4)   ADULT(PETER)

Defaults (1) and (2) clearly conflict. We get two extensions, one of them contains MARRIED, the other one ¬MARRIED. We probably want to give the more specific first default priority over the second one. What we need is a way of blocking the applicability of a default in certain circumstances, without explicitly asserting the negation of its justification. Reiter and Criscuolo propose to use *semi-normal* defaults of the form

$\qquad$ A(x): B(x) ∧ C(x)/C(x)

to avoid unwanted extensions. Generally, a default P:Q/R is semi-normal if its conclusion is implied by the single justification, i.e. if ⊦ (Q ⊃ R). This has the advantage that the default is guaranteed to be inapplicable whenever the negation of its conclusion has been derived. The same effect can also be achieved with a somewhat less restrictive form of defaults which are semi-normal with respect to W, the first order part of a default theory (D,W). We say a default is *semi-normal with respect to* W whenever W ⊦ (Q ⊃ R).

Generally, we can give a default d_1 priority over a conflicting default d_2 by adding the negation of d_1's prerequisite to the justification of d_2. In our example (2) can be represented as

(2') $\text{ADULT}(x) : \neg\text{STUDENT}(x) \wedge \text{MARRIED}(x)/\text{MARRIED}(x)$

Now we can only derive that an adult is married if we cannot derive that he is a student.

Our priority problem is solved with this representation but, the defaults do not look very natural if all situations where they should not be applied are explicitly mentioned in their justifications. Moreover, whenever additional knowledge requires blocking of a default, the default has to be rewritten.

A somewhat more elegant solution involves the introduction of names for defaults. It can be done by using logical constants as names which then allow us to reason explicitly about a default's applicability. For this purpose a standard predicate can be used, say APPL for 'applicable'. More precisely we need a set of predicates APPL_i, where i is the number of free variables, the 'arity' of the default. For sake of simplicity this index is left implicit. This technique was first suggested by McDermott (McDermott 82).

Let us introduce the constant R_1 to denote the above default. We can rerepresent it as follows:

(2'a) $\text{ADULT}(x): \text{APPL}(R_1,x) \wedge \text{MARRIED}(x)/\text{MARRIED}(x)$

Now we can use simple logical implications to block the applicability of this default; in our case the blocking formula is

(BF) $\forall x.\text{STUDENT}(x) \supset \neg\text{APPL}(R_1,x)$

With this representation the unwanted extension disappears. In the example, since Peter is a student, $\text{APPL}(R_1,\text{PETER})$ cannot consistently be assumed, i.e. R_1 is blocked. If we later learn about other situations in which the default has to be blocked, it can be done without changing the default. We only have to add new formulae containing information about (non-) applicability of the default.

A naming technique similar to the one discussed here has independently been used by Poole (Poole 88), see Section 5.1. He uses predicates as names; instead of $\text{APPL}(R_k,x)$ he writes $R_k(x)$. The advantage of using constants is that we can reason about the defaults in the logic and not just express the fact that they are applicable. We can, for instance, define classes of defaults and block all defaults belonging to a certain class in specific circumstances.

As we show in Section 3.4 the expressiveness of semi-normal defaults partly rests upon the fact that the logic is not semi-monotonic. Semi-monotonicity guarantees that a default applied to generate an extension of (D,W) remains applicable in an extension of (D ∪ D', W), that is adding defaults can never make applicable defaults inapplicable in all extensions. But this is what is needed to represent priorities adequately.

Contrary to other authors, e.g. (Lukaszewicz 88), we therefore do not see semi-monotonicity as a desirable property unless the idea of coding priorities into the defaults is given up. And in the latter case normal defaults seem to be sufficient. We return to this topic in Section 3.4.

It must be mentioned that semi-normal defaults introduce the danger of 'odd loops', i.e. cases where the consequent of a default conflicts - possibly via a long chain of derivations - with its own justification. In other words, the existence of extensions of semi-normal default theories is not guaranteed. A simple example is the following one (Reiter, Criscuolo 81):

(1) $: A \wedge \neg B / \neg B$

(2) $: B \wedge \neg C / \neg C$

(3) $: C \wedge \neg A / \neg A$

The use of semi-normal defaults was motivated by the need to represent priorities. There are other possible ways to achieve this. Instead of coding priorities into the defaults we can take the idea underlying prioritized circumscription (Section 4.4) and apply it to default logic, defining an iterated version; prioritized default logic (PDL).

Definition 3.4: *Let Di (i=1,...,n) be sets of defaults, W a set of formulae. E is a PDL-extension of T = (D1,...,Dn,W) iff there exist sets of formulae E1,...,En such that*

> *E1 is an extension of (D1,W)*

> *E2 is an extension of (D2, E1)*

> ...

> *E = En is an extension of (Dn, En-1).*

We omit the 'PDL' when it is clear from context that a PDL-extension is meant. In this definition defaults in Di have higher priority than those in Dj if i<j. Every 'layer' of defaults in a default theory can produce multiple extensions, each extension can be used as basis for the generation of extensions in the next layer, giving us a tree with W as root and where every son of a node is a DL-extension of its father and the leaves are PDL-extensions. Now we can state priorities, but we are not forced to do so, as was the case with HAEL (Section 2.3) where missing priorities between defaults led to an inconsistency.

Assume we represent the Nixon example as follows:

> D1 = {REP: ¬PAC/¬PAC}

> D2 = {QUA: PAC/PAC}

> W = {REP, QUA}

Then we get E1=Th({REP, QUA, ¬PAC}) and E2 = E = E1, i.e. we have assigned higher priority to the default 'republicans are not pacifists'.

It should be noted that the definition of PDL-extensions works as intended only if (1) all defaults are normal, and (2) no prerequisite of a default with higher priority is derived in a later level.

If we allow general defaults it may be the case that we derive formulae in a later layer that are inconsistent with the justification of a default that has been applied in an earlier layer. This means that a PDL-extension is not necessarily a DL-extension of the default theory (D1 ∪ ... ∪ Dn, W). Fortunately, since we have other means of expressing priorities now, normal defaults seem sufficient for most practical applications.

But even with normal defaults a problem arises; if a prerequisite of a default d with priority i can be derived in a later layer j then this default, according to our definition, is never applied. These problems disappear for defaults of the form :p/p, that is normal defaults without prerequisite. Some authors call such defaults supernormal. We shall see in Chapter 5 that Poole's approach to default reasoning is equivalent to the use of default logic restricted to this type of defaults. The expressiveness of his simple framework is astonishing and makes it interesting enough to consider the possibility of introducing priorities to supernormal defaults.

3.3: The Relation Between DL and AEL

At a first view DL seems to be much less expressive than AEL since there is no possibility of nesting defaults in DL. We cannot write defaults whose consequents are themselves defaults for instance, or derive defaults from some other formulae since defaults are not part of the language.

Konolige (Konolige 88a) has shown however that, surprisingly, AEL and DL are equivalent. The term *equivalent* here has to be read with some caveats in mind. It means that the extensions of a default theory are exactly the first order part, that is the formulae not containing L, of a *certain class* of AEL extensions, the strongly grounded extensions. The notion of strong groundedness guarantees that every ordinary sentence ϕ has a derivation that does not depend on $L\phi$. It turns out that the definition in (Konolige 88a, p. 360) leads to counterexamples. One such counterexample is to be found in (Marek, Truszczynski 89). We use in this section Konolige's corrected definition (Konolige, personal communication).

Konolige first shows that every AEL theory can be represented equivalently in a normal form where all sentences have the form

$$\neg L\alpha \lor L\beta 1 \lor ... \lor L\beta n \lor \omega$$

where α, $\beta 1$, ..., βn, ω do not contain a modal operator ($\neg L\alpha$ or/and $L\beta i$ may be missing). Such a formula is represented as the default α: ¬β1,..., ¬βn / ω

and vice versa. AEL formulae not containing L become members of W in the default theory. If ¬Lα is missing TRUE becomes the prerequisite. It should be noted that the default representation we used in Chapter 2

GERMAN(PETER) ∧ ¬L¬DRINKS-BEER(PETER) ⊃ DRINKS-BEER(PETER)

becomes in the translation

: DRINKS-BEER(PETER) / GERMAN(PETER) ⊃ DRINKS-BEER(PETER)

The defaults corresponding to the standard DL defaults with prerequisites are of the form

LGERMAN(PETER) ∧ ¬L¬DRINKS-BEER(PETER) ⊃ DRINKS-BEER(PETER)

The main difference between these two types of defaults is that the first one allows for indirect forms of contraposition whereas the second does not. In both cases we cannot derive ¬GERMAN(PETER) given ¬DRINKS-BEER(PETER). In some more complicated cases however we get different results. Compare for instance

(1)   : DRINKS-BEER(PETER) / GERMAN(PETER) ⊃ DRINKS-BEER(PETER)

(2)   : DRINKS-WINE(PETER) / ITALIAN(PETER) ⊃ DRINKS-WINE(PETER)

with

(1')   GERMAN(PETER) : DRINKS-BEER(PETER) / DRINKS-BEER(PETER)

(2')   ITALIAN(PETER) : DRINKS-WINE(PETER) / DRINKS-WINE(PETER)

If additionally ¬DRINKS-BEER(PETER) v ¬DRINKS-WINE(PETER) is given, then with the first pair of defaults we obtain ¬GERMAN(PETER) v ¬ITALIAN(PETER). This conclusion cannot be obtained using the second pair of defaults.

We shall next present Konolige's corrected definition of strongly grounded AEL extensions:

Definition 3.5: *Let A be a set of AEL sentences in normal form, and let T be an extension of A. Let A' be the set of sentences ¬Lα v Lβ1 v ... v Lβn v ω of A such that none of β1 ... βn is contained in T. Then T is strongly grounded in A iff*

$$T = \{p \mid A' \cup LA' \cup \neg L T_0 \models_{SS} p\}$$

As defined in Section 2.2 LA' denotes the set of formulae {Lp | p ∈ A'}, ¬LT_0 the set {¬Lp | p ∉ T and ordinary}. ⊨SS stands for entailment with the restriction of modal indices to stable sets (see Section 2.2).

With this definition Konolige was able to prove:

Theorem 3.3: *For any set of sentences A of AEL, there is an effectively constructible default theory (W, D), and vice versa, for every default theory (D, W) there is an effectively constructible set of sentences A of AEL, such that E is a default extension of (W, D) iff it is the first order subset of a strongly grounded extension of A.*

Note that the possibility of multiple justifications in a DL-default is required for this result. In a recent paper (Reiter 87b) Reiter restricted DL to defaults with exactly one justification. With this restriction the equivalence does no longer hold, since a formula having more than one unnegated modal disjunct Lβi in its normal form cannot be translated. Konolige handled the case where the normal form of a formula does not contain any disjunct Lβ separately by introducing an extended normal form. If we admit defaults with no justification then this is not necessary. We shall argue in Chapter 9 that such defaults are useful all the same.

In a more recent paper (Marek, Truszczynski 89) the opposite way of obtaining equivalence has also been explored; instead of strengthening the notion of AEL extension the notion of DL extension can be weakened. This leads to similar equivalence results. See the original paper for the details.

3.4: Cumulative Default Logic

Many commonsense examples can be handled adequately in DL. There are however, some cases discussed in the literature where DL does not produce the expected answers. Poole gives the following example (Poole 89):

(1)   :USABLE(X) $\wedge$ $\neg$BROKEN(X)/USABLE(X)

(2)   BROKEN(LEFTARM) v Broken(RIGHTARM)

This default theory has exactly one extension containing both USABLE(RIGHTARM) and USABLE(LEFTARM) although we know that at least one of the arms is broken. The reason is that there is nothing in the definition of extensions which forces the justifications of all applied defaults to be consistent with each other and with what is believed. The result is conclusions which are too strong. This problem arises in the case of non-normal defaults only, i.e. defaults where the justification is not equivalent to the consequent.

Some readers may argue against the example that implicit knowledge is not made explicit here: if we add the information

(3) $\forall$X.BROKEN(X) $\supset$ $\neg$USABLE(X)

then of course two extensions are generated, as intended. In this case non-normal defaults are not needed at all and we can simply replace (1) by the normal default :USABLE(X)/USABLE(X). This type of 'hard' exceptions to a default, i.e. exceptions for which the negation of the default's consequent can be proven, are handled by normal defaults without any problem.

The basic assumption underlying the broken-arms example, however, is that (3) does i hold: we want to make (1) inapplicable if we know that a given x is broken, but without stating that x is not usable in this case. This is a weaker type of exception to a default: we want to block a default but we do not assert the negation of its consequent.

Such weak exceptions have also been used in Section 3.2 for representing priorities. To express this type of exceptions only, non-normal defaults are needed and the above-mentioned problem arises. Given this intended use of non-normal defaults it seems unreasonable to conclude that both arms are usable in the above example. We agree absolutely with Poole here who writes (Poole 89, p. 334):

I would argue that this is definitely a bug, being able to conclude both arms are usable given we know one of his arms is broken. The problem is we have implicitly made an assumption, but have been prevented from considering what other assumptions we made as a side effect of this assumption.

A second problem, probably even more serious, has been pointed out by David Makinson (Makinson 89). He studied general properties of nonmonotonic inference relations. One of the properties an inference relation, even a nonmonotonic one, is usually expected to have is cumulativity. Cumulativity means that adding a theorem of a set of premises to the premises does not change the derivable formulae. More formally cumulativity can be expressed as the condition:

If $W \mid\sim y$ then $W \mid\sim x$ iff $W \cup \{y\} \mid\sim x$.

$\mid\sim$ here denotes an arbitrary, possibly nonmonotonic, inference relation. This usual formulation of the cumulativity condition is adequate for default logic only if the skeptical notion of derivability is used. For the arbitrary choice notion of derivability where each extension is considered as a possible belief set we need a reformulation. Assume a default theory has an extension containing a formula y. Adding y to W certainly should give us all former extensions containing y, but it also should not produce any new extensions. The natural formulation of choice cumulativity therefore is:

If there is at least one extension of $A = (D,W)$ containing y, then E is an extension of A containing y iff E is an extension of $A' = (D,W \cup \{y\})$.

Note that cumulativity in the choice sense implies skeptical cumulativity if the existence of extensions is guaranteed.

It turns out that Reiter's default logic is not cumulative, neither in the skeptical nor in the choice sense. Makinson gives the following example:

(1) :p/p   (2) p v q: ¬p/¬p

From these defaults (W={}) we get the single extension Th({p}). This extension clearly contains p v q. But adding p v q to the premises gives rise to an additional extension Th({¬p, q}).

Let us first discuss a similar, but less abstract example to understand better what is happening here. Take the following example:

(1) DOG v BIRD⊃ PET   (4) Sings : BIRD/ BIRD

(2) DOG ⊃ ¬ BIRD   (5) Sings

(3) PET : DOG/ DOG

From this default theory we obtain the single extension Th(W $\cup$ {BIRD}). This extension contains PET. Adding PET to the premises however, makes (3) applicable and gives rise to an additional extension where the object is a DOG.

Why was this default not applicable before? The only reason to believe PET was that BIRD was believed. This, of course, is inconsistent with DOG. If we add PET to the premises this implicit information is lost. Now there might be independent information that PET is true. It is far from obvious that these cases actually should yield the same results if the reasons for believing something are taken into account. Default logic distinguishes these cases and hence is more a logic of reasoned belief than just plain belief. It turns out that cumulativity of a version of default logic can be obtained if this implicit reasoning about reasons is made explicit.[2]

We shall now define cumulative default logic, CDL, a new version of default logic. Instead of simple first order formulae this logic will use more complicated structures, called assertions, which contain the justifications and consequents of defaults used to derive a belief. This allows us to distinguish between believing PET because BIRD is consistent, and hence believed, and just believing PET independently. Moreover, since the consistency conditions are part of the formulae the applicability condition can easily be strengthened to handle mutually inconsistent justifications adequately.

Definition 3.6: *Let* $p, r_1, ..., r_n$ *be first order formulae.* $<p:\{r_1,...,r_n\}>$ *is called an assertion, and* $\{r_1,...,r_n\}$ *the support of this assertion.*

The intuitive meaning of the assertion is as follows: p is believed, since $r_1 \wedge ... \wedge r_n$ is consistent with what is believed and the consistency conditions of other believed formulae.

Definition 3.7: *Let W be a set of assertions.*

Form(W), the asserted formulae of W, is the set $\{p \mid <p:\{r_1,...,r_n\}> \in W\}$.
Supp(W), the support of W, is the set $\{r \mid <p:\{r_1,..., r , r_n\}> \in W\}$.

Definition 3.8: *An assertion default theory is a pair (D,W), where D is a set of defaults in the sense of Reiter, and W is a set of assertions.*

We shall also speak simply of a default theory if it is clear from the context that we mean an assertion default theory. As the next step the classical inference relation of first order logic has to be extended to assertions in an obvious way:

Definition 3.9: *Let A be a set of assertions.* $Th_s(A)$, *the supported theorems of A, are the smallest set of assertions such that*

(1) $A \subseteq Th_s(A)$,

---

[2] There certainly is an argument for preferring default (4) to (3) in this example even if there is independent information that Pet is true. (4) is more specific than (3) since singers are typically birds, and birds are pets. The idea of preferring the most specific information is missing from default logic and the other nonmonotonic formalisms discussed in Chapters 2-5. This idea plays a major role in our discussion of inheritance systems (Chapter 8).

(2)   if <p₁:J₁>, ..., <pₖ :Jₖ> ∈ Thₛ(A) and p₁, ..., pₖ |- q,

then <q:J₁ ∪ ... ∪Jₖ> ∈ Thₛ(A).

|- here stands for classical derivability in first order logic. When it is clear from the context that A is a set of assertions we shall omit the index from Thₛ. We are now in a position to define the extensions of a default theory:

Definition 3.10: *An extension of an assertion default theory (D,W) is a fixed point of the operator Γ which, given a set of assertions S, produces the smallest set of assertions S' such that*

(1)   W ⊆ S',

(2)   S' is deductively closed, i.e. Thₛ(S') = S',

(3)   if A:B₁,...,Bₙ/C ∈ D, <A:{J₁,...,Jₖ}> ∈ S', and {B₁,...,Bₙ,C} ∪ Form(S) ∪ Supp(S) is consistent, then <C:{J₁,...,Jₖ,B₁,...,Bₙ,C}> ∈ S'.

There are two differences between Reiter's original logic and our modified version:

(1)   In every derivation of an asserted formula the justification and the consequent of every default needed for the derivation are recorded,

(2)   The applicability condition for a default requires its justification and its consequent to be consistent not only with what is believed but also with the support of believed formulae, i.e. the set of justifications and consequents of all other applied defaults.

We shall first show that the earlier examples are handled correctly in the new logic.

It is not difficult to see that the broken-arms example yields the desired results. Let us assume that BROKEN(LEFTARM) v BROKEN(RIGHTARM) is believed for no further reason, i.e. with empty support. The example becomes

(1)   :USABLE(x) ∧ ¬BROKEN(x)/USABLE(x)

(2)   BROKEN(LEFTARM) v BROKEN(RIGHTARM):{ }

We get two extensions. One extension contains

<USABLE(LEFTARM):{USABLE(LEFTARM) ∧ ¬BROKEN(LEFTARM)}>. [3]

The support of this formula blocks the application of the default instance with x=RIGHTARM since ¬BROKEN(RIGHTARM) is not consistent with the support of the above formula and BROKEN(LEFTARM) v BROKEN(RIGHTARM).

The other extension contains

<USABLE(RIGHTARM):{USABLE(RIGHTARM) ∧ ¬BROKEN(RIGHTARM)}>.

For similar reasons the default instance with x=LEFTARM is blocked in this case. As intended in none of the extensions both arms are usable.

Here is the new version of the pet example:

---

[3] We omit subsumed formulae from supports.

(1)   <DOG ∨ BIRD⊃ PET:{ }>   (4)   SINGS: BIRD/ BIRD

(2)   <DOG ⊃ ¬ BIRD:{ }>   (5)   <SINGS:{ }>

(3)   PET: DOG / DOG

We derive <BIRD:{BIRD}> and, via (1), <PET:{BIRD}>. Adding this last formula to the premises no longer makes default (3) applicable, as was the case in the original version of DL, since DOG is inconsistent with BIRD. On the other hand, adding <PET:{ }>, which is not a theorem of the former theory, to the premises in fact changes the results. This is reasonable since the premises now state that the object at hand is a PET independent from being a BIRD.

The question might arise why in CDL justifications *and* consequents of applied defaults are recorded. It is obvious that we need the default justifications since we want their joint consistency, but do we also need the consequents? The answer is yes. It turns out that this is necessary to give us the desired cumulativity. Assume we would change condition (3) in Definition 3.10 in such a way that only default justifications become part of an assertion. The following simple example shows non-cumulativity of this modification:

(1)   TRUE: TRUE / p

(2)   p ∨ q: ¬p / ¬p

With the above modification this default theory has one extension containing <p:{ }> and hence <p ∨ q:{ }>. However, adding this last formula to the premises leads to an extension containing <¬p:{ }>. This shows that it is necessary to record consequents as in our Definition 3.10. In CDL <p ∨ q:{p}> is contained in the single extension, and adding this formula causes no problem.

It should be noted that with our definition of CDL-extensions it makes no difference whether two formulae A and B or their conjunction A ∧ B are contained in the support of a formula. This observation and the fact that consequents of defaults are part of the generated supports of formulae show that all defaults implicitly become semi-normal. A default A:B/C can equivalently be replaced by A:B∧C/C, or the other way around, a normal default A:B/B can be replaced by A:TRUE/B.

We now present some formal results about CDL, in particular that the logic deserves its name. All proofs are to be found in (Brewka 90a). We shall first define an interesting subclass of assertion default theories and prove two useful lemmata:

Definition 3.11: *An assertion default theory (D,W) is well based iff Form(W) ∪ Supp(W) is consistent.*

Lemma 3.1: *Let Δ = (D,W) be a well based assertion default theory and E an extension of Δ. Then Form(E) ∪ Supp(E) is consistent.*

Lemma 3.2: *Let $\Delta = (D,W)$ be a well based assertion default theory. Let E be an extension of Δ containing $<p:J>$. Then $\Delta' = (D,W \cup \{<p:J>\})$ is a well based assertion default theory.*

The first proposition provides us with a quasi-inductive characterization of CDL similar to the one of Proposition 3.1.

Proposition 3.4: *E is a CDL-extension of an assertion default theory (D,W) iff*

$$E = \bigcup_{i=0}^{\infty} E_i \text{ where}$$

$E_0 = W, \text{ and for } i \geq 0$

$E_{i+1} = Th_s(E_i) \cup \{<C:\{J_1,...,J_k,B_1,...,B_n,C\}> \mid$
$\qquad A:B_1,...,B_n/C \in D, <A:\{J_1,...,J_k\}> \in E_i,$
$\qquad \text{and } \{B_1,...,B_n,C\} \cup Form(E) \cup Supp(E) \text{ is consistent}\}.$

The next proposition shows that the results of CDL and DL are equivalent (modulo supports) if all defaults are normal, i.e. of the form A:B/B, and if all formulae in W have empty supports.

Proposition 3.5: *Let D be a set of normal defaults and W a set of assertions with empty supports. If E is a CDL-extension of (D,W) then Form(E) is a DL-extension of (D, Form(W)). Vice versa, if E' is a DL-extension of (D, Form(W)) then there exists a CDL-extension E of (D,W) such that Form(E) = E'.*

The last proposition can be seen as a partial 'rehabilitation' of Reiter's logic. Another property of CDL is semi-monotonicity.

Proposition 3.6: *CDL is semi-monotonic, i.e. for every extension E' of an arbitrary assertion default theory (D',W) and every set of defaults D such that $D' \subseteq D$ there exists an extension E of (D,W) such that $E' \subseteq E$.*

The existence of extensions is an immediate consequence of Proposition 3.6. since all assertion default theories (D, W) with empty D obviously have an extension, namely $Th_S(W)$.

Proposition 3.7: *Every CDL default theory has an extension.*

We now present our main result; CDL actually is cumulative.

Proposition 3.8: *If there is at least one extension F of (D,W) containing $<p:J>$, then E is a CDL-extension of (D,W) containing $<p:J>$ iff E is a CDL-extension of (D, W $\cup$ $\{<p:J>\}$).*

In the rest of this section we shall argue that semi-monotonicity is not a desired property from the representational point of view. As discussed in Section 3.2 semi-normal defaults are needed to represent priorities between defaults, but part of this expressiveness is destroyed if the logic is semi-monotonic. Consider a slightly extended version of the student example from Section 3.2:

(1)   STUDENTMARRIED $(x):\neg$MARRIED$(x)/\neg$MARRIED(x)

(2)   ADULT(x):MARRIED(x) ∧ ¬STUDENT (x)/MARRIED(x)

(3)   BEARD(x):STUDENT (x)/STUDENT (x)

(4)   BEARD(x):ADULT(x)/ADULT(x)

(5)   BEARD(PETER)

CDL generates two extensions in this case. Since the justification of (2) can block (3) from being applied we obtain an extension where PETER is not a student, and hence married. Our representation of a priority between two defaults which makes the prerequisite of the preferred default a weak exception of the other one fails since it affects a default used to derive the weak exception. The basic reason for this is the semi-monotonicity of CDL. If we want to give the student default (1) priority over the adult default (2) even if STUDENT is derived by another default (3), then (3) must override (2) and not vice versa. Semi-monotonicity just means that this is impossible. (Note that to obtain the 'representational' priority of (1) over (2) default (3) must have 'technical' priority over (2')).

In other words, CDL destroys part of the additional expressiveness of semi-normal defaults. Can CDL be changed in a way such that this problem is avoided? The answer is yes. What we have to do is consider only some of the generated extensions, those respecting the intended priorities. If, for example, we have defaults :B/B and :¬B∧C/C, then we are interested only in the extension containing B, i.e. we expect the logic to behave more like DL in this case. To achieve this we have to treat consequents and justifications differently. If there is a default d inapplicable with respect to an extension E, but only because its consequent contradicts the justifications of applied defaults, then we know that the default d should have been applied and we reject E. This motivates the following definitions:

Definition 3.11: *Let E be a CDL-extension of (D,W). GD(E), the set of generating defaults of E, is the set*

$$\{A:B_1,...,B_n/C \in D \mid A \in Form(E), \{B_1,...,B_n,C\} \cup Form(E) \cup Just(E) \text{ consistent}\}.$$

Definition 3.12: *Let E be a CDL-extension of (D,W). E is called priority-preserving if for no $A:B_1,...,B_n/C \in D\backslash GD(E)$: $A \in Form(E)$, $\{B_1, ..., B_n, C\} \cup Form(E)$ is consistent, and $\{C\} \cup Form(E) \cup Supp(E)$ is inconsistent.*

If we only consider priority-preserving extensions then the student example yields the desired results. The extension with generating defaults {(4), (2)} is not priority-preserving. Default (3) was not applied in this extension, but for one reason only; its consequent is inconsistent with the justification of (2). Therefore the extension is rejected.

The other fixed point generated by {(4), (3), (1)} is priority-preserving and we derive <¬MARRIED(PETER):{STUDENT(PETER),¬MARRIED(PETER)}> as intended.

This shows that priorities can be expressed in the way proposed by Reiter. In this respect CDL$_F$, i.e. CDL with the additional filter on extensions, is closer to Reiter's original logic than CDL without filter. On the other hand, since all CDL$_F$-extensions are CDL extensions, we keep the property of joint consistency of justifications, that is DL and CDL$_F$ still differ in their treatment of the broken-arms example.

As the example shows CDL$_F$ is not semi-monotonic. Moreover, the existence of priority-preserving extensions is not guaranteed. Consider as an example the assertion default theory $(\{B{:}A/A, :{\neg}A{\wedge}B/B\}, \{\})$ which has the single non-priority-preserving CDL-extension Th($\{<B{:}\{\neg A{\wedge}B\}>\}$). This is the price we have to pay if we want to use semi-normal defaults to represent priorities. Proposition 3.5 still holds since the property of being priority-preserving trivially holds for all extensions of normal theories: If E is an extension of a normal default theory then Form(E) $\cup$ Supp(E) = Form(E) and hence the consequent of a default cannot at the same time be consistent with Form(E) but inconsistent with Form(E) $\cup$ Supp(E).

Let us conclude this section with the discussion of some related work. Lukaszewicz (Lukaszewicz 88) recently presented a modified version of DL. His logic is based on a two-place fixed point operator. The second argument of the operator is used to keep track of justifications of applied defaults. Lukaszewicz describes his applicability criterion for defaults as follows (Lukaszewicz 88, p.3):

If the prerequisite of a default is believed (its justification is consistent with what is believed), and adding its consequent to the set of beliefs neither leads to inconsistency nor contradicts the justification of this or any other already applied default, then the consequent of the default is to be believed.

It is not difficult to see why this applicability condition fails to handle the broken arms example correctly. Lukaszewicz is concerned only with conflicts between a consequent and a justification, not with conflicts between justifications. We argued above that the consequent should win in this case. His applicability condition is too weak to guarantee consistency between the justifications of all applied defaults. Moreover, his logic is semi-monotonic. Lukaszewicz does not consider this as a problem, however, and hence has lost part of the additional expressiveness of non-normal defaults. Cumulativity is not discussed in his paper.

Since we had to make the justifications used for derivations explicit in order to obtain cumulativity we did not need a second argument for the fixed point operator in our approach. With a stronger applicability condition we were able to define a cumulative default logic which handles the problem of inconsistent justifications adequately. CDL also turned out to be semi-monotonic, but the full ability to represent priorities between defaults was restored by filtering out some of the generated extensions, those preserving the intended priorities.[4]

---

[4] There is an interesting relation between our two-step definition of priority preserving extensions and some recent approaches to make de Kleer's ATMS (Chapter 9) nonmonotonic (Dressler 89), (Junker 89). Both authors encode defaults

Our main concern in this section was to show that the basic idea underlying default logic, the representation of defaults as nonstandard inference rules, is not undermined by some recent criticisms. Default logic should be seen as a logic of reasoned plausible belief. If this is made explicit, then the logic can be made cumulative and the 'misbehaviour' of DL disappears.[5]

---

with explicit Out-assumptions. The resulting ATMS labelings correspond to extensions of the underlying default theory. As in CDL there are too many extensions generated this way and an additional test checks, among other things, whether priority is preserved or not. This test clearly corresponds to our priority criterion. It is a topic of further research whether the existing nonmonotonic ATMS can be modified such that they can be used for computing CDL-extensions.

[5] For a more detailed introduction to default logic see (Besnard 89).

CHAPTER 4: CIRCUMSCRIPTION

Circumscription, a formalization of nonmonotonic reasoning introduced by John McCarthy and further developed mainly by Vladimir Lifschitz, is quite different from the logics described so far. Instead of extending the logical language or adding nonmonotonic inference rules McCarthy defines the formulae nonmonotonically derivable from a set of premises as the set of formulae monotonically derivable from a certain superset of the premises. The nonmonotonicity arises from the fact that the (set of) formula(e) added to the premises depends on the premises, that is what is added to P is different from what is added to a superset of P.

Circumscription allows the set of objects for which a predicate (or a formula) holds to be minimized in certain ways. From the semantic point of view this corresponds to disregarding certain models, namely those which are not minimal in a specific sense. As mentioned in Section 1.4 we restrict our presentation to predicate, variable and prioritized circumscription. The other variants proposed in the literature seem more experimental. Formula circumscription as described in (McCarthy 84) is not described here since, as McCarthy himself has suggested, the ability to minimize arbitrary predicate expressions is inessential. We can always define predicates equivalent to the predicate expressions and minimize them instead.

Different versions of circumscription have been defined either in terms of a first order schema, e.g. (McCarthy 80), or in terms of a second order formula, e.g. (McCarthy 84). We follow the presentations in the original papers and describe predicate circumscription in first order, and variable and prioritized circumscription in second order form. Second order logic is not very popular among AI researchers because it is more difficult to implement systems based on it. In fact, there is provably no sound and complete proof procedure for second order logic. However, its additional expressiveness which allows more general conclusions, not restricted to predicates for which symbols in the logical language exist, is needed to fully capture the semantics of circumscription. The second order versions of circumscription are complete with respect to their semantics, the first order versions are not (Lifschitz 85b). Soundness and completeness here is to be read in the sense that the models of the premises A together with the circumscription axiom are exactly the minimal models of the premises A alone.

This kind of completeness is the reason why the second order approach is commonly favoured. But see (Perlis, Minker 86) for a different view. For an introduction to second order logic see (Benthem, Doets 83).

4.1: Predicate Circumscription

There are predicates which typically do not hold for objects. Take as an example the predicate red-haired. Not many people have red hair. It, therefore, might be reasonable to assume that people do not belong to the class of red-haired objects as long as there is no information to the contrary. For this purpose we need a technique that allows us to derive that the objects which are provably red-haired are the *only* red-haired objects.

Semantically, we can model such a minimization of the extension of a predicate if we do not, as usual, use *all* models to define entailment, but instead a certain subset of the models. In our example we might want to consider only models with the smallest possible extension for the predicate red-haired.

Generally we can define a partial ordering on the models of a set of first order premises A depending on the predicate P to be minimized. The models under consideration are first order models where the domain is the set of individuals and where predicates are represented by their extensions. The ordering can be defined as follows:

Definition 4.1: *Let A be a set of formulae and M and N models of A. M $\leq_P$ N iff*

(1)   M and N have the same domain,

(2)   all predicate symbols of A besides P have the same extensions in M and N,

(3)   the extension of P in M is contained in its extension in N.

We say M is $\leq_P$-*minimal* iff for all M': M' $\leq_P$ M => M' = M.

Based on the minimal models we can define a new notion of entailment:

Definition 4.2: *A set of premises A minimally entails q (with respect to P) iff q holds in all $\leq_P$-minimal models of A.*

Take as an example the set of premises

$$A_1 = \{\text{MARY} \neq \text{PETER, RED-HAIRED(MARY)}\}$$

There are certainly models of A_1 in which RED-HAIRED is true for PETER. But for all of them smaller models (with respect to $\leq_{\text{RED-HAIRED}}$) can be found. Hence ¬RED-HAIRED(PETER) is minimally entailed by the premises (with respect to RED-HAIRED).

It is interesting to compare this minimal entailment semantics with the semantics defined by Etherington for DL (Section 3.1). As observed by him (Etherington 87a, p. 497f) there are three main differences. Firstly, rather than an ordering on sets of models we have in minimal entailment semantics an ordering on individual models. Secondly, instead of defining the ordering in terms of accessability via a default it is defined in terms of general criteria and intrinsic features of the models. And finally, the definition of minimal entailment is based on all minimal models, whereas in Etherington's semantics each single extremum of his ordering corresponds to an extension.

The question now is: How can the minimally entailed formulae be characterized syntactically? In predicate circumscription (McCarthy 80) this is achieved by augmenting the premises in a specific way. The additional premises eliminate the uninteresting models. The nonmonotonic theorems of a set of premises A are defined to be the classical theorems of A » X. The choice of the right X guarantees that only minimal models of A are models of A » X.

Definition 4.3: *Let A be a first order formula (i.e. the conjunction of the premises) containing an n-place predicate symbol P. Let A(ϕ) be the result of replacing all occurrences of P in A by the predicate parameter ϕ. The predicate circumscription of P in A is the sentence schema*

$$A(\phi) \wedge (\forall x.\phi(x) \supset P(x)) \supset (\forall x.P(x) \supset \phi(x))$$

where $x = x_1,...,x_n$.

All instances of this schema together with A can be used for derivations. The predicate parameter in the schema can be replaced by any predicate expression with 'arity' n, i.e. by any formula possibly containing free variables (the arguments of ϕ have to be substituted for free variables during instantiation accordingly). More precisely, we note predicate expressions as usual in the form of lambda expressions:

$$\lambda x_1, ..., x_n.F$$

where F is an arbitrary formula. $\lambda x_1, ..., x_n.F(arg_1, ..., arg_n)$ then represents the expression obtained when all occurrences of the x_i ($i \in \{1,...,n\}$) in F are replaced by arg_i. It has been shown (Besnard et al. 89) that it is necessary to allow predicate expressions containing more than n free variables to be substituted for the parameter in the circumscription schema, and that it must be possible to use the circumscribed predicate P in the substituted predicate expression.

The interesting case is an instance of the schema with true antecedents. The first antecedent then guarantees that everything that has been said about P in A also holds for the substituted predicate. The second antecedent guarantees that only those objects which can be proven to be P belong to the extension of the substituted predicate. In this case the instance of the circumscription schema allows us to derive that P is equivalent to the substituted predicate.

Predicate circumscription of RED-HAIRED in our example gives the following schema:

$$\text{MARY} \neq \text{PETER} \wedge \phi(\text{MARY}) \wedge$$

$$(\forall x.\phi(x) \supset \text{RED-HAIRED}(x))$$

$$\supset$$

$$(\forall x.\text{RED-HAIRED}(x) \supset \phi(x))$$

Substituting for ϕ the expression $\lambda x.x=\text{MARY}$ and applying the lambda expression, which means replacing the x by ϕ's argument in each case, yields:

$$\text{MARY} \neq \text{PETER} \wedge (\text{MARY} = \text{MARY}) \wedge$$

$$(\forall x.(x=\text{MARY}) \supset \text{RED-HAIRED}(x))$$

$$\supset$$

$$(\forall x.\text{RED-HAIRED}(x) \supset (x=\text{MARY}))$$

It follows from the premises A_1 that the antecedents of the implication hold and we can derive:

$$(\forall x.\text{RED-HAIRED}(x) \supset (x=\text{MARY}))$$

We have derived that Mary is the only object for which the predicate RED-HAIRED holds. Together with PETER $\neq$ MARY we get as we intended $\neg$RED-HAIRED(PETER).

Here is another example taken from (McCarthy 80):

$$T = \text{ISBLOCK}(A) \wedge \text{ISBLOCK}(B) \wedge \text{ISBLOCK}(C)$$

Predicate circumscription of ISBLOCK in T yields the schema

$$\phi(A) \wedge \phi(B) \wedge \phi(C) \wedge (\forall x.\phi(x) \supset \text{ISBLOCK}(x)) \supset (\forall x.\text{ISBLOCK}(x)\supset\phi(x))$$

If we substitute for ϕ the expression $\lambda x.(x=A \vee x=B \vee x=C)$, then we get

$$(A=A \vee A=B \vee A=C) \wedge$$

$$(B=A \vee B=B \vee B=C) \wedge$$

$$(C=A \vee C=B \vee C=C) \wedge$$

$$(\forall x.(x=A \vee x=B \vee x=C) \supset \text{ISBLOCK}(x))$$

$$\supset$$

$$(\forall x.\text{ISBLOCK}(x)\supset(x=A \vee x=B \vee x=C))$$

It follows from T that the antecedents are true and we get

$$\forall x.\text{ISBLOCK}(x) \supset (x=A \vee x=B \vee x=C)$$

We have been able to derive that A, B and C are the only blocks. If we add the premise that D is also a block, we get

$$T' = \text{ISBLOCK}(A) \wedge \text{ISBLOCK}(B) \wedge \text{ISBLOCK}(C) \wedge \text{ISBLOCK}(D)$$

and our circumscription schema becomes

$\phi(A) \wedge \phi(B) \wedge \phi(C) \wedge \phi(D) \wedge (\forall x.\phi(x) \supset \text{ISBLOCK}(x))$

$\supset$

$(\forall x.\text{ISBLOCK}(x) \supset \phi(x))$

Now our old substitution does *not* make the antecedents of the implication true. We now have to use another substitution, namely

$\lambda x.(x=A \vee x=B \vee x=C \vee x=D)$

With this substitution we derive

$\forall x.\text{ISBLOCK}(x) \supset (x=A \vee x=B \vee x=C \vee x=D)$

Our former conclusion that A, B and C are the only blocks is no longer derivable, that is circumscription is in fact nonmonotonic.

It is also possible to circumscribe several predicates jointly. In this case we need a different predicate parameter for each circumscribed predicate and the second antecedent and the consequent of the circumscription schema have to be repeated for each of the parameters. We shall encounter an example of joint (parallel) variable circumscription in the next section.

It has to be mentioned that the definition of the circumscription schema presupposes that the sets of premises are finite, a restriction that does not hold for the other logics described in this book.

Predicate circumscription can be shown to be correct (McCarthy 80) with respect to minimal entailment. However, the first order version is not complete, that is there are cases where a formula true in all minimal models cannot be derived using predicate circumscription. Nevertheless, for very broad classes of theories completeness results have been established (Perlis, Minker 86).

How can this very general technique be used to model default reasoning? In (McCarthy 84) the use of a predicate AB ('abnormal') is proposed as a uniform principle. Defaults are represented in the form:

(1) $\forall x.\text{GERMAN}(x) \wedge \neg\text{AB}(x) \supset \text{DRINKS-BEER}(x)$

Intuitively: Germans who are not abnormal like beer. AB then is circumscribed to make as few objects as possible abnormal. Of course, a person may be abnormal with respect to drinking beer but normal in some other aspect. Thus we need different abnormality predicates AB_i for different aspects, i.e. usually one for each default.

Unfortunately, it turns out that predicate circumscription is too weak to yield the results we expect from a formalization of default reasoning. If we have, in addition to default (1) above

(2) $\text{GERMAN}(\text{PETER})$

then the predicate circumscription of AB yields

$(\forall x.\text{GERMAN}(x) \wedge \neg\phi(x) \supset \text{DRINKS-BEER}(x)) \wedge$

$\text{GERMAN}(\text{PETER}) \wedge$

$(\forall x.\phi(x) \supset AB(x))$

$\supset$

$(\forall x.AB(x) \supset \phi(x))$

The left hand side of this schema is true if we substitute for ϕ

$\lambda x.(\text{GERMAN}(x) \wedge \neg\text{DRINKS-BEER}(x))$

We get $(\forall x.AB(x) \equiv \text{GERMAN}(x) \wedge \neg\text{DRINKS-BEER}(x))$, but this is less than we expect as it does not generate the desired conclusion DRINKS-BEER(PETER).

This is not an accident. In fact, Etherington, Mercer and Reiter (Etherington et al. 84) have shown that predicate circumscription yields

* no new positive or negative ground instances of predicates which have not been circumscribed (as DRINKS-BEER above),

* only new negative ground instances of circumscribed predicates.

This is certainly not what we were hoping for from a formalization of default reasoning. A stronger version of circumscription with a larger set of conclusions is needed.

4.2: Variable Circumscription

Variable circumscription is a generalization of predicate circumscription which allows certain other predicates to vary during the minimization, i.e their extensions may change as an effect of the minimization. This is achieved by the following definition[1]:

Definition 4.4: *Let A(P;Q) be a formula (the conjunction of the premises of a theory) containing the n-ary predicate symbol P ($x=x_1,...,x_n$), and the predicate symbols from Q = {$Q_1, ... , Q_m$}. Let A($\phi,\theta_1,...,\theta_m$) be the result of replacing all occurrences of P, $Q_1, ..., Q_m$ with predicate variables $\phi,\theta_1,...,\theta_m$. Then the variable circumscription of P in A with variable predicates $Q_1,...,Q_m$ - denoted CIRC(A;P;Q) - is the second order formula*

$$A(P;Q) \wedge \forall\phi,\theta_1,...,\theta_m.A(\phi,\theta_1,...,\theta_m) \wedge (\forall x.\phi(x)\supset P(x)) \supset (\forall x.P(x)\supset\phi(x))$$

The second conjunct of this formula is called the circumscription axiom. If multiple predicates are to be minimized in parallel, a different variable for each of them has to be substituted and the second conjunct of the precondition, as well as the conclusion of

---

the circumscription axiom, have to be repeated accordingly. An example involving the minimization of two abnormality predicates follows below.

The semantics of variable circumscription is a slight modification of the semantics for predicate circumscription. Condition 2) in the definition of ≤P (Definition 4.1) is replaced by

(2')   all predicate symbols of A other than P, Q_1, ..., Q_m have the same extensions.

This has the effect that more models are comparable. Thus the number of minimal models decreases and the set of formulae true in all minimal models increases.

Here is our example using the new version of circumscription:

(1) $\forall x.\text{GERMAN}(x) \wedge \neg\text{AB}_1(x) \supset \text{DRINKS-BEER}(x)$

(2) $\text{GERMAN}(\text{PETER})$

If we circumscribe AB1 allowing DRINKS-BEER to vary (omitting the outer universal quantifier in this and the following examples) we get:

$(\forall x.\text{GERMAN}(x) \wedge \neg\phi(x) \supset \theta(x)) \wedge$

$\text{GERMAN}(\text{PETER}) \wedge$

$(\forall x.\phi(x) \supset \text{AB}_1(x))$

$\supset$

$(\forall x.\text{AB}_1(x) \supset \phi(x))$

Substitution of $\lambda x.\text{FALSE}$ for ϕ and $\lambda x.\text{GERMAN}(x)$ for θ in the second order formula gives $(\forall x.\text{AB}_1(x) \supset \text{FALSE})$, i.e. nobody is AB_1 and we get DRINKS-BEER(PETER).

Adding the premises

(3) $\forall x.\text{EATS-PIZZA}(x) \supset \neg\text{DRINKS-BEER}(x)$

(4) $\text{EATS-PIZZA}(\text{PETER})$

yields

$(\forall x.\text{GERMAN}(x) \wedge \neg\phi(x) \supset \theta(x)) \wedge \text{GERMAN}(\text{PETER}) \wedge$

$(\forall x.\text{EATS-PIZZA}(x) \supset \neg\theta(x)) \wedge \text{EATS-PIZZA}(\text{PETER}) \wedge$

$(\forall x.\phi(x) \supset \text{AB}_1(x))$

$\supset$

$(\forall x.\text{AB}_1(x) \supset \phi(x))$

In this case the substitution of $\lambda x.(\text{GERMAN}(x) \wedge \text{EATS-PIZZA}(x))$ for ϕ and $\lambda x.\neg\text{EATS-PIZZA}(x)$ for θ gives the conclusion that the objects being AB_1 are exactly the Germans who eat pizza. Peter is one of them and does not like beer.

Let us now replace (3) by the default

(3') $\forall x.\text{EATS-PIZZA}(x) \land \neg \text{AB}_2(x) \supset \neg \text{DRINKS-BEER}(x)$

Parallel circumscription of AB_1 and AB_2 using DRINKS-BEER as variable yields the formula

$(\forall x.\text{GERMAN}(x) \land \neg \phi_1(x) \supset \theta(x)) \land$

GERMAN(PETER) $\land$

$(\forall x.\text{EATS-PIZZA}(x) \land \neg \phi_2(x) \supset \neg \theta(x)) \land$

EATS-PIZZA(PETER) $\land$

$(\forall x.\phi_1(x) \supset \text{AB}_1(x)) \land$

$(\forall x.\phi_2(x) \supset \text{AB}_2(x))$

$\supset$

$(\forall x.\text{AB}_1(x) \supset \phi_1(x)) \land$

$(\forall x.\text{AB}_2(x) \supset \phi_2(x))$

With the substitutions

$\lambda x.(\text{GERMAN}(x) \land (\neg \text{EATS-PIZZA}(x) \lor \text{AB}_2(x)))$ for θ

$\lambda x.(\text{GERMAN}(x) \land \text{EATS-PIZZA}(x) \land \neg \text{AB}_2(x))$ for ϕ_1

$\lambda x.(\text{GERMAN}(x) \land \text{EATS-PIZZA}(x) \land \text{AB}_2(x))$ for ϕ_2

we can derive

$(\forall x.\text{AB}_1(x) \equiv \text{GERMAN}(x) \land \text{EATS-PIZZA}(x) \land \neg \text{AB}_2(x))$

and

$(\forall x.\text{AB}_2(x) \supset \text{GERMAN}(x) \land \text{EATS-PIZZA}(x))$

We have a situation where Germans who eat pizza are the abnormal objects, and each of them is abnormal exactly in one of two different aspects. It is not derivable in which aspect Peter is abnormal, however.

The last example illustrates that circumscription deals with conflicting defaults in a way corresponding to the fixed point intersection approach of McDermott & Doyle, and not to Reiter's single extension approach. In the case of conflicting defaults, minimal models corresponding to the different conflicting conclusions exist. Minimal entailment requires validity in all minimal models and as a consequence we get the skeptical behavior of circumscription.

It has recently been shown (DeKleer, Konolige 89) that the ability to have fixed predicates which are not allowed to vary does not increase the power of variable circumscription. The effect of fixing a predicate P can be modelled by the introduction of a new predicate P*. Adding the formula

$\forall x.P(x) \equiv \neg P^*(x)$

and including P and P* in the predicates to be minimized yields exactly the same results. This is important since, as we will see, a theorem about the relationship between DL and circumscription without fixed predicates has been proven (Section 4.4) and proof procedures for this case exist (Section 7.2).

In many cases circumscription yields the desired results only under an additional assumption, the unique names assumption which states that different constants denote different objects. If we know that a typical German likes beer, Peter is a German, and there is Hans who does not like beer, then we have to show that Peter is different from Hans in order to derive by circumscription that Peter likes beer. Circumscription cannot be used to minimize the equality predicate (Etherington et al. 84). It is not difficult to see the reason for this. To be comparable models must have the same domain. If it is logically possible that two terms are equal then we can always construct a minimal model where they actually are equal. Hence, circumscription cannot produce new facts about equality not already derivable from the premises, and the extra assumption is necessary. For a modification of circumscription that handles the problem see (Rathmann, Winslett 89).

The examples we have just looked at have raised some important questions. The first is: How do we know which predicates to vary? The results of (Etherington et al. 84) give at least a hint (Section 4.1): if we require that circumscription can possibly yield new ground instances of a certain predicate, then we have to include it in the list of varying predicates.

The choice of varying and fixed predicates also allows us to control unwanted effects of the contraposition of defaults in certain cases. Obviously, the default (A ∧ ¬AB ⊃ B) is equivalent to the contraposed default (¬B ∧ ¬AB ⊃ ¬A). If we fix A, however, then we never can derive ¬A from ¬B by default. This is often an advantage: 'A's are typically B's' does not always imply 'non-B's are typically non-A's'. Take for example 'objects typically don't fly'. This does certainly not mean the same as 'flying things are typically not objects'. This fixing technique, however, cannot be applied in general. If, for instance, we have a chain of defaults 'A's are typically B's' and 'B's are typically C's', then fixing B to avoid the contraposition of the second default certainly conflicts with the intended use of the first default. Note that DL does not have this problem. Since defaults in DL are inference rules it is impossible to use a default for deriving the negation of its prerequisite.

The second, probably more serious question is: how do we find the right substitutions for the circumscription schema or axiom which will allow us to derive anything useful? Even for examples as simple as the ones we have discussed it is not always easy, and for large knowledge bases containing hundreds or thousands of formulae it is an extremely difficult task.

These problems have led McDermott to criticize circumscription very severely (McDermott 86) (McDermott 87). He argues that guessing the right instances of the schema makes it necessary to know what can be derived before circumscription can be used to verify it. His proposal is to keep the nice semantics of circumscription but to dispense with its syntactical counterpart completely.

The situation is not always unmanageable, however. As we shall see in Chapter 7, a variety of proof techniques for circumscription have been developed. For a broad class of theories circumscription can even be reduced to first order logic. For such theories standard first order proof techniques can be used. The computational aspects of circumscription will be discussed in detail in Chapter 7.

The mathematical properties of the two versions of circumscription have been studied intensively. In the rest of this section we shall briefly state some of the important results which have been established.

Circumscription does not preserve consistency (Etherington et al. 84); in other words it may be the case that a theory for which models exist does not have minimal models. Lifschitz (Lifschitz 86a) has shown that predicate circumscription is consistency preserving for a very broad class of theories, the so-called almost universal theories. Variable circumscription is consistency preserving for universal theories; that is theories whose prenex normal form does not contain existential quantifiers. The second of these results has been proven independently in (Etherington 86). Mott (Mott 87) has proposed a slight modification of circumscription which guarantees that consistency is preserved in all cases.

Lifschitz has shown (Lifschitz 85a) that under the domain closure assumption (each object is denoted by a constant) and the unique names assumption (different constants denote different objects) the closed world assumption (Definition 1.1) is equivalent to the predicate circumscription of all predicates if the CWA does not lead to an inconsistency.

We now turn to a third, even more general version of circumscription.

4.3: Prioritized Circumscription

We discussed ways of introducing default priorities in default logic in Chapter 3. Expressing priorities is also useful in the case of circumscription when multiple predicates are to be minimized. Before we show how this can be done we shall give an alternative definition of variable circumscription. The definition and the notation are taken from (Lifschitz 85b).

If U, V are n-ary predicates, then $U \leq V$ stands for $\forall x. U(x) \supset V(x)$, where $x = x_1, ..., x_n$. This notation is extended to tuples $U = U_1, ..., U_m$ and $V = V_1, ..., V_m$. $U \leq V$ stands for $U_i \leq V_i$, $i = 1, ..., m$. $U = V$ stands for $U \leq V \wedge V \leq U$, $U < V$ for $U \leq V \wedge \neg(V \leq U)$.

With this notation the circumscription of a predicate tuple $P = P_1,...,P_n$ with variable predicates $Z = Z_1,...,Z_m$ in a theory $A(P,Z)$ can equivalently be written as

$$A(P,Z) \wedge \neg\exists p,z.A(p,z) \wedge p < P$$

where $p = p_1,...,p_n$ and $z = z_1,...,z_m$ are tuples of predicate variables such that the arity of each p_i (z_i) corresponds to the arity of P_i (Z_i).

This alternative definition is useful for introducing priorities. Assume the tuple P of predicates to be minimized is divided into a partition K of disjoint subsets $P1,...,Pk$, with the intention that Pi is to be minimized at higher priority than $Pi+1$. Let pi, qi be tuples of predicate variables corresponding to Pi, and let p,q stand for the tuples $p1,...,pk$ and $q1,...,qk$, respectively. We define $p \leq_K q$ as:

$$\bigwedge_{i=1}^{k} \left(\bigwedge_{j=1}^{i-1} pj = qj \supset pi \leq qi \right)$$

If we replace $\leq$ in the definition of variable circumscription by our new order $\leq_K$ then we get prioritized circumscription; denoted $CIRC(A;P1>...>Pk;Z)$.

Lifschitz (Lifschitz 85b) has shown that any prioritized circumscription can equivalently be written as the conjunction of ordinary circumscriptions, i.e. $CIRC(A;P1>...>Pk;Z)$ is equivalent to

$$\bigwedge_{i=1}^{k} Circum(A; Pi; Pi+1,..., Pk, Z)$$

This means that we can interpret prioritized circumscription as a sequence of circumscriptions where predicates with highest priority are minimized first (the other predicates to be circumscribed may vary) and the minimization of the other predicates is iteratively performed on the results of the former minimizations.

Take as a simple example a degenerate form of the Nixon problem where:

$$A = \{\neg AB_1(\text{NIXON}) \supset PAC(\text{NIXON}), \neg AB_2(\text{NIXON}) \supset \neg PAC(\text{NIXON})\}$$

Assume the first default has higher priority, so we are interested in

$$CIRC(A; AB_1 > AB_2; PAC)$$

which, according to Lifschitz's result, is equivalent to

$$CIRC(A; AB_1; AB_2, PAC) \wedge CIRC(A; AB_2; PAC)$$

It is not difficult to see that the first of these two circumscriptions yields $\forall x.\neg AB_1(x)$ and hence $PAC(\text{NIXON})$ and $AB_2(\text{NIXON})$. This is what we expect from giving priority to the first default.

See (Lifschitz 85b) for more illustrating examples of prioritized circumscription.

Without going into the technical details we would like to present briefly the ideas behind two further generalizations of circumscription developed by Vladimir Lifschitz. The versions of circumscription we have examined so far require that a circumscription policy be selected for each particular application. The policy must

specify the predicates to be minimized, the varying predicates, and the priorities
between circumscribed predicates. In (Lifschitz 89a) an approach is developed where
all this information is expressed in the logical axioms themselves. Accordingly it
becomes possible to reason about the policy in the same way as about the domain of
discourse. Technically, it is achieved by introducing for each pair of predicates
(P,C) an additional predicate constant V_{PC} expressing, intuitively, that C may vary
during the minimization of P.

Circumscribing a predicate P corresponds, very roughly, to the use of a normal
prerequisite-free default :¬P/¬P, or to the use of an AEL-axiom (¬Lp ⊃ ¬P). Non-
normal defaults seem to have no counterparts in circumscription. Based on (Perlis
88) Lifschitz defines a version of circumscription called introspective
circumscription which combines the full power of circumscription with the
additional expressiveness of AEL's introspective capabilities (Lifschitz 89b). Instead
of using a modal operator as in AEL, Lifschitz introduces for each predicate P an
additional predicate LP. This turns out to be sufficient for his purpose. Introspective
circumscription subsumes prioritized circumscription as a special case, and as in the
approach mentioned above, the minimization policy is completely described by
axioms. Interestingly, introspective circumscription has a fixed point semantics, not
a semantics based on an ordering of the models.

We have seen in the last sections three different versions of circumscription; some
others were mentioned briefly. Is there one version to be preferred over the others?
Certainly not. They all differ in their expressiveness and the choice depends on the
expressiveness needed for a particular application. So all we can say is: the most
appropriate form of circumscription is the simplest one which is expressive enough
to solve a problem.

4.4: The Relation Between Circumscription and DL/AEL

Unfortunately, the relationship between circumscription and other approaches is not
as simple as that between DL and AEL. It was mentioned in Section 4.2 that circumscription is not capable of minimizing equality. In this respect circumscription is
weaker than DL since we can use DL-defaults to derive inequality statements.
Imielinski (Imielinski 85) has shown that, in general, it is not possible to translate
even normal DL-defaults to circumscription in a modular way. Modularity of a
translation TRANS usually means that TRANS(A ∪ B) = TRANS(A) ∪ TRANS(B),
where A and B are sets of formulae. Imielinsky uses a much weaker notion of
modularity requiring only that the addition of a new specific fact does not lead to the
recomputation of the translation. Not even translations satisfying this weak notion of
modularity are possible.

On the other hand, nothing in DL corresponds to the possibility that in circumscription the predicates can be specified which are allowed to vary while all others remain fixed. However, using de Kleer and Konolige's technique mentioned in Section 4.2, fixed predicates can be eliminated from a circumscription, so this is not a principle obstacle to representing circumscription in AEL.

The ability to eliminate fixed predicates increases the importance of the following theorem (Etherington 87b) which shows that in a very restricted case DL is equivalent to circumscription:

Theorem 4.1: *Assume there is a set of ground terms $g1, ..., gn$ such that*

(1) $T \vdash \forall x.\ x=g1\ v\ ...\ v\ x=gn$

(2)   for all i, j either $T \vdash gi=gj$ or $T \vdash gi \neq gj$

then the formulae contained in every extension of the default theory are exactly the theorems obtained by circumscribing P in T allowing all predicates to vary.

The restrictions require that the domain be finite and that every individual be denotable by a ground term. Moreover, T must contain complete information about equality of terms. This last requirement is due to the different treatment of equality in circumscription and DL. If b is a constant of the language then circumscribing P in T = P(c) does not yield ¬P(b). Circumscription takes the possibility into account that b might be equal to c. The single extension of the default theory ({:¬Px/¬Px}, {P(c)}), however, contains ¬P(b). If T contains full information about equality this problem disappears.

Konolige recently generalized Etherington's result, in the framework of AEL, to non-finite domains (Konolige 89). He first extended AEL to allow for quantification into the scope of the modal operator. Then he showed that variable circumscription can be translated to this generalized form of AEL in the following way:

(1)   for each circumscribed predicate P_i add to the premises W the AEL formula

   $\forall x.\neg LP_i(x) \supset \neg P_i(x),$

(2)   for each fixed predicate Q_j add to the premises W the formulae

   $\forall x.\neg LQ_j(x) \supset \neg Q_j(x),$

   $\forall x.\neg L\neg Q_j(x) \supset Q_j(x),$

(3)   to model the handling of the equality predicate in circumscription adequately add

   $\forall x,y.\neg L(x=y) \supset \neg(x=y),$

   $\forall x,y.\neg L\neg(x=y) \supset (x=y).$

Konolige proved that the first order sentences true in every extension of the resulting AEL-theory are exactly those sentences true in all P-minimal models of W. AEL with Konolige's modifications is thus more general than variable circumscription.

4.5: Preferential Entailment: A Semantical Framework

Yoav Shoham (Shoham 86) (Shoham 87) generalized the notion of minimal entailment in order to provide a unifying semantical framework for the definition of nonmonotonic logics. A related, somewhat less general approach has been investigated in (Bossu, Siegel 85).

In circumscription a specific ordering of models was introduced and in the definition of minimal entailment some models, the non-minimal ones, were disregarded. This idea can be generalized. Starting from any standard logic with a model-theoretic semantics, such as first order logic or a modal logic, a *preference logic* is obtained by adding an arbitrary strict partial preference order on interpretations to the logic. This ordering is used to focus on a subset of the models of a set of formulae. The preferred models are those minimal with respect to the given ordering. We can now define preferential entailment.

Definition 4.5: *Let A be a set of formulae, p a formula. A preferentially entails p iff the models of p are a superset of the preferred models of A.*

An example of a useful preference criterion very different from those implicit in circumscription is Shoham's chronological minimality ordering for temporal reasoning (Shoham 86). Shoham uses a modal temporal logic and investigates an ordering preferring models where properties persist as long as possible. In Section 10.2 we shall describe this idea in somewhat more detail.

Shoham first claimed that all of the known nonmonotonic logics could be viewed as special cases of his simple framework. For circumscription it can be seen quite easily since its semantics is defined in terms of minimal (preferred) models. (Shoham 86) also describes how a variant of AEL due to Halpern and Moses (Halpern, Moses 84) fits into the framework. DL poses more difficulties. Shoham first translates default theories to modal logic in a way quite similar to Konolige's translation. He then develops different, more and more complicated preference orders not all of which, however, precisely capture DL.

In the meantime it was proven that DL cannot be captured by the preferential model semantics (Makinson 89). As discussed in Section 3.4, DL is not cumulative; in other words the addition of theorems of a default theory (D,W) to the premises W may produce changes in the derivable formulae. DL, taken in the liberal sense where any extension is seen as an acceptable set of beliefs, even violates half of the cumulativity property, the property of cumulative transitivity defined as:

A |- x whenever A |- y and A ∪ {y} |- x.

Makinson has shown that every preferential logic satisfies this property, even when Shoham's notion is further generalized as in (Makinson 89).

Shoham states (Shoham 86, p. 108):

In fact, this model-theoretic analysis raises the question whether Reiter's particular definition, which is most ingenious technically, is well-motivated.

However, the fact that DL does not fit into the preferential entailment framework does not allow us to conclude that DL is not well-motivated. Etherington's definition of a semantics for DL has shown that it is actually possible to give a model-theoretic characterization of DL, a characterization outside Shoham's framework.

General frameworks are very useful since they provide insights in common and distinguishing features of their subsumed instances. But they should not be used for arguing against approaches which do not fit in.

So far not many concrete preference orderings on models have been investigated besides those implicit in circumscription. One exception, Shoham's chronological minimality criterion, has been mentioned before. Other useful orderings have yet to be detected.

CHAPTER 5: PREFERRED SUBTHEORIES

Intelligent agents must certainly be able to draw plausible conclusions based on in-complete information and they must handle rules with exceptions in a reasonable way. In addition, they must be able to deal with inconsistent information. The approaches to formalizing nonmonotonic reasoning we examined so far require the set of premises to be consistent, otherwise they give no interesting result at all. In each case the infer-ence relation is extended to yield more than just the classically derivable formulae. In circumscription, for instance, this is achieved by adding a second order formula. In DL non-standard inference rules are introduced. In AEL the definition of extensions forces Lp to be in an extension whenever p is and ¬Lp whenever p is not. For incon-sistent sets of premises the derivable formulae consist of the whole language.

In this chapter we present an approach based on an alternative view. What makes a piece of knowledge *default* knowledge? What distinguishes it from a fact? Mainly our attitude towards it in the case of a conflict, that is in the case of an inconsistency. If we take this view seriously then the idea of default reasoning as a special case of inconsistency handling seems quite natural.[1] There is no problem with inconsistent premises as long as we provide ways to handle the inconsistency adequately, in other words, if we modify the inference relation in such a way that in the case of an incon-sistency less than all the formulae are derivable. As we shall show in this chapter, it is possible to specify strategies for handling inconsistency which can be used to model default reasoning.

We first present a simple general framework for defining nonmonotonic systems. Section 5.2 presents Poole's approach to default reasoning (Poole 88) and shows how it fits into this framework. Moreover, we discuss some limitations of Poole's approach which are caused by the inability to represent priorities between defaults adequately. Section 5.3 presents a more general instance of our framework which uses several layers of possible hypotheses to represent different degrees of reliability. A second further generalization based on a partial ordering between premises is described in Section 5.4. In both approaches a formula is provable from a theory if it is possible to construct a consistent argument for it based on the most reliable hypotheses.

---

[1] This idea has also been proposed in (Bibel 85).

5.1: A Framework for Nonmonotonic Systems

A standard way of handling inconsistent premise sets uses maximal consistent subsets of the premises at hand. Since, in general, there is more than one maximal consistent subset, provability is defined as provability in all such sets. The idea behind the requirement of maximality is clear: we want to modify the available information as little as possible. The notion of maximal consistent subsets per se, however, does not give us the possibility to express, say, that *Tweety flies* should be rejected rather than *Tweety is a penguin*, when we know that penguins do not fly. To be able to express such preferences we have to consider not *all* maximal consistent subsets, but only some of them, the *preferred* maximal consistent subsets, or more briefly, *preferred subtheories*. This idea is similar to preferential entailment, where not all but only a subset of the models is taken into account.

The notion of a preferred maximal consistent subset; is not new; it dates back to (Rescher 64). Rescher has defined a particular ordering of subtheories which will be briefly discussed in Sect. 5.4. He did not, however, apply this idea to default reasoning.

In this section we leave open the exact definition of what the preferred subtheories are. As in Shoham's framework (Section 4.5), where a concrete nonmonotonic logic is defined by a specific preference ordering, in our framework a nonmonotonic logic is obtained by defining the preferred subtheories. Several possible ways to do this are presented in the rest of this chapter.

Based on the notion of preferred subtheory we can define a weak and a strong notion of provability:

Definition 5.1: *A formula p is weakly provable from a set of premises T iff there is a preferred subtheory S of T such that S |- p.*

Definition 5.2: *A formula p is strongly provable from a set of premises T iff for all preferred subtheories S of T we have S |- p.*

These notions correspond roughly to containment in at least one or in all extensions in the fixed point approaches to default reasoning. In fact, we can also introduce the notion of extension in the following way:

Definition 5.3: *E is an extension of a set of premises T iff there is a preferred subtheory S of T and E = Th(S).*

To specify the preferred subtheories we shall impose in the rest of the chapter a certain structure on the premises T. In one approach (Section 5.3), for instance, we split T into several levels $T_1, ..., T_n$. This additional structure is used to define the preferred subtheories of T. For sake of simplicity we also speak of preferred subtheories (and extensions) of these structures and leave the premise set T implicit.

One important aspect of this approach should be noted; the provable formulae of our theories depend on the syntactic form of the premises. It makes an important difference whether, for instance, a set of premises contains both A and B, or the equivalent single formula A ∧ B. Assume there is a preferred subtheory S inconsistent with A, but not with B. If both A and B are given, then B must be contained in S. If, however, our premise is A ∧ B, then this is not the case.

We could avoid this by introducing a certain normal form for formulae. However, we do not see this unusual behaviour as a drawback at all. It increases the expressive power of the logic in that we can express that two formulae A and B must be accepted or given up *together*. It makes perfect sense to distinguish between situations where A and B are two possibly unrelated hypotheses or where A ∧ B is a single hypothesis.

Consider the following example. Someone tells you that Michael was sitting in a bar drinking beer. Call 'Michael was in the bar' A and 'Michael was drinking beer' B. Now someone else gives you the more reliable information 'Michael was working at the university'. Call this information C. Clearly, C is inconsistent with A, but not with B. However, it seems reasonable in this case to give up B also. In our approach this can be achieved by using the premise A ∧ B. Note that replacing a single premise P by an equivalent single premise Q does not change the resulting preferred subtheories.

What we defined so far is just a general framework. To obtain a specific instance of the framework, that is a real nonmonotonic system, it remains for us to define what the preferred subtheories are. We shall first show that Poole's approach to default reasoning can be seen as such an instance.

5.2: Poole's System: Default Reasoning as Theory Construction

David Poole (Poole 88) presents an approach to default reasoning based on the viewpoint that nonmonotonicity, rather than being a problem with logic, is a problem of how logic is used. A similar viewpoint has also been expressed in (Bibel 85, p.198).

Poole considers defaults as possible hypotheses used to form theories about the world, and (Poole 88, p.28):

If one allows hypothetical reasoning, then there is no need to define a new logic to handle nonmonotonic reasoning.

In Poole's framework it is assumed that the user provides

(1)   a consistent set F of closed formulae, the facts about the world,

(2)   a set Δ of, possibly open, formulae, the possible hypotheses.

The open formulae in Δ are just for notational convenience. They are used to represent all of their ground instances, that is having an open formula p in Δ is equivalent to having all ground instances of p in Δ.[2]

Definition 5.4: *A scenario of F and Δ is a set D ∪ F where D is a set of ground instances of elements of Δ such that D ∪ F is consistent.*

Definition 5.5: *A formula g is explainable from F and Δ iff there is a scenario of F and Δ which implies g.*

Definition 5.6: *An extension of F and Δ is the set of logical consequences of a (set inclusion) maximal scenario of F and Δ.*

The terminology reflects the way Poole uses his framework not only for prediction; but also for explanation; of observed facts. Since our main interest here is default reasoning we shall also call Δ the set of defaults. The party example can be represented as follows:

Δ = {GERMAN(x) ⊃ DRINKS-BEER(x)}

F = {GERMAN(PETER)}

DRINKS-BEER(PETER) is explainable from the scenario F ∪ {GERMAN(PETER) ⊃ DRINKS-BEER(PETER)}. Adding to F the formulae

EATS-PIZZA(PETER)

∀x.EATS-PIZZA(x) ⊃ ¬DRINKS-BEER(x)

makes DRINKS-BEER(PETER) unexplainable. If we remove the last formula and add instead the default

EATS-PIZZA(x) ⊃ ¬DRINKS-BEER(x)

to Δ, then we get two extensions, one containing the formula DRINKS-BEER(PETER), the other one its negation. Note the important difference between having an open and a universally quantified formula in Δ. The universally quantified formula cannot be used for explanations if there is a single exception to it mentioned in F. Assume we have:

Δ' = {∀x.GERMAN(x) ⊃ DRINKS-BEER(x)}

F' = {GERMAN(PETER), GERMAN(HANS), ¬DRINKS-BEER(HANS)}

Now we cannot explain DRINKS-BEER(PETER) since the universally quantified formula in Δ' is inconsistent with F' and hence cannot be contained in a scenario.

In spite of the very different views underlying Poole's and Reiter's approach there is a close connection between the resulting systems; Poole's system is equivalent to DL with the restriction to 'supernormal' defaults, that is normal defaults without prereq-

---

[2] Schema would have been the better name. We did not want to change Poole's terminology, however. In our generalizations we will speak of schemata rather than open formulae.

uisites. If we define a default theory (Δ', F) such that $\Delta' = \{:w/w \mid w \in \Delta\}$, then the extensions in Poole's system and DL are identical.

These restrictions seem, at first view, very drastic. However, Poole has shown that many of the standard examples involving defaults can be handled adequately with this simple and elegant approach (Poole 88). He uses a naming technique similar to the one presented in Section 3.3. Instead of using constants as names together with a standard applicability predicate he uses new predicates as names. For a hypothesis $w(x) \in \Delta$ with free variables x he introduces a new predicate symbol p_w of the same arity. Poole shows that $w(x)$ can equivalently be replaced by $p_w(x)$, if the formula

$$\forall x.p_w(x) \supset w(x)$$

is added to F. Poole uses the notation $p_w(x):w(x)$ as an abbreviation for that case. Thus, the power of the system is not restricted if only atoms are allowed in Δ.

The use of names makes it possible to block the applicability of a default when needed. If we want a default $p_w(x)$ to be inapplicable in situation s we simply have to add

$$\forall x.s \supset \neg p_w(x)$$

to our facts.

Assume we have a default $\mathrm{BIRDS\_FLY}(x): \mathrm{BIRD}(x) \supset \mathrm{FLIES}(x)$. We want to block the applicability of this default to penguins without stating that all penguins do not fly. We therefore add the fact $\forall x.\mathrm{PENGUIN}(x) \supset \neg \mathrm{BIRDS\_FLY}(x)$, that is we have

$$\Delta = \{\mathrm{BIRDS\_FLY}(x)\}$$
$$F = \{\forall x.\mathrm{BIRDS\_FLY}(x) \supset (\mathrm{BIRD}(x) \supset \mathrm{FLIES}(x)), \forall x.\mathrm{PENGUIN}(x) \supset$$
$$\neg\mathrm{BIRDS\_FLY}(x)\}$$

Given $\mathrm{BIRD}(\mathrm{TWEETY})$ as an additional fact we derive $\mathrm{FLIES}(\mathrm{TWEETY})$. Given the additional facts $\mathrm{BIRD}(\mathrm{TWEETY})$ and $\mathrm{PENGUIN}(\mathrm{TWEETY})$ it remains open whether Tweety flies or not.

(Poole 88) contains many interesting examples showing how this technique can be used.

What has Poole's system to do with the preferred subtheory framework? It turns out that Poole's approach is a simple instance of our framework. Let Δ' be the set obtained from Δ by replacing open formulae with all of their ground instances. Now define the preferred subtheories of $\Delta' \cup F$ as those subtheories which contain F. It is not difficult to see that with this definition of preferred subtheories our notion of weak provability and Poole's explainability coincide.

In Poole's system the default *A's typically are B's* is equivalent to the default *non-B's typically are non-A's*. It is a consequence of the fact that defaults have no prerequisites as in DL. In many cases the equivalence may be useful, e.g. if we have *birds fly* we may want also to have *non-fliers are not birds*. But there are cases where this behavior is not desired, e.g. from *objects typically don't fly* we certainly do not want to conclude *fliers typically are not objects*, or from *people on this planet typically do not know about nonmonotonic reasoning* we do not want to conclude *those who know about nonmonotonic reasoning are typically not people on this planet*.[3]

Poole extends his definition of scenarios to handle this problem. He introduces an additional set C of constraints which are used in the consistency check but not necessarily explainable themselves:

Definition 5.7: *A scenario of F, Δ and C is a set $D \cup F$ where D is a set of ground instances of elements of Δ such that $D \cup F \cup C$ is consistent.*

If we now have a default d: $b \supset c$, that is if $d \in \Delta$ and $d \supset (b \supset c) \in F$, then we can prevent the contraposition of d from being used by adding the constraint $\neg c \supset \neg d$.

Poole also proposes the use of constraints for approximating Reiter's semi-normal defaults of the form

$$\frac{A(x): B(x) \wedge C(x)}{C(x)}$$

Such a DL-default can be modelled with the default $D(x): A(x) \supset C(x)$ together with the constraints $\forall x. \neg C(x) \supset \neg D(x)$ and $\forall x. \neg B(x) \supset \neg D(x)$. The approximation is, however, not exact. It corresponds more to the - still semi-normal - Reiter default

$$\frac{: B(x) \wedge C(x)}{A(x) \supset C(x)}$$

Poole argues that when the two systems differ his system produces better results than Reiter's. In particular, in his system extensions always exist if $F \cup C$ is consistent.

We do not find all of his examples entirely convincing, however. For instance, in his example 8.1 (Poole 88) he criticizes the fact that RUNS(POLLY) cannot be derived from the defaults

$$\frac{EMU(x):RUNS(x)}{RUNS(x)} \qquad \frac{OSTRICH(x):RUNS(x)}{RUNS(x)}$$

together with the fact

EMU(POLLY) v OSTRICH(POLLY).

But the defaults can easily be reformulated to yield the desired result. We just have to remove the prerequisites and replace the consequents by implications. The defaults

$$\frac{:RUNS(x)}{EMU(x) \supset RUNS(x)} \qquad \frac{:RUNS(x)}{OSTRICH(x) \supset RUNS(x)}$$

yield the desired conclusion.

In fact, it is not difficult to extend Poole's result about the relation between his approach and DL to default theories with constraints. If C is finite and $F \cup C$ consistent then the default theory (Δ', F) with

$$\Delta' = \{: \text{CONJ}(C) \wedge w \ / \ w \mid w \in \Delta\}$$

---

[3] This example is due to Nic Wilson.

has exactly the same extensions as Poole's system. CONJ(C) here denotes the conjunction of all elements of C. Poole's default theories with constraints are, under the conditions mentioned, a very special class of prerequisite-free semi-normal defaults. All the properties of DL criticized by Poole are due to DL's additional expressiveness.

It is easy to extend our preferred subtheory framework accordingly to capture constraints. We can add to the premises T a set of constraints C, determine the preferred subtheories from T ∪ C, but use only the formulae in T to define weak and strong provability. The formal definitions are rather straightforward and can be found elsewhere (Brewka 90b). In Section 5.5 we discuss a possible use of constraints for theory revision.

Poole's approach is simple and elegant, and its expressiveness is astonishing. Moreover, an efficient Prolog-implementation exists (Poole et al. 86). There seem to be two drawbacks, however. First, the number of defaults needed to represent a situation may become very large when exceptions to exceptions must be represented, and second, it is possible to block the applicability of defaults in certain circumstances, but there does not seem to be a way to express priorities between defaults adequately. In fact, we shall see that the first drawback is a consequence of the second one.

We shall use an example from to Ulrich Junker to illustrate the problems. Assume we have the following commonsense facts:

> *Usually one has to go to a project meeting.*

> *This rule does not apply if one is sick, unless the sickness is only a cold.*

> *The rule is also not applicable if one is on vacation.*

Let us first see how this example can be represented in DL. Using R1 as a name for the first rule we can use the following defaults and formulae to represent these facts:

(1)   :R1 ∧ MEETING / MEETING   (2)   SICK: ¬COLD ∧ ¬R1/¬R1

(3)   VACATION ⊃ ¬R1   (4)   COLD ⊃ SICK

With this representation we do not derive MEETING given SICK. If we additionally have COLD then MEETING is derivable, however, unless VACATION is also given. To obtain similar results in Poole's system we need, besides formulae (3) and (4), a default

(1')   R1: MEETING

together with the fact

(2')   SICK⊃ ¬R1

which blocks the applicability of R1 when SICK is known. This blocking cannot be achieved by another default: if we choose to have the default Ri: SICK ⊃ ¬R1 rather than (2'), then, given SICK, two extensions are generated, one containing ¬Ri.

As a consequence we have to introduce a *new* default

(5)   R2: COLD ⊃ MEETING

to achieve the desired behavior. But this is not sufficient. As a side effect of the inability to use defaults to block defaults we need another fact; since we want to stay home when on vacation even if we have a cold, we have to block the applicability of R2 in this case, i.e. we further need

(6)   VACATION ⊃ ¬R2

This seems awkward, since we have to look 'down' in the hierarchy of exceptions and block defaults lower in the hierarchy. It is not difficult to imagine that the number of needed defaults may increase heavily in cases where more exceptions and exceptions to exceptions are involved.

The inability to use defaults to block other defaults seems to be the heart of the problem. It *is* possible to block a default's applicability in Poole's system, e.g. the default *birds fly* can be blocked for penguins. But this requires that the exceptional condition, in this case, penguin, be a certain fact. It is *not* possible to express that default d_1 should have priority over a conflicting default d_2 in the sense that d_2 is not applicable if d_1 can be applied. Adding the fact $d_1 \supset \neg d_2$ does not help; that is equivalent to $d_2 \supset \neg d_1$. But adding a default, say d_3: $d_1 \supset \neg d_2$ together with the constraint $d_2 \supset \neg d_3$ to prevent the use of the contraposition does not help either: d_2 still can be applied and its application then blocks d_1 and d_3. This is the reason why in our meeting example it was necessary to block R1 in the case of a sickness, then to add a new default handling cold, the exceptional sickness, correctly, and then to handle the repercussions of this addition.

In the next section we present a generalization of Poole's approach which allows us to represent such priorities easily. The important contribution of Poole's work is that he demonstrated the close relation between hypothetical and default reasoning.

5.3: First Generalization: Levels of Reliability

The following figure illustrates Poole's basic idea. There are two levels in a theory, the basic level which can be seen as set of premises which must be true and consistent, and a second level consisting of hypotheses which are less reliable.

Δ	Hypotheses
F	Facts

We shall generalize these ideas in two respects. First, we do not require the most reliable formulae (T1) to be consistent. In our generalization every formula is in principle refutable. And second, we introduce more than just two levels. This can be illustrated by the following figure:

Tn	Hypotheses
Tn-1	Hypotheses
...	
T2	Hypotheses
T1	Hypotheses

The idea is that the different levels of a theory represent different degrees of reliability. The innermost part is the most reliable one. If inconsistencies arise the more reliable information is preferred. Intuitively, a formula is provable if we can construct an argument for it from the most reliable available information. Of course, there may be conflicting information with the same reliability. In this case we get multiple extensions, i.e. two contradicting formulae can be provable in the weak sense. The fact that there are no principally unrefutable 'premises' makes it possible to treat all levels uniformly. For instance, we can add to any theory information which is even more reliable than the current lowest level.

We now show how these intuitive ideas can be made precise in the preferred subtheory framework. First we define default theories.

Definition 5.8: *A level default theory T is a tuple $(T_1, ..., T_n)$, where each T_i is a set of classical first order formulae.*

We shall often simply speak of a default theory when it is clear from the context that a level default theory is meant. Intuitively, information in T_i is more reliable than information in T_j if $i < j$. As in Poole's approach a default like *birds fly* can be represented as the set of all ground instances of the schema BIRD(x) $\supset$ FLIES(x). For notational convenience we write

$$T_i = \{..., P(x), ...\}$$

to express that T_i contains all ground instances of P(x). Note again the important difference between universally quantified formulae and schemata containing free variables. It remains for us to define the preferred subtheories:

Definition 5.9: *Let $T=(T_1,...,T_n)$ be a level default theory. $S = S_1 \cup ... \cup S_n$ is a preferred subtheory of T iff for all k $(1 \leq k \leq n)$ $S_1 \cup ... \cup S_k$ is a maximal consistent subset of $T_1 \cup ... \cup T_k$.*

In other words, to obtain a preferred subtheory of T we have to start with an arbitrary maximal consistent subset of T_1, add as many formulae from T_2 as can be consistently added, in any possible way, and continue to do so for T_3, ..., T_n.

The following simple examples show how the different levels can be used to express priorities between defaults:

(a) Good old Tweety:

T1 = {BIRD(TWEETY), ∀x.PENGUIN(x) ⊃ ¬FLIES(x)}

T2 = {BIRD(x) ⊃ FLIES(x)}

FLIES(TWEETY) is strongly provable.

T1 = {BIRD(TWEETY), ∀x.PENGUIN(x) ⊃ ¬FLIES(x), PENGUIN(TWEETY)}

T2 = {BIRD(x) ⊃ FLIES(x)}

¬FLIES(TWEETY) is strongly provable. This example can also be used to illustrate again the importance of the distinction between schemata and universally quantified formulae. If we replace the schema in T2 by a corresponding quantified formula, then the formula is not contained in any preferred subtheory if there is a single nonflying bird. When a schema is used only the ground instance where x is the exceptional bird is 'disabled', all other ground instances remain usable.

If there is a penguin who does fly, then we can use the following representation where *penguins don't fly* is given higher priority than *birds fly*:

T1 = {BIRD(TWEETY), PENGUIN(TWEETY), PENGUIN(TIM), FLIES(TIM)}

T2 = {PENGUIN(x) ⊃ ¬FLIES(x)}

T3 = {BIRD(x) ⊃ FLIES(x)}

(b) Nixon example:

T1 = {REP(NIXON), QUAK(NIXON)}

T2 = {REP(x) ⊃ ¬PAC(x), QUAK(x) ⊃ PAC(x)}

Both PAC(NIXON) and ¬PAC(NIXON) are weakly provable. None of them is strongly provable. If we want to give priority to - say - *Quakers are Pacifists*, this can be achieved as follows:

T1 = {REP(NIXON), QUAK(NIXON)}

T2 = {QUAK(x) ⊃ PAC(x)}

T3 = {REP(x) ⊃ ¬PAC(x)}

Now PAC(NIXON) is strongly provable.

(c) Meeting example:

In this example we use named defaults and adopt Poole's notation. R:Q ∈ Ti stands for R ∈ Ti and R ⊃ Q ∈ T1.

T1 = {VACATION ⊃ ¬R1, COLD ⊃ ¬R2, COLD ⊃ SICK}

T2 = {R2: SICK⊃ ¬R1}

T3 = {R1: MEETING }

Now we find that MEETING is strongly provable. If we add VACATION to T1 then MEETING is no longer strongly or weakly provable. The same happens if we add SICK. If, however, we add COLD (without VACATION) then again MEETING is strongly provable. And finally, if both COLD and VACATION are added, then again MEETING is not derivable.

In some applications it is possible to generate the levels of reliability automatically. Assume we want to prefer the most specific information.[4] Assume the user provides a consistent set of facts F and a finite set of open defaults D of the form $P(x) \supset Q(x)$ where x may be a tuple of variables. To define the theorems of such a theory we translate (F, D) into a level default theory $(T_1, T_2, ...,T_n)$ in the following way:

$T_1 = F$

$T_2 = \{P(x) \supset Q(x) \in D \mid$
    there is no $R(x) \supset Z(x) \in D$ with
    $F \vdash \forall x.R(x) \supset P(x)$ and not $F \vdash \forall x.P(x) \supset R(x)\}$

$T_{i+1} = \{P(x) \supset Q(x) \in D - (T_2 \cup ... \cup T_i) \mid$
    there is no $R(x) \supset Z(x) \in D - (T_2 \cup ... \cup T_i)$ with
    $F \vdash \forall x.R(x) \supset P(x)$ and not $F \vdash \forall x.P(x) \supset R(x)\}$

n is the smallest integer such that $T_2 \cup ... \cup T_n = D$.

Each default level T_i, $i \geq 2$, consists of the defaults which have not been put into a lower level already and for which no remaining defaults with more specific precondition exist. A precondition R(x) is more specific than P(x) if we can prove from F that all R's are P and not vice versa. Here is another bird example:

F = {BIRD(TWEETY), PENGUIN(HANSI), $\forall$x.PENGUIN(x) $\supset$ BIRD(x)}

D = {BIRD(x) $\supset$ FLIES(x), PENGUIN(x) $\supset$ ¬FLIES(x)}

The translation into a level default theory yields

T1 = F

T2 = {PENGUIN(x) $\supset$ ¬FLIES(x)}

T3 = {BIRD(x) $\supset$ FLIES(x)}

From this theory ¬FLIES(HANSI) and FLIES(TWEETY) is strongly provable.

5.4: Second Generalization: Partially Ordered Defaults

For many problems the introduction of levels of reliability is sufficient to express the necessary priorities between defaults. Sometimes, however, we want to leave open the

---

[4] Specific here means strictly, undefeasibly more specific, that is A is more specific than B if the extension of A is a proper subset of the extension of B. This, of course, is an enormous simplification. Specificity in general will be the main topic of Chapter 8.

judgement whether a formula p is of more, less or the same reliability as another formula q. Here is a political example that reflects the ideas of different groups in Germany about how to handle unemployment. The Social Democrats (SPD) tend to believe that there are not enough jobs and we should share them out, that is that everybody should work less. However, reducing everybody's salary is believed to be bad for the economy. There is a subgroup of the Social Democrats associated with the politician Lafontaine, however, which agrees with the first, but not with the second position since, according to their view, working less without reducing the salaries would make work too expensive. According to company owners the problem is not that we do not have enough to do; they believe that salaries are too high. We can formalize these ideas using the following defaults:

(1)   SPD ⊃ LESS -WORK ∧ ¬LESS -MONEY

(2)   LAF⊃ LESS -WORK ∧ LESS -MONEY

(3)   COMP-OWNER ⊃ ¬LESS -WORK ∧ LESS -MONEY

LAF represents a subclass of the SPD, i.e. information about Lafontaine-supporters is more specific than information about social democrats in general. We certainly want to give (2) priority over (1) in this case. But how about (3)? Choosing exactly one reliability level for each formula forces us to specify a priority either between (1) and (3) or between (2) and (3). There seems to be no good reason for such a decision.

The problem can be avoided if we allow the degrees of reliability to be represented via an arbitrary partial ordering of the premises rather than via different levels. Again we have to define the preferred subtheories to obtain weak and strong provability based on a partial ordering:

Definition 5.10: *Let < be a strict partial ordering on a finite set of premises T. S is a preferred subtheory of T iff there exists a strict total ordering $(t_1, t_2, \ldots , t_n)$ of T respecting < (i.e. $t_j < t_k => j < k$) such that $S = S_n$ with*

$S_0 := \{\}$, *and for $0 \leq i < n$*

$S_{i+1} := $ *if t_{i+1} consistent with S_i then $S_i \cup \{t_{i+1}\}$ else S_i.*

Basically the partial reliability ordering is handled by considering all possible linearizations. The generalization to the infinite case is straightforward.

If we define in our political example the ordering to be (2) < (1), then LESS-WORK ∧ LESS-MONEY is strongly provable from SPD and LAF. 'From SPD and LAF' here means that these formulae are smaller than (1), (2) and (3) with respect to the partial ordering <. From SPD and COMP-OWNER both LESS-WORK ∧ ¬LESS-MONEY and ¬LESS-WORK ∧ LESS-MONEY are weakly provable. The two corresponding preferred subtheories are generated from different total orderings respecting <. Similarly, we obtain two preferred subtheories given LAF and COMP-OWNER. In this case LESS-WORK ∧ ¬LESS-MONEY is provable from one preferred subtheory.

What this example shows is that we are able to express the wanted preference between (2) and (1) without having to introduce any unwanted preference involving (3).

This approach can be applied to the formalization of frame systems (Section 1.1) with multiple inheritance and a strict subclass hierarchy. Frames can be interpreted as unary predicates, and slots as functions. If a frame F has a slot S with value V, this can be represented as $F(x) \supset S(x) = V$. The ordering $<$ has to be defined such that

$$(F_1(x) \supset S(x) = V_1) < (F_2(x) \supset S(x) = V_2)$$

whenever F_1 is below F_2 in the frame hierarchy and both F_1 and F_2 have the slot S.

Given the car example from Section 1.1 we obtain:

(1) CAR(x) $\supset$ WHEELS(x) = 4

(2) CAR(x) $\supset$ SEATS(x) = 5

(3) CAR(x) $\supset$ CYLINDERS(x) = 4

(4) SPORTSCAR(x) $\supset$ SEATS(x) = 2

(5) SPORTSCAR(x) $\supset$ CYLINDERS(x) = 6

The superclass specification translates to

(6) $\forall$x.SPORTSCAR(x) $\supset$ Car(x)

Instance definitions become atomic formulae

(7) SPORTSCAR(SPEEDY)

We extend the relation $<$ to sets of formulae such that S $<$ T stands for s $<$ t for all s $\in$ S and t $\in$ T. Now let (5) $<$ (3), (4) $<$ (2) and {(6), (7)} $<$ {(1), ..., (5)}. There is a single preferred subtheory containing SEATS(SPEEDY) = 2, CYLINDERS(SPEEDY) = 6, and WHEELS(SPEEDY) = 4.

Note, however, that the translation of the frame hierarchy is not modular. We cannot translate each definition of a frame independently. To determine the relation $<$ correctly we have to look at the translations of the other available frame definitions, that is a global view is necessary. A modular translation from frames to circumscription is examined in Section 8.

5.5: Related Work

As mentioned in Section 5.2 Poole's system without constraints is equivalent to DL restricted to prerequisite-free normal defaults. The relation between our approach and Reiter's is - as expected - less simple. In Section 3.4 we briefly introduced a modification of default logic, called prioritized default logic (PDL). It turns out that the relation between PDL and our first generalization (Section 5.3) is the same as that between DL and Poole's system.

It is not difficult to show that our default theories $T=(T_1,...,T_n)$ can be translated to PDL default theories $D=(D_1,...,D_n,\{\})$, where D_i is the set of prerequisite-free normal defaults obtained from T_i (i.e. $(:p/p) \in D_i$ iff $p \in T_i$). A formula then is strongly provable from T iff it is contained in all PDL extensions of D, and weakly provable from T iff it is contained in at least one PDL extension of D.

The idea of introducing different levels of subtheories into a nonmonotonic formalism also underlies Konolige's HAEL (Konolige 88). As we saw in Section 2.3 in HAEL a modal operator in one level is allowed to refer to lower levels only. This makes it possible to represent priorities between conflicting defaults. Unfortunately, it also forces us to specify priorities, producing inconsistent results from conflicting defaults for which no priority has been defined. This major drawback of Konolige's approach does not arise in our framework.

It is also interesting to compare our framework with circumscription. There one starts with a consistent set of formulae (otherwise no interesting results are obtained) and select some of the models of the premises. We start with an inconsistent set of formulae T1 ∪ ... ∪ Tn (otherwise the approach produces the same results as classical logic) and select some of the maximal consistent subsets of the premises. The way our general framework (Section 5.1) generalizes Poole's approach is similar to the way Shoham's preferential logics framework (Section 4.5) generalizes McCarthy's circumscription; we abstract from the specific way of defining preferred subtheories whereas Shoham abstracts from the specific way of defining preferred models. The analogy goes even further: the motivation behind the development of prioritized circumscription (Section 4.3) seems to be the same as the motivation for our generalization from Section 5.3.

As mentioned in Section 5.1 the idea of preferred subtheories was developed in (Rescher 64). Instead of ordering the premises Rescher introduces an ordering of the whole logical language. Every formula belongs to a modal category M_i. Each category represents a different degree of something like 'willingness to accept'. The categories are used to select certain maximal consistent subsets of premises as follows: we start with those premises belonging to the lowest category and add as many formulae of the same category as consistenly possible. Generally there are different possible consistent additions and we obtain multiple sets from the first category. Interestingly, the added formulae do not have to be theorems of any of the given premises. Then we add to each of these sets as many of the premises belonging to the next category as consistently possible. After that, all formulae of the next category which can be added consistently are added and so on. When the last category has been handled, then each resulting set contains a 'preferred' maximal consistent subset of the premises (for the details see (Rescher 64), p.50f).

It is difficult to see, however, how this ordering could be used in a framework for default reasoning. It seems unnecessary to base the notion of default inference on a given ordering of all formulae of the logical language. Ordering the given premises is entirely sufficient.

There is also a close relation between our approach and recent research in the area of theory revision (Gärdenfors 88) (Gärdenfors, Makinson 88). Default reasoning investigates the principles of drawing plausible conclusions given a set of premises and defaults. Theory revision investigates the principles of rationally changing beliefs in the light of new information. The basic question is: Given an epistemic state S and an arbitrary piece of information p, what is the epistemic state S' a rational agent should be in after p is added to or removed from S? Epistemic states are often modelled as belief sets, i.e. deductively closed sets of logical formulae, and p is taken to be a logical formula. The new epistemic state after the addition (revision) or removal (contraction) of a piece of information is required to be unique. To determine it Gärdenfors and Makinson use the notion of epistemic entrenchment; an ordering on propositions. There is obviously much common intuition behind epistemic entrenchment and our partial ordering on premises.

From the standpoint of Artificial Intelligence the description of an epistemic state in terms of deductively closed logical theories is somewhat unsatisfactory. First of all, AI is interested in finite descriptions of the beliefs of an agent. Moreover, there seems to be an important distinction missing from this characterization of epistemic states: the distinction between derived and underived beliefs. Researchers in theory revision have felt this lack (Gärdenfors 88, p 67):

However, belief sets cannot be used to express that some beliefs may be reasons for other beliefs. ... And intuitively, when we compare degrees of similarity between different epistemic states, we want the structure of reasons or justifications to count as well.

In AI the standard way to obtain finite descriptions of an agent's beliefs is to use finite sets of premises instead of their deductive closure. Moreover, the distinction between underived and derived beliefs is, often implicitly, introduced by interpreting the premises as underived and their theorems as derived beliefs.

If we adopt this simple view then theory changes can be modelled in a straightforward manner in our framework. Our premises, that is the underived beliefs, will be default theories. The epistemic states are the extensions of the premises, that is we admit alternative possible epistemic states. This makes it possible to adopt either a skeptical or a credulous view. We can either take the intersection of all extensions as 'the' epistemic state, or we can pick out an arbitrary extension.

The problem of revising and contracting epistemic states therefore reduces to the problem of revising and contracting default theories. For sake of simplicity we restrict our presentation to the reliability level approach. All necessary generalizations to partially ordered defaults are straightforward.

We will start with revisions, that is the addition of possibly inconsistent information. We are looking for a function, *, which, given a level default theory T and a formula p, produces a level default theory 'containing' p. As usual we will use infix notation and denote this new default theory by T*p.

Since our default theories consist of several layers of formulae there is some additional expressiveness not available in standard approaches to theory revision. We can specify a degree of reliability of the information to be added. We will express this by indexing p accordingly.

Definition 5.11: *Let T = (T$_1$,...,T$_n$) be a level default theory, p a formula, j a natural number.*

The revision of T with respect to p, T*p, is the level default theory ({p}, T$_1$, ...,T$_n$).

The (insert-) revision of T with respect to p at degree j, T*$^{(j)}$p, is the level default theory (T$_1$, ..., T$_j$ ∪ {p}, ... , T$_n$).

The (minus-) revision of T with respect to p at degree -j, T*$^{(-j)}$p, is the level default theory (T$_1$, ..., T$_{j-1}$, {p}, T$_j$, ... ,T$_n$).

Definition 5.11 is straightforward. Everything is left to the logical machinery of the underlying nonmonotonic formalism. Note that the other nonmonotonic logics examined so far, for example DL, are not able to model theory revisions in a similar way. The reason is that they are unable to handle arbitrary new information. If, for example, we add new information p to a DL default theory (D,W) and p is inconsistent with W, then the set of all formulae is the single extension, that is we end up with an inconsistent belief state. In this sense possible inconsistencies have to be anticipated in DL. We must know in advance where possible exceptions may arise. Only if we have represented our information adequately will the logical machinery accommodates new conflicting information. In case of an unanticipated inconsistency DL breaks down to inconsistency. In the preferred subtheory approach this is not the case and thus arbitrary changes can be modelled easily.

Note that, among others, Gärdenfors' postulate K*2 (Gärdenfors 88) for revisions does not generally hold in our approach. This postulate requires that the new information p is believed in the new epistemic state. In our approach the new information may be less reliable than conflicting old information. Even if we revise without specifying a degree of reliability the postulate is violated if p is inconsistent.

In the definition of T*p old information is never forgotten, even if it is currently ruled out by more reliable conflicting information. This is very useful since it is always possible that this conflicting information itself is overridden. Let us illustrate this with the following example:

T= (T$_1$,T$_2$) with

T$_2$ = {B}

T$_1$ = {A}

We now revise this default theory with respect to $\neg A \vee \neg B$. According to Definition 5.11 this yields

$T^*(\neg A \vee \neg B) = (T'_1, T'_2, T'_3)$ with

$T'_3 = T_2 = \{B\}$

$T'_2 = T_1 = \{A\}$

$T'_1 = \{\neg A \vee \neg B\}$

This new default theory has a single extension: $Th(\{A, \neg A \vee \neg B\})$. If we now revise with respect to $\neg A$ we obtain

$(T^*(\neg A \vee \neg B))^* \neg A = (T''_1, T''_2, T''_3, T''_4)$ with

$T''_4 = \{B\}$

$T''_3 = \{A\}$

$T''_2 = \{\neg A \vee \neg B\}$

$T''_1 = \{\neg A\}$

This default theory again has a single extension: $Th(\{\neg A, B\})$. Note that B is recovered.

Generally, a formula which is not contained in any extension of a default theory may become weakly or even strongly provable if, as a consequence of some revisions, arguments against this formula are themselves overridden by better information.

The definition of contractions is somewhat more difficult. Contraction means that a formula is removed from a belief set without the assertion of its negation. It turns out that we can adopt Poole's constraints (Section 5.2) to model contractions in our framework. Basically, we split each level of a default theory into two sets, a set of premises and a set of constraints. Premises and constraints are used to determine preferred subtheories, but only the premises are used to define the extensions. The contraction of a default theory T with respect to a formula p, denoted T–p, is the default theory obtained by adding $\neg p$ as a constraint in the appropriate level. We shall give a simple example and refer to (Brewka 90b) for the exact formal definitions. To distinguish constraints from formulae we underline them . Let T = (T1,T2) with

T2 = {BIRD(TWEETY) $\supset$ FLIES(TWEETY)}

T1 = {BIRD(TWEETY)}

This default theory has a single extension Th(T1 $\cup$ T2) which contains FLIES(TWEETY). Now contract this theory with respect to FLIES(TWEETY), that is add the constraint $\neg$FLIES(TWEETY) in a new level:

T–FLIES(TWEETY) = (T'1,T'2,T'3) with

T'3 = {BIRD(TWEETY) $\supset$ FLIES(TWEETY)}

T'2 = {BIRD(TWEETY)}

T'1 = {¬FLIES(TWEETY)}

The new default theory has a single preferred subtheory:

{¬FLIES(TWEETY), BIRD(TWEETY)}

The single extension is:

Th({BIRD(TWEETY)})

We have thus made FLIES(TWEETY) underivable without asserting ¬FLIES(TWEETY).

Again some of Gärdenfors' postulates for contraction are violated, for instance postulate (-2) (Gärdenfors 88). It requires that, for any belief set K and formula A, K–A ⊆ K. The natural reformulation for default theories is: every extension of a default theory T–A is contained in an extension of T. This requirement is clearly violated since our approach is able to memorize currently unused information and T–A may have extensions containing formulae not contained in any extension of T. We do not consider this an indication of irrationality of our approach. The Gärdenfors postulates are devised especially for changes of epistemic states seen as deductively closed theories. The distinction between derived and underived beliefs, and the view of epistemic states as implicitly given as the nonmonotonic consequences of a set of premises, seem to require different rationality criteria.

We have presented in this chapter two generalizations of David Poole's approach to default reasoning. The first generalization extends his original approach in two respects: (1) we allow several levels of reliability instead of only two and (2) we treat all levels uniformly, i.e. there are no unrefutable premises. The second approach generalizes the reliability levels to an arbitrary partial ordering on the premises. In Poole's theory the applicability of a default can be blocked, but there is no way of representing priorities between defaults in the sense that one of two conflicting defaults is not applied if the other one can be applied. Our systems provide a natural means of representing such priorities.

At the heart of our approach lies the notion of preferred subtheory. The different levels of a default theory and the partial ordering on premises can be seen as ways to define specific preference orderings on maximal consistent subsets useful for default reasoning. Further research will reveal whether other interesting orderings can be found, such as for example an ordering corresponding to Shoham's chronological minimality principle (Shoham 86), discussed in Chapter 10.

There is always a tradeoff between expressiveness and simplicity. We have seen that in order to increase expressiveness and to allow for the representation of default priorities we had to give up some of the simplicity and elegance of Poole's system. But still we are much closer to classical logic than many other systems; we do not need modal operators, nonstandard inference rules, fixed point constructions, second order logic or abnormality predicates for the representation of defaults. This should make it simpler to integrate default reasoning with other forms of commonsense reasoning.

Take as an example the representation of counterfactual reasoning (Section 1.2). The truth of a counterfactual A > B ('if A were true, B would be true'), for instance, can be determined by

(1)   adding to the default theory representing our world knowledge the premise A with higher reliability than all others premises (in the reliability level approach this corresponds to introducing a new level {A} with highest reliability), and

(2)   checking whether B is strongly provable from the new theory.

Moreover, the problem of handling inconsistent information - a problem every commonsense reasoner has to deal with anyway - is implicitly solved. I hope therefore that the above approach will prove to be a good compromise between simplicity and expressive power.

CHAPTER 6: A CONDITIONAL APPROACH

6.1: Delgrande's Logic N

Another approach to formalizing default reasoning (Delgrande 87) (Delgrande 88) is based on a conditional => which is used to represent default implication: if A and B are formulae not containing the conditional, then A => B is also a formula with the intuitive meaning 'if A is true then typically B is true'. Nesting of conditionals is not allowed.

Conditionals are binary connectives which are different from logical implication in an important aspect. They are not truth functional. The truth value of A => B is not just a function of the truth values of A and B. The usual way of defining truth values for conditionals, and thus their semantics, is based on possible worlds. The possible worlds represent different alternative forms the actual world might take. An accessibility relation between worlds indicates which world is 'visible' from which other world. On the syntactical side additional axioms and inference rules are used to obtain the semantically justified derivations. For an overview see (Nute 84) or (Veltman 75).

Delgrande develops a possible worlds semantics and corresponding axioms for => in order to give the conditional the properties needed for default reasoning. He observes that in all approaches to default reasoning we have examined so far it is impossible to reason about defaults adequately. For instance, from 'all A's are B' it should follow that the default 'A's are typically not B' is false. Nevertheless in all the logics we have seen in Chapters 2 - 5 these sentences can consistently be asserted. In DL for instance, the default is simply never applied.

To avoid the drawback Delgrande distinguishes between reasoning about defaults and reasoning with defaults. The former is the (monotonic) derivation of defaults from other defaults, the latter the (nonmonotonic, revisable) derivation of plausible conclusions from defaults. He introduces the monotonic first order conditional logic N which allows us to express and reason about defaults. Then, in a second step, the defaults derivable in the logic are used for nonmonotonic inferences. We start with the definition of N.

The language of N is that of first order logic with an additional binary connective =>. The intuitive meaning of A => B is 'if A then normally B'. N consists of classical first order logic with the following additional axiom schemata:

N_1. $\alpha => \alpha$

N_2. $((\alpha => \beta) \wedge (\alpha => \gamma)) \supset (\alpha => (\beta \wedge \gamma))$

N_3. $(\alpha => \beta) \supset (((\alpha \wedge \beta) => \gamma) \supset (\alpha => \gamma))$

N_4. $\neg(\alpha => \beta) \supset ((\alpha => \gamma) \supset ((\alpha \wedge \neg\beta) => \gamma))$

N_5. $((\alpha => \gamma) \wedge (\beta => \gamma)) \supset ((\alpha \vee \beta) => \gamma)$

N_6. $\forall x.(\alpha => \beta) \supset (\alpha => \forall x.\beta)$ if x does not occur free in α

Moreover, N has the new inference rule

R_N.   From $\beta \supset \gamma$ infer $(\alpha => \beta) \supset (\alpha => \gamma)$

This logic has a possible worlds semantics with an accessibility relation E between worlds. E(w1,w2), intuitively, says that world w1 is at least as exceptional as w2. In (Delgrande 87) it is argued that in order to capture this informal notion E has to be reflexive, transitive and forward connected, i.e. if E(w1,w2) and E(w1,w3) then either E(w2,w3) or E(w3,w2). This accessibility relation is used to establish truth in the 'least exceptional' worlds. We shall not present the semantics formally here but simply state that N is provably complete and sound with respect to this semantics.

6.2: Using N for Nonmonotonic Inference

N is monotonic. How can we use N to draw nonmonotonic default inferences? Delgrande presents two equivalent approaches. The starting point for both is a default theory (D, C), where D is a set of formulae of the logic N and C a consistent set of classical formulae. The idea is that D represents general relations between objects, laws and definitional (strict or default) relationships like 'ravens are birds' or 'ravens are typically black' whereas C contains the contingent facts. In Delgrande's equivalent definitions of the nonmonotonic theorems either C is augmented according to specific rules depending on D, or D is augmented according to rules depending on C. Two basic assumptions underly both approaches:

Assumption of Normality: The world being modelled is among the least exceptional worlds according to D where the sentences of C are true.

Assumption of Relevance: Only those sentences known to bear on the truth value of a conditional relation are assumed to have a bearing on that relation's truth value.

The first approach is to augment D nonmonotonically: if we have

RAVEN(x) => BLACK(x)

we can, according to the assumption of relevance, add

RAVEN(x) ∧ HAS-WINGS(x) => BLACK(x)

to D if nothing indicates that the property HAS-WINGS is relevant to the colour of ravens. The conditionals added to D contain additional, and according to the mentioned assumption non-relevant, preconditions.

The following definitions make the idea precise. Interestingly, specificity information is used to solve possible conflicts. Delgrande's approach is the first approach examined so far in this book where the idea of preferring more specific information is implicit.

To avoid confusion we use $\vdash_{FOL}$ here to denote classical derivability. $\vdash_N$ stands for derivability in N.

Definition 6.1: *Let Γ be a set of formulae of N. $\alpha => \gamma$ is supported in Γ if there is a formula β such that:*

(1) $\vdash_{FOL} \alpha \supset \beta$,

(2) $\Gamma \vdash_N \beta => \gamma$,

(3) *if there is β' such that $\vdash_{FOL} \alpha \supset \beta'$ and $\Gamma \vdash_N \neg (\beta' => \gamma)$, then*
$\vdash_{FOL} \beta \supset \beta'$.

Delgrande describes the intuition behind this definition as follows (Delgrande 88, p.74):

Thus basically $\alpha => \gamma$ is supported in Γ if there is a conditional $\beta => \gamma$ where β follows from α and there is no conditional in Γ with a stronger antecedent that denies γ.

The following diagram illustrates this idea:

This notion is used to define default extensions:

Definition 6.2: *Let (D,C) be a default theory, and $\beta_1, \beta_2,...$ an ordering of formulae of first order logic. A maximal default extension $E(D_C)$ of D is defined by:*

$E_0 = D$,

$E_{i+1} =$
$E_i \cup \{(\alpha \wedge \beta_i) => \gamma /\ D \vdash_N (\alpha => \gamma), (\alpha \wedge \beta_i) => \gamma \text{ supported in } C \cup D\} \cup$
$\quad \{(\alpha \wedge \neg\beta_i) => \gamma /\ D \vdash_N (\alpha => \gamma), (\alpha \wedge \beta_i) => \gamma \text{ not supported in } C \cup D\}$,

$E(D_C) = \overset{\infty}{\underset{i=0}{\cup}} E_i$.

Delgrande has shown that in each case a single extension only is produced, independent of the ordering. Moreover, $E(D_C)$ is consistent if D is. Here is the definition of the theorems of a default theory:

Definition 6.3: *Let (D,C) be a default theory. A formula p is derivable from (D,C) iff $E(D_C) /-_N C => p$.*

The second, equivalent approach can be seen as dual to the first: instead of augmenting D, $\alpha \supset \gamma$ is added to C if it is contingently supported. This notion is defined as follows:

Definition 6.4: $\alpha \supset \gamma$ *is contingently supported in a default theory $T = (D,C)$ iff*

(1) $D /-_N \alpha => \gamma$,

(2) $C \cup D \cup \{\alpha \supset \gamma\}$ is consistent,

(3)   if there is α' such that $/-_{FOL} C \supset \alpha'$ and $C \cup D /-_N \neg(\alpha' => \gamma)$, then $/-_{FOL} \alpha \supset \alpha'$.

Delgrande says:

This means that $\alpha \supset \gamma$ is added to C, if $C \cup D \cup \{\alpha \supset \gamma\}$ is consistent and for any α' implied by C and which conflicts with γ, α' is implied by α. So, in a similar fashion to the first approach, only the strongest 'reasonable' conditionals are contingently supported.

Based on this definition the notion of maximal contingent extensions is introduced.

Definition 6.5: *Let (D,C) be a default theory. E is a maximal contingent extension of (D,C) iff there is a sequence $C_0, C_1, ...$ such that*

(1) $C_0 = C$,

(2) $C_{i+1} = C_i \cup \{\alpha \supset \gamma\}$, where $\alpha \supset \gamma$ is contingently supported in (D, C_i),

(3) $E = \bigcup\limits_{i=0}^{\infty} C_i$.

In this approach a default theory may have more than one extension. The theorems are defined as the intersection of all extensions.

Definition 6.5: *Let (D,C) be a default theory. Let EXT be the set of maximal contingent extensions of (D,C). p is derivable from (D,C) iff $p \in Th(E)$ for all $E \in EXT$.*

Delgrande's original papers provide a number of illustrative examples. He shows that his approach behaves skeptically in the case of conflicting information. However, as mentioned above, specificity information is used to solve conflicts whenever possible. For instance, from the defaults

(1) $\forall x.\text{ADULT}(x) => \text{EMPLOYED}(x)$

(2) $\forall x.\text{STUDENT}(x) => \neg\text{EMPLOYED}(x)$

together with the facts

(3)   STUDENT(PETER)

(4)   ADULT(PETER)

we cannot derive whether Peter is employed or not. If, however, we add the default

(5) $\forall$x.STUDENT(x) => ADULT(x)

then the situation changes and (2) gets priority over (1).

The separation of reasoning *about* and reasoning *with* defaults is an appealing idea and certainly has intuitive advantages. Moreover, it allows us to represent the principle that more specific defaults should override more general ones within the logic. Delgrande has shown that many of the standard examples of default reasoning are adequately handled. On the other hand, there seem to be tremendous computational problems involved with his approach. It has still to be shown whether an efficient implementation of a default reasoning system based on it is possible.

Nicholas Asher and Michael Morreau recently presented a formalization of default reasoning and generics which extends Delgrande's ideas in various aspects. They introduce, besides a conditional, a modal operator N (normally) and present a possible worlds semantics for their logic. (Asher, Morreau 90) gives a first description of the approach, which seems promising but is still under development.

CHAPTER 7: NONMONOTONIC THEOREM PROVING

7.1: Expressiveness Versus Tractability

We briefly mentioned in Chapter 1 that the nonmonotonic logics which subsume first order logic are not semi-decidable in their general form. This means that we either have to give up soundness and/or completeness or we have to restrict the logics in some way in order to get theorem provers for them. In this chapter we want to pursue the latter possibility.

Of course, there is always a tradeoff between expressiveness and efficiency. Some researchers have concentrated on what they call *stratified* theories: Gelfond (Gelfond 86) discusses stratified AEL-theories and their relation to stratified logic programs, Gelfond and Lifschitz (Gelfond, Lifschitz 89) discuss the relation between circumscription and stratified logic programs, Konolige's HAEL (see Section 2.3) can also be seen as a version of AEL enforcing stratification.

Stratification, intuitively, means that the predicates or formulae of a theory are partitioned into different layers such that each layer depends on deeper layers only. In such theories no cyclic dependencies can exist. As a consequence, there can be no conflicting defaults which generate multiple extensions or fixed points. An exact definition of stratified logic programs is given in Section 7.2.

It is not astonishing that for stratified theories quite efficient proof techniques exist. In our view, however, stratification forms a restriction which is too strong for many applications. Interacting defaults inducing multiple extensions are very common and cannot always be excluded. We shall therefore present in somewhat more detail a proof procedure for a decidable subset of a modal nonmonotonic logic which is able to handle multiple extensions. It turns out that with the proposed restrictions the procedure can be seen as a proof procedure for NML as well as for AEL. A first version of it was implemented in the FAULTY system (Brewka/Wittur 84), (Brewka 86).

Before examining the proof procedure we shall look at proof techniques developed for the other logics. For circumscription, a number of interesting results have been established, which is not surprising since circumscription is a formalization of non-monotonic reasoning quite close to classical logic. After looking at these results and techniques in Section 7.2 we go on to describe two algorithms for Reiter's DL in Section 7.3. In Section 7.4 our own modal proof procedure is presented.

7.2: Circumscriptive Theorem Proving

In Chapter 4 different forms of circumscription were examined. Generally, a circumscriptive theorem prover needs as input not only a set of formulae and a goal, but also a circumscription policy describing the set of predicates to be minimized, the set of varying predicates, and possibly a preference relation between minimized predicates. Restrictions can be put on all these different input data to permit efficient implementations.

We discuss in this section four different approaches to the computation of circumscription: (1) reduction to first order logic, (2) compilation to logic programs, (3) a special type of resolution, called MILO resolution, and (4) an approach based on de Kleer's ATMS.

(1) Reduction to first order logic

A very important result for the mechanization of circumscription has been established by Vladimir Lifschitz (Lifschitz 85b). He was able to show that for a broad class of theories consisting of so-called separable formulae predicate circumscription is equivalent to a first order formula. This is very helpful since it allows us to use standard first order theorem proving techniques to compute circumscription.

Assume we want to circumscribe the n-place predicate P in A. Lifschitz first observes that the circumscription axiom is equivalent to

$$\forall x. \neg P(x)$$

(x stands for $x_1,...,x_n$) whenever A contains no positive occurrences of P, i.e. whenever P appears only within the scope of a negation symbol in the clausal form of A. Additionally, if A can be written in the form

$$\forall x. Q(x) \supset P(x)$$

where Q is any predicate not containing P (remember that a predicate can be any expression of the form $\lambda x.F$ where F is a formula), then the circumscription of P in A is equivalent to

$$\forall x. Q(x) \equiv P(x).$$

We use the notation $(Q \leq P)$ for $\forall x. Q(x) \supset P(x)$, $(Q = P)$ for $\forall x. Q(x) \equiv P(x)$ and also apply these relation symbols to tuples of predicates $(Q_1,...,Q_n)$ and $(P_1,...,P_n)$ representing the conjunction of the formulae $\forall x. Q_i(x) \supset P_i(x)$, respectively the conjunction of the formulae $\forall x. Q_i(x) \equiv P_i(x)$.

Lifschitz investigates formulae constructed from subformulae of these two types using conjunction and disjunction. Moreover, he considers cases where a tuple P of predicates $P_1, ..., P_m$ is minimized.

Definition 7.1: *A formula A is called solitary with respect to P = $(P_1,...,P_m)$ if it is a conjunction of*

(i)   *formulae containing no positive occurrences of $P_1,...,P_m$,*

(ii)   *formulae of the form $U_i \leq P_i$, where U_i is a predicate not containing $P_1,...,P_m$.*

Any solitary formula A can be written as

$$N(P) \wedge (U \leq P)$$

where N(P) contains no positive occurrence of $P_1,...,P_m$ and U is a tuple of predicates not containing $P_1,...,P_m$. The result of circumscribing P in A without varying predicates then is

$$N(U) \wedge (U = P)$$

where N(U) is obtained from N(P) by replacing each P_i with U_i. Here is a simple example. Assume P is circumscribed in

$$A = P(a) \wedge \neg P(b) \wedge \forall x.Q(x) \supset P(x)$$

A is solitary since it can be transformed to

$$\neg P(b) \wedge \forall x.Q(x) \vee (x = a) \supset P(x)$$

which in the notation of Definition 7.1 is

$$\neg P(b) \wedge (\lambda x.Q(x) \vee (x = a) \leq P).$$

The result of circumscribing P in A hence is

$$\neg(Q(b) \vee (b = a)) \wedge \forall x.Q(x) \vee (x = a) \equiv P(x).$$

The next definition introduces a generalization of solitary formulae.

Definition 7.2: *A formula is called separable (with respect to P) if it is a disjunction of solitary formulae (with respect to P).*

Lifschitz has proven the following theorem:

Theorem 7.1: *If A is separable, i.e. can be written in the form*

$$\bigvee_i (N_i(P) \wedge (U_i \leq P))$$

then the circumscription of P in A is equivalent to

$$\bigvee_i (D_i \wedge (U_i = P))$$

where D_i is

$$N_i(U_i) \wedge \bigwedge_{j \neq i} \neg (N_j(U_j) \wedge (U_j < U_i)).$$

$\bigvee_i F_i$ and $\bigwedge_i F_i$ represent the disjunction and conjunction, respectively, of the formulae F_i.

Lifschitz goes on to extend his results to the case where predicates are allowed to vary and where priorities among circumscribed predicates are introduced. We look only at the main ideas. Varying predicates are handled by showing that every variable circumscription can be reduced to a circumscription without variables. More precisely, CIRC(A(P,Z); P; Z), that is the circumscription of predicates P in A(P,Z) with variable predicates Z, is equivalent to

$$A(P,Z) \land CIRC(\exists z.A(P,z);P)$$

Lifschitz discusses cases where the existential second order quantifier in the new formula can be eliminated.

Prioritized circumscription is reducible to the conjunction of circumscriptions without priorities. An excellent overview on these and further results together with illustrating examples can be found in (Genesereth, Nilsson 87).

(2) Compilation to logic programs

Another approach uses logic programs to compute circumscription. In a recent paper (Gelfond, Lifschitz 89) it has been shown how circumscriptive theories can under certain circumstances, be compiled to logic programs. This approach works - as we shall see - only if the logic program resulting from the compilation is of a certain form. To be more precise, it has to be stratified. We start with the definition of the necessary terminology. The definitions are taken from (Gelfond, Lifschitz 89).

Definition 7.3: *A rule is a formula of the form*

$$L_1 \land ... \land L_m \supset A$$

where L_i are literals and A is an atom, the head of the rule.

Definition 7.4: *A logic program Π is a finite set of rules.*

Definition 7.5: *The definition of a predicate P in Π is the set of rules containing P in the head.*

Definition 7.6: *A stratification of Π is a partition $P_1; ... ;P_k$ of its predicates into disjoint parts such that for every predicate P from P_i ($1 \leq i \leq k$)*

(i)   all predicates that occur in the definition of P belong to $P_1,...,P_i$,

(ii)   all predicates that occur negated in the definition of P belong to $P_1,...,P_{i-1}$.

A program is said to be stratified if it has a stratification. Assume there is a logic programming interpreter which behaves according to the semantics of logic programs given in (Przymusinski 89b). The answer of the interpreter to a query w given a logic program Π is denoted Ans(Π,w).

In order to develop the main theorem of Gelfond and Lifschitz, the following restrictions on the circumscription under consideration are imposed.

(1)   A is a set of clauses without function symbols.

(2)   Uniqueness of names is assumed.

(3)   Each predicate is either minimized or varied.

(4)   Each clause contains at most one literal with a varied predicate.

It is possible to state priorities among the predicates to be minimized. The circumscription can be denoted

$$\text{CIRC } (\forall A \wedge U; P_1 > ... > P_k; Z)$$

where $\forall A$ denotes the universal closure of A, U is the conjunction of the uniqueness of names axioms, P_i are lists of predicates, predicates in P_j are to be minimized with higher priority than predicates in P_{j+1}, and Z is the list of all predicates not contained in $P_1,...,P_k$. We abbreviated this term as CIRC.

The clauses in A are translated to rules. If there are clauses without positive literals this compilation requires the introduction of new predicate symbols representing the negation of predicates. The negation of Q is denoted Q*.

Replace(A) denotes the result of replacing in A each occurrence of $\neg Z_i$ ($Z_i \in Z$) by Z_i*. Resolve(A) denotes the set of clauses obtained by resolving a pair of clauses from A upon an atom whose predicate symbol belongs to Z. We can now state the main theorem:

Theorem 7.2: *Let Π be a logic program obtained from Replace(A) $\cup$ Resolve(A) by writing each clause as a rule. Let w be an atomic ground formula whose predicate symbol occurs in A. If the partition*

$$P1; ...; Pk; Z, Z^*$$

is a stratification of Π, then the following holds:

(a)   *CIRC |= w iff Ans(Π,w) = yes,*

(b)   *if the predicate symbol of w belongs to P1,...,Pk, then CIRC|=$\neg$w iff Ans(Π,w) = no,*

(c)   *if the predicate symbol of w belongs to Z, then CIRC |= $\neg$w iff Ans(Π,Replace($\neg$w)) = yes.*

The main restriction of this theorem is that the priorities between predicates to be minimized have to be a stratification of P. Intuitively, there can be no conflicting defaults unless the conflict is broken in favour of one of them. Let us see what this means for a simplified version of the Nixon example. Assume A is:

(1) AB_1(NIXON) v PAC(NIXON)

(2) AB_2(NIXON) v $\neg$PAC(NIXON)

Assume there is no priority stated between (1) and (2), i.e. we circumscribe (AB_1, AB_2) in the theory without priorities letting PAC vary. Replace(A) $\cup$ Resolve(A) yields

(1') AB_1(NIXON) v PAC(NIXON)

(2') AB_2(NIXON) v PAC*(NIXON)

(3') $AB_1(NIXON) \lor AB_2(NIXON)$

We now have to translate these clauses to rules. Since there is more than one positive literal in each clause the translation can be done in different ways. But independent of the possible solution we choose, there is no stratification (AB_1, AB_2); (PAC, PAC^*) of the resulting program. Either AB_1 appears negated in the definition of AB_2, or vice versa. So we see that the theorem cannot be used for the intended circumscription.

The theorem can be used, however, if we break the conflict between our defaults. The different possible ways of writing the rules reflect the different ways of doing this. If we choose the rules

(R1) $\neg AB_1(NIXON) \supset PAC(NIXON)$

(R2) $\neg AB_2(NIXON) \supset PAC^*(NIXON)$

(R3) $\neg AB_1(NIXON) \supset AB_2(NIXON)$

then AB_1; AB_2; PAC, PAC^* is a stratification. Now we have assigned higher priority to the minimization of AB_1 than to that of AB_2. $PAC(NIXON)$ is in this case derivable from the program and, according to the theorem, from the corresponding prioritized circumscription. If we write instead of (R3)

(R3') $\neg AB_2(NIXON) \supset AB_1(NIXON)$

we give higher priority to minimizing AB_2.

To conclude, application of the theorem of Gelfond and Lifschitz forces us to break all conflicts between defaults. There is no possibility to remain agnostic in case of conflicting evidence.

(3) MILO resolution

Przymusinski (Przymusinski 86) (Przymusinski 89a) describes an algorithm for answering circumscriptive queries. The algorithm assumes uniqueness of names, but otherwise only requires (first order) decidability of the circumscribed theory T. Our presentation assumes that all formulae are ground clauses, but as shown in (Przymusinski 89a), the algorithm can easily be generalized to the non-ground case.

We start with the necessary notation. Let $P=(P_1,...,P_n)$ and $Z=(Z_1,...,Z_m)$ be tuples of predicates. $CIRC(T;P;Z)$ denotes the circumscription of predicates P in T with varying predicates Z. By P^- we denote the set of all negative literals whose predicate symbols are in P. Moreover, Z and P are also used to denote the set of all literals with predicate symbols in Z and P respectively.

Przymusinski defines MILO-resolution (minimal model linear ordered resolution), a slightly modified version of ordered linear resolution (Chang, Lee 73). An *extended clause* is an ordered list of literals, some of which may be framed. A *framed literal* k is denoted [k]. The purpose of framed literals is merely to record resolved-upon literals.

Definition 7.7: *Given a theory T and a clause C, a MILO-deduction of a clause C_n from T+C is a sequence of extended clauses $C_0, ..., C_n$ such that $C_0 = C$ and C_{i+1} is generated from C_i according to the following rules:*

(i)   *An extended clause D_{i+1} is constructed which is the ordered resolvent of $C_i = \{l_1,...,l_m\}$ and some input clause $B = \{k_1,...,k_s\}$ from T upon the first literal l_j in C_i that belongs to $Z + P^-$, i.e.*

$$D_{i+1} = \{l_1,...,l_{j-1},k_1,...,k_{u-1},k_{u+1},...,k_s, [l_j], l_{j+1},...,l_m\}$$

   where $k_u = \neg l_j$;

(ii)   *C_{i+1} is obtained from D_{i+1} by*

   (a)   *deleting any unframed literals k in D_{i+1} for which there exists a framed literal $[\neg k]$ in D_{i+1};*

   (b)   *merging any identical literals to the right;*

   (c)   *removing any framed literals in D_{i+1} not preceded by unframed literals from $Z + P^-$.*

(iii)   *None of the clauses C_i can be a tautology and none can be subsumed by any of the previous clauses C_j, $j < i$.*

Definition 7.8: *A clause for which a MILO-deduction from $T + C$ exists and which does not contain literals from $Z + P^-$ is called a MILO-leaf of $T + C$. The conjunction of all MILO-leaves of $T + C$ is called MILO-derivative of $T + C$, denoted by DERIV(T,C).*

The following two theorems, theorems 3.4 and 3.9 in (Przymusinski 89a), state the relationship between MILO-resolution and circumscription:

Theorem 7.3: *Suppose that F is any formula not containing literals from Z and that F is represented in conjunctive normal form as $F = D_1 \wedge ... \wedge D_m$, where the D_i are clauses. Then $CIRC(T;P;Z) \models F$ iff $T \models DERIV(T,D_i)$, for every $i \leq m$.*

Theorem 7.4: Let F be any formula. Then,

   $CIRC(T;P;Z) \models F$ iff $CIRC(T;P;Z) \models \neg DERIV(T,\neg F)$.

These theorems are the basis for the following algorithm to determine whether a given formula F is implied by CIRC(T; P; Z):

(1)   Check if F contains literals from Z. If it does go to 2, else go to 3.

(2)   (a) Represent F in conjunctive normal form, i.e. let $F = G_1 \wedge ... \wedge G_m$, where G_i are clauses.

   (b) For all j ($1 \leq j \leq m$) determine DERIV(T, G_j).

   (c) For all j ($1 \leq j \leq m$) verify whether $T \models DERIV(T, G_j)$.

   (d) If there is a j such that not $T \models DERIV(T, G_j)$ then return NO, else return YES.

(3) (a) Represent F in disjunctive normal form, i.e. let $F = K_1 \lor \ldots \lor K_m$, where the K_i are conjunctions of literals.

(b) Set $T_1 = T$ and for all i ($1 \leq i \leq m$) determine DERIV(T_i, $\neg K_i$), where $T_{i+1} = T_i + \neg K_i$.

(c) Use step 2 of this algorithm to determine whether

CIRC(T; P; Z) $\models \neg$[DERIV(T_1, $\neg K_1$) $\land \ldots \land$ DERIV(T_m, $\neg K_m$)]

(d) If yes, then return YES, else return NO.

Step 2 of the algorithm applies Theorem 7.3, step 3 Theorem 7.4. Since MILO-leaves do not contain literals from Z step 2 can be invoked in step 3c. In the general case the algorithm does not necessarily terminate since it is not always possible to determine DERIV(T,S) and to decide whether a formula is classically derivable from a given theory. In special cases, for instance if the logical language does not contain function symbols, the algorithm is guaranteed to terminate and is then a decision procedure.

(Przymusinski 89a) contains a number of illustrative examples. In addition he shows how his approach can be used to compute prioritized circumscription.

(4) Circumscription and Confirmation

Ginsberg has developed a circumscriptive theorem prover based on an assumption-based truth maintenance system (Ginsberg 89). His prover presupposes the following restrictions on the possible circumscriptions CIRC(T; P; V):

(i) T contains no function symbols.

(ii) Uniqueness of names and domain closure is assumed, that is different constants denote different objects, and for each object in the domain there exists a denoting constant.

(iii) V contains all predicates which are not minimized.

For a set of sentences D a relation $\leq_D$ between models is defined such that M1 $\leq_D$ M2 iff the set of elements of D valid in M1 is a subset of those valid in M2. From results in (Lifschitz 85) it follows that, under the three given conditions, q is a consequence of CIRC(T; P; V) iff q is valid in all $\leq_D$-maximal models of T, where D is the set of all negated ground literals with predicate symbol P.

Ginsberg introduces the following concept of confirmation.

Definition 7.9: *A sentence q is confirmed by p for D and T iff:*

(i) $T \cup \{p\}$ *is satisfiable*

(ii) $T \cup \{p\} \models q$

(iii) *p is in disjunctive normal form with respect to D, i.e. p is a disjunction of conjunctions of elements from D.*

Ginsberg's main result is the following:

Theorem 7.5: *A sentence q holds in all ≤D-maximal models of T iff there is some p that confirms q such that ¬p is unconfirmed.*

Together with the above mentioned result on the relation between circumscription and ≤D-maximal models this constitutes the theoretical basis of his algorithm.

The task now is to determine the sentences confirming a query q. Ginsberg observes that it is sufficient to consider only the weakest such sentence and its negation. An assumption-based truth maintenance system, ATMS, (de Kleer 86) (Reiter, de Kleer 87) - see also Section 9.3 - is used to determine the weakest sentence p confirming q (Intuitively, the ATMS assumptions are the sentences in D, contexts are their conjunctions, environments are disjunctions of such conjunctions). The environment of ¬p then is used to check whether ¬p is unconfirmed.

Ginsberg's ATMS differs from de Kleer's in two important ways: it uses a technique examined in (Ginsberg 87c) to achieve backward chaining behavior, and it allows for quantified assumptions in contexts. The details together with some examples are to be found in (Ginsberg 89).

In (Baker, Ginsberg 89) the results are extended to handle the prioritized circumscription CIRC(T; $P_n < ... < P_1$; V). Interestingly, a proof for a formula q can be seen as a dispute between a proponent trying to establish a valid argument for q and an opponent trying to undermine the proponent's argument.

Definition 7.10: *A sentence p is an argument for q iff*

(1) p is a disjunction of conjunctions of negated ground literals containing predicates from Pi,

(2) T ∪ {p} is satisfiable,

(3) T ∪ {p} |= q.

The *priority of* p is the least k such that p contains a literal with predicate symbol from P_k.

Definition 7.11: *Let p and q be arguments. Then, p rebuts q iff p is an argument for ¬q and the priority of p is greater than or equal to the priority of q; p refutes q iff p rebuts q and q does not rebut p, i.e. the priority of p is greater than that of q.*

Definition 7.12: *Let p and q be arguments. Then, p ultimately rebuts q iff p rebuts q, and p is not ultimately refuted; p ultimately refutes q iff p refutes q, and p is not ultimately rebutted.*

Definition 7.12 is well-founded, since a refuting argument must always have higher priority than the refuted argument. Baker and Ginsberg have shown the following:

Theorem 7.6: *Let q be a sentence, T a finite set of sentences without function symbols which includes domain closure and uniqueness of names assumptions. Moreover, let V* *be the set of all predicates not contained in $P_1, ..., P_n$. Then $CIRC(T; P_n < ... < P_1; V)$ |= q iff there is an argument for q that is not ultimately rebutted.*

Again, the weakest arguments in disjunctive normal form correspond exactly to ATMS labels. In each case it is sufficient to consider only those assumptions whose priorities are high enough.

It turns out that this approach to computing prioritized circumscription can be used directly for the generalization of Poole's approach introducing levels of reliability (Section 5.3). We have only to generalize the notion of argument somewhat: instead of a disjunction of conjunctions of negated literals with predicates from P, an argument becomes a disjunction of a conjunction of formulae in any of the available levels. The priority of an argument is the level of its least reliable part (in Definitions 5.8 and 5.9 high numbers indicated low reliability). The necessary modifications of the other definitions are straightforward.

It is certainly also possible to generalize the approach to partially ordered defaults. But this has not been worked out, so far.

7.3: Theorem Proving in Default Logic

In his original DL-paper (Reiter 80) Reiter presents a proof procedure for normal defaults. We restrict this presentation to the case of closed normal default theories, which are theories whose defaults contain no free variables. The generalization to arbitrary normal default theories is not difficult but involves some additional technicality that we prefer to avoid here. For the details see (Reiter 80).

Reiter introduces the concept of a default proof:

Definition 7.13: *Let $\Delta=(D,W)$ be a closed normal default theory, and β a closed wff. Let CONSEQUENTS(D) denote the consequents, PREREQUISITES(D) the prerequisites of a set of defaults D. A finite sequence $D_0,...,D_k$ of finite subsets of D is a default proof of β with respect to Δ iff*

(i) $W \cup CONSEQUENTS(D_0)$ |- β

(ii)   For $1 \leq i \leq k$
* $W \cup CONSEQUENTS(D_i)$ |- PREREQUISITES(D_{i-1})*

(iii) $D_k = \emptyset$

(iv) $\bigcup\limits_{i=0}^{k} CONSEQUENTS(D_i)$ is satisfiable.

Reiter is able to show that if Δ is consistent there exists an extension E containing β iff β has a default proof with respect to Δ.

The open question is how to determine the sequence $D_0,...,D_k$. Reiter proposes using for that purpose a modified version of linear resolution (Chang, Lee 73) where each clause is indexed with the set of defaults which gave rise to its derivation. If β is provable, i.e. if the empty clause is derivable from

$$W \cup \{\neg\beta\} \cup \text{CONSEQUENTS(D)}$$

then the index D_j of the empty clause is the set of defaults used for the proof of β. We will say the proof returns D_j in this case.

Reiter's procedure for testing whether a formula β is contained in an extension of a closed normal default theory (D,W) starts with a proof for β. If a proof returning D_0 is found, another proof is generated for the prerequisites of the defaults in D_0. This proof returns D_1, a new proof for D_1's prerequisites is generated and so on. The generation of proofs continues until a proof with empty index is found. The last step consists of a consistency check. It has to be tested whether W together with the consequents of all defaults contained in one of the returned D_i is satisfiable. If this is the case, β is contained in an extension of (D,W).

Unfortunately, this proof procedure is not extendable to non-normal defaults, since only normal defaults allow for the local view inherent in the procedure: the restriction to the normal case guarantees that defaults not considered in the procedure are irrelevant to the existence of an extension. In the general case the local view on defaults is impossible. Here a default can block the applicability of another default in every extension. Take as an example the default theory $(\{d_1, d_2\}, \{\})$ with $d_1=(\text{True:A/A})$, $d_2=(\text{True:}\neg A \wedge B/B)$; d_1 makes the application of d_2 impossible in all extensions.

Etherington (Etherington 87) presents a nondeterministic procedure for constructing extensions of arbitrary finite default theories (D,W). Finiteness here means that the number of variables, constants, predicate symbols and defaults is finite, and that no functions are allowed. The procedure constructs a sequence of successive approximations by applying defaults with 'known' prerequisites and 'currently' consistent justifications. Etherington shows that there is a converging computation with two subsequent identical approximations H_i and H_{i+1} iff $\text{Th}(H_i)$ is an extension. The nondeterminism of the procedure is necessary to allow for the generation of different extensions.

Unfortunately, in the general case the procedure admits cycling and hence nonterminating computations. Etherington (Etherington 87) describes classes of theories for which this cannot happen.

It is difficult to see how a theorem prover could efficiently use Etherington's general procedure. Of course, it is possible generate extensions one after the other using all different possible choices admitted by the procedure. But this is a hopelessly inefficient process.

What seems to be needed, then, is a procedure which can handle more general cases than Reiter's approach and on the other hand is more efficient (and therefore presumably less general) than Etherington's procedure. In the next section we present a proof procedure for NML and AEL whose generality lies between the two extremes. Konolige's equivalence result allows also us to interpret this proof procedure as an algorithm for default logic.

7.4: A Modal Default Prover

In this section we look at a simple modal default prover. A first version of the proof procedure has been described in (Brewka, Wittur 84) and (Brewka 86). In these papers the system was presented as a prover for NML. We will see that with the restrictions imposed on the language the objective part of each NML fixed point corresponds exactly to the objective part of an AEL expansion and vice versa. Hence we can also interpret the prover as an AEL prover.

Here are the restrictions on the language.

(I)   We assume a standard first order language with a finite set of constant symbols and without function symbols. It should be noted that this makes the Herbrand universe finite and the first order logic, for that reason, decidable.

(II)   This language is extended to contain the M-operator[1], but - and this is essential - the operator is only admitted in defaults of the form

$$A \wedge M\, B_1 \wedge ... \wedge M\, B_n \supset C$$

where A, B_i and C are ordinary formulae, i.e. they do not contain M.

(III)   In order to avoid the problems of quantifying into the scope of a modal operator (see Section 2.2) we do not allow B_i to contain free variables. We admit default schemata, however. The schema

$$BIRD(x) \wedge M\, FLIES(x) \supset FLIES(x)$$

for instance, represents all formulae obtained by replacing parameter x by a ground-term.

In addition to the restrictions on the form of the allowed premises we restrict the formulae which may be tested for derivability; we are only interested in the derivability of ordinary formulae.

With these restrictions no statements about the consistency or inconsistency of a formula p can be made explicitly. All we can express is that p is derivable if some other formulae are consistent. And the only way to find out whether a formula actually is consistent is to try to prove its negation.

The following theorem has been proven in (Brewka 89):

---

[1] Remember that M is equivalent to $\neg L \neg$.

Theorem 7.7: *Let A be a set of premises with restrictions I, II, and III. Then the ordinary formulae of each NML fixed point of A are exactly those of a corresponding AEL extension of A and vice versa.*

With this result in mind we base our argument in the the rest of this section exclusively on NML. This makes the presentation of our results somewhat easier.

In order to explain our proof procedure we will start with a simple example. How about Tweety?

(1)   BIRD(TWEETY)

(2)   BIRD(TWEETY) ∧ M FLIES(TWEETY) ⊃ FLIES(TWEETY)

We try to prove FLIES(TWEETY) from these premises. We run a standard resolution refutation proof where Mq for all q is treated as a literal. We cannot derive the empty clause but we get the interesting unit clause

(3)   ¬M FLIES(TWEETY)

This formula is interesting because it only contains literals starting with ¬M. We will call such clauses M-clauses.

Definition 7.14: *A clause l_1 v ... v l_n is an M-clause iff each literal l_i is of the form ¬Mp, where p is an ordinary formula.*

From the definition of NML fixed points we know that they must contain the formula Mq if they do not contain ¬q. In our example the question is: is M FLIES(TWEETY) contained in the fixed point(s), or, in other words, is ¬FLIES(TWEETY) not derivable within the fixed point(s)? Because if this is the case we can use (3) to derive the empty clause.

The only way to find that out is to start a new resolution proof for ¬FLIES(TWEETY). This new refutation proof does not yield the empty clause and, moreover, it does not yield an M-clause. This tells us that even with the addition of any formulae of the form Mq we cannot derive ¬FLIES(TWEETY). Therefore every fixed point must contain M FLIES(TWEETY), i.e. we are allowed to use this additional formula in our first proof and the proof now succeeds.

In our simple example the success of one proof depended on the failure of another proof. The dependency between success and failure of proofs can be more complicated, however. Here is the Nixon example:

(1)   QUAK(NIXON) ∧ M PAC(NIXON) ⊃ PAC(NIXON)

(2)   REPUBL(NIXON) ∧ M ¬PAC(NIXON) ⊃ ¬PAC(NIXON)

(3)   QUAK(NIXON)

(4)   REPUBL(NIXON)

Trying to prove PAC(NIXON) yields the M-clause ¬M PAC(NIXON) (let us call this proof P1). This leads to the creation of a second proof P2 for ¬PAC(NIXON). This proof generates the M-clause ¬M¬PAC(NIXON). The proof necessary to decide on the consistency of ¬PAC(NIXON), P1, is already there.

We are now in a situation where success and failure of both proofs depend on each other. P1 succeeds if and only if P2 fails and vice versa. These two cases correspond exactly to the two fixed points of our theory: one fixed point contains M PAC(NIXON) and, therefore, PAC(NIXON). This fixed point corresponds to the case where P1 succeeds and P2 fails. The other fixed point containing M¬PAC(NIXON) and ¬PAC(NIXON) corresponds to the success of P2 and failure of P1.

We take McDermott and Doyle's view here and remain agnostic in the case of conflicting evidence, that is when more than one fixed point exists a formula will be derivable only if it is contained in all fixed points. In our proof procedure the proof for the tested formula must succeed independently of the possible ways of assigning success and failure to the constructed proofs.

To make this precise we need the following definitions:

Definition 7.15: *A (refutation) proof P_i for a formula q from a set of premises A is the smallest set of clauses such that*

(1)   the clausal form of A is a subset of P_i,
(2)   the clausal form of ¬q is a subset of P_i,
(3) P_i is closed with respect to the resolution rule.

Definition 7.16: *Let $P = \{P_1, ..., P_n\}$ be a set of proofs from a set of premises A. P is dependency complete if P contains a proof for ¬p whenever there exists P_i ($1 \leq i \leq n$) with an M-clause containing ¬Mp as a literal.*

Intuitively, a set of proofs is dependency-complete if and only if failure and success of each proof in the set depend only on proofs in the same set.

Definition 7.17: *Let $P = \{P_1, ..., P_n\}$ be a set of proofs for the formulae $p_1, ..., p_n$, respectively, and L: P -> {SUCCESS, FAILURE} a labelling of P which assigns to each of the proofs in P exactly one of SUCCESS or FAILURE. Moreover, let ADDCLAUSES(L) = {M¬p_i / L(P_i) = FAILURE}. L is admissible iff for all i*

     $P_i \cup ADDCLAUSES(L)$ *is inconsistent <=> L(P_i) = SUCCESS.*

Definition 7.18: *A formula q is derivable from a set of premises A iff its proof Q is labelled SUCCESS in all admissible labellings of a dependency complete set of proofs containing Q.*

We are now in a position to describe the proof procedure. It consists of two main steps. The first step, the generation of a dependency complete set of proofs containing the proof for the original goal, can semi-formally be described as follows:

    push the goal onto the agenda
    until the agenda is empty do
        remove the top element from the agenda
        start a refutation proof for it
        if the empty clause is derived, mark this proof with SUCCESS

>   *else   if no M-clause is derived mark this proof with FAILURE*
>   *else   for each literal ¬Mq in each derivable M-clause*
>   *unless ¬q is in the agenda or a proof for it exists already*
>   *push ¬q onto the agenda.*

This proof construction phase is guaranteed to terminate since our restriction to a finite Herbrand universe implies that there is only a finite number of possible instances of literals beginning with ¬M.

The second main step of our proof procedure consists of finding all admissible labellings for the constructed proofs and checking whether the proof for the main goal is labelled with SUCCESS in all of them. It is interesting to see that the dependencies between proofs can be expressed in terms of propositional formulae. Using the names of the proofs as propositional constants such that P stands for 'proof P succeeds' we can, for instance, express the dependencies from our Nixon example where two proofs P1 and P2 are created with the formula

$$P1 \equiv \neg P2$$

It is not difficult to see that the propositional models of this formula correspond exactly to admissible labellings of the proofs. The models $\{P1, \neg P2\}$ and $\{\neg P1, P2\}$ correspond to the admissible labellings which assign SUCCESS to P1 and FAILURE to P2, and respectively FAILURE to P1 and SUCCESS to P2.

According to the skeptical view the formula PAC(NIXON) for which P1 was generated is derivable if P1 is true in all models of the dependency formula. In other words, if P1 logically follows from the formula. In our example this is not the case. We remain agnostic with respect to Nixon's pacifism.

The second step of the proof procedure generates a set of propositional formulae, the dependency propositions, and invokes a propositional prover on them.

Definition 7.19: *Let $P=\{P_1,...,P_n\}$ be the set of proofs for formulae $p_1, ..., p_n$, respectively, generated in the proof construction phase. For each P_i we define $DP(P_i)$, the dependency proposition of P_i, as follows:*

>   *if P_i is marked with SUCCESS then $DP(P_i) := P_i$*

else

>   *if P_i is marked with FAILURE then $DP(P_i) := \neg P_i$*

else

> $DP(P_i) := P_i \equiv (\neg P_{11} \wedge ... \wedge \neg P_{1k}) \vee ... \vee (\neg P_{j1} \wedge ... \wedge \neg P_{jm})$,

where $\{\neg M \neg p_{11} \vee ... \vee \neg M \neg p_{1k}, ... , \neg M \neg p_{j1} \vee ... \vee \neg M \neg p_{jm}\}$ is the set of all M-clauses derivable in P_i. .

We extend the definition of DP to sets of proofs and define

> $DP(P)=\{DP(P_i) \mid P_i \in P\}$.

Here is an example. Assume the M-clauses generated for proof P1 are

> $\{\neg Ma \vee \neg Mb, \neg Mc\}$

and the empty clause is not derivable in P1. Let P2, P3, P4 be the proofs for ¬a, ¬b, ¬c respectively. Then the dependency proposition for P1 is

$$P1 \equiv (\neg P2 \wedge \neg P3) \vee \neg P4 .$$

Intuitively this can be read as 'P1 succeeds iff P2 and P3 fail or P4 fails'.

As we have just said propositional models of the dependency propositions of a set of proofs correspond exactly to admissible labellings which in turn correspond to fixed points of the theory. Since we are interested in formulae contained in all fixed points the question is whether their proofs are 'true' in all models, i.e. whether the corresponding constant logically follows from the dependency propositions. This can be checked by a standard propositional prover.

Let us illustrate the two steps with a slight extension of the Nixon example. Read R as 'Nixon is Republican', Q as 'Nixon is Quaker', D as 'Nixon is a dove', H as 'Nixon is a hawk', and P as 'Nixon is politically interested'. Assume our premises are:

(1)	R	R
(2)	Q	Q
(3)	$R \wedge M H \supset H$	$\neg R \vee \neg M H \vee H$
(4)	$Q \wedge M D \supset D$	$\neg Q \vee \neg M D \vee D$
(5)	$H \supset \neg D$	$\neg H \vee \neg D$
(6)	$H \wedge M P \supset P$	$\neg H \vee \neg M P \vee P$
(7)	$D \wedge M P \supset P$	$\neg D \vee \neg M P \vee P$

The right hand column shows the premises in clausal form. We want to know whether Nixon is politically interested and generate P1, a refutation proof for P. P1 yields exactly three M-clauses, namely

$$\{\neg M H \vee \neg M D, \neg M H \vee \neg M P, \neg M D \vee \neg M P\}.$$

The first M-clause is obtained from (1), (2), (3), (4) and (5), the second from (1), (3), (6), and the negated goal ¬P, the third from (2), (4), (7), and the negated goal.

This leads to the generation of three new proofs: P2 for ¬H, P3 for ¬D, and P4 for ¬P. P2 yields the M-clauses

$$\{\neg M H \vee \neg M D, \neg M D\}.$$

The second clause (which subsumes the first) is obtained from (2), (4), (5) and the negated goal H. P3 yields

$$\{\neg M H \vee \neg M D, \neg M H\}.$$

The second M-clause (which also subsumes the first) is obtained from (1), (3), (5) and the negated goal D. P4 yields only the M-clause which can already be obtained from the premises, namely

{¬M H v ¬M D}

Neither P2, P3 nor P4 lead to further proofs as the set of proofs generated is dependency-complete.

We now generate the dependency propositions. For P1 we get

(D1) P1 ≡ (¬P2 ∧ ¬P3) v (¬P2 ∧ ¬P4) v (¬P3 ∧ ¬P4).

For P2 correspondingly

P2 ≡ (¬P2 ∧ ¬P3) v ¬P3,

which is equivalent to

(D2) P2 ≡ ¬P3.

Subsumed M-clauses can be omitted from the construction of the dependency proposition according to the laws of propositional logic. The dependency formula for P3 is equivalent to that of P2. For P4 we get

(D4) P4 ≡ (¬P2 ∧ ¬P3).

P1 is logically entailed by these formulae. Substituting P2 for ¬P3 in (D4) yields

P4 ≡ false,

substituting false for P4 in (D1) leads together with (D2) to the desired result. Hence 'Nixon is politically interested' is derivable. The two models of the formulae, {P1,P2,¬P3,¬P4} and {P1,¬P2,P3,¬P4}, correspond to the two fixed points of the premises containing 'Nixon is a dove' and 'Nixon is a hawk', respectively.

As we have mentioned we do not admit quantifying into the scope of M. We do allow default schemata, however, representing the set of their ground instances. For the sake of simplicity we did not distinguish syntactically between meta-linguistic parameters and logical variables (apart from the fact that default schemata never have a quantifier). We have to be somewhat careful with such parameters in our procedure, however. Take the following theory about birds:

(1)   CANARY(TWEETY)

(2)   PENGUIN(JOE)

(3)   ¬FLIES(JOE)

(4)   ¬M FLIES(x) v FLIES(x)

The question is ∃x.FLIES(x). We negate this formula and add the clause ¬FLIES(x) to the premises. We get the M-clause ¬M FLIES(x). This is *not* to be interpreted as ¬M∀x.FLIES(x). Generating a new proof for the negation of ∀x.FLIES(x), that is a proof for ∃x.¬FLIES(x), would lead to the derivation of the empty clause, so this new proof would be successful and the original proof would fail.

We have to remember that whenever there is an M contained in a clause this clause is a schema. If JOE and TWEETY are the only constants the M-clause schema represents the set of clauses {¬M FLIES(TWEETY), ¬M FLIES(JOE)}, i.e. we have to generate two new proofs for ¬FLIES(TWEETY) and ¬FLIES(JOE). The first of these fails without producing an M-clause. Therefore our original proof succeeds and we get the right answer, ∃x.FLIES(x) is derivable.

Another problem has to be addressed here: the derivable formulae of NML and AEL depend on the language of the logic. If we remove (1) from the above example and admit JOE as the only constant ∃x.FLIES(x) is no longer derivable as there is no constant c such that M FLIES(c) can be contained in a fixed point.

As a consequence we have to be careful with Skolemization since Skolemization introduces new constants. Take the following two premises:

(1)   ¬FLIES(JOE)

(2)   ¬M FLIES(x) v FLIES(x)

The goal is ∀x.FLIES(x). For our refutation proof we have to negate this formula and skolemize with let us say sk1, i.e. we add the clause ¬FLIES(sk1). If we now proceed as usual we obtain the M-clause ¬M FLIES(sk1). The new proof for ¬FLIES(sk1) fails without producing an M-clause. The original proof, therefore, is successful. But this, obviously, is not the right answer with respect to our goal. (It would be the right answer to FLIES(sk1), however, if sk1 were a constant of the language. Not the procedure is wrong but the use of Skolemized formulae).

Where did we go wrong? In fact the default schema does not represent the instance ¬M FLIES(sk1) v FLIES(sk1) since sk1 does not belong to the logical language. Therefore, we cannot resolve ¬FLIES(sk1) with the schema. Generally, whenever a Skolem-constant is contained in a clause we are not allowed to build the resolvent from the formula and a schema. In our example this means that there is no M-clause and the proof for the goal correctly fails.

We now discuss some fundamental properties of the proof procedure. The following soundness result has ben shown in (Brewka 89):

Theorem 7.8: *Let A be a set of premises, F an ordinary formula. The proof procedure yields 'provable' only if F is derivable from A in NML, i.e. only if F is contained in all fixed points of A.*

Unfortunately, the converse of the theorem does not hold, that is the proof procedure is incomplete. If there is a fixed point then there must be a corresponding admissible labelling of proofs generated by the procedure. But, on the other hand, there may be admissible labellings that do not correspond to fixed points. This can be the case when the addition of assumptions Mq leads to the 'collapse' of a fixed point candidate, although none of the assumptions contributes to the success or failure of the generated proof. We use an example from (Reiter, Criscuolo 81) to illustrate this possibility.

(1)   ¬M(A ∧ ¬B) v ¬B

(2)   ¬M(B ∧ ¬C) v ¬C

)3)   ¬M(C ∧ ¬A) v ¬A

This premise set has no fixed point, a result which can be shown with our procedure. If the goal is ¬B proof P1 for that goal generates the single M-clause ¬M(A ∧ ¬B). This leads to proof P2 for ¬(A ∧ ¬B). P2 produces as single M-clause ¬M(C ∧ ¬A). We therefore generate proof P3 for ¬(C ∧ ¬A). Again we get one M-clause, namely ¬M(B ∧ ¬C). Proof P4 for ¬(B ∧ ¬C) then, correspondingly, generates the M-clause ¬M(A ∧ ¬B). The needed proof P2 is already there. Together this yields the dependency propositions

$$\{P1 \equiv \neg P2, P2 \equiv \neg P3, P3 \equiv \neg P4, P4 \equiv \neg P2\}$$

This set is inconsistent, i.e. there is no admissible labelling and thus no fixed point of the premise set. Therefore, ¬B is derivable.

But what if the goal is D? Obviously, D is derivable since there is no fixed point. But our procedure does not generate an M-clause in the proof for D. Therefore it does not generate new proofs at all; the single dependency proposition ¬P1 has an admissible labelling that marks P1 with failure. Thus the procedure returns 'unprovable'. The problem is that the nonexistence of the fixed point corresponding to this admissible labelling has only to do with formulae which are irrelevant to the derivability of the empty clause in P1.

This problem can only arise if there are 'odd loops' in the theory, that is if there are cases where the derivability of a formula depends in some way on the non-derivability of the same formula. The simplest example is {Mq ⊃ ¬q} where the derivability of ¬q depends on the consistency of q, i.e. the non-derivability of ¬q.

This problem could be cured in principle, but at a high price. Since there is no way to decide which formulae contribute to an 'odd loop', completeness can only be guaranteed if a proof for ¬q is generated for every literal ¬Mq that appears in any clause of the theory. We hope that odd loops do not occur very often in practical applications and that, therefore, the tremendous loss of efficiency necessary to ensure completeness can be avoided.

The situation is somewhat different, however, if the set of premises used in an application does not change frequently. In this case the premise set can be prepro-cessed. The complete set of proofs induced by any literal ¬Mq in the premise set and all dependency propositions can be generated in advance. In this case for each goal the proof procedure has only to generate one resolution proof plus one propositional proof.

It should be noted that incompleteness and soundness of the procedure depend on the fixed point intersection approach we pursued. If the single fixed point view is adopted, then the situation changes. In that case step 2 of the procedure has to be changed. The question becomes: Is there an admissible labelling which marks the proof for the goal with SUCCESS? Now exactly the opposite properties hold. Since for all fixed points there exists a corresponding admissible labelling, we have completeness, but soundness is lost since the labelling that has been found might not correspond to a fixed point.

It remains to be noted that Junker and Konolige have recently explored ways of using a truth maintenance system (TMS, see Chapter 9) for an implementation of an AEL prover (Junker, Konolige 90). Defaults are coded to TMS-justifications. A classical theorem prover is used to establish the necessary first order dependencies between the different parts of the defaults. These dependencies are made available to the TMS by adding appropriate justifications. In other words, the TMS is made as first order complete as necessary. The purpose of the truth maintenance system is roughly the same as that of our propositional prover. It computes admissible labellings corresponding to AEL fixed points.

A decision procedure for propositional NML based on the semantic tableau method is described in (McDermott, Doyle 80).

Until now there has been little practical experience with this and other approaches to nonmonotonic theorem proving. Not much is known therefore about their relative advantages and disadvantages and, in particular, about their efficiency for solving practical problems. The application of some of the examined techniques to real world problems remains a challenge.

CHAPTER 8: INHERITANCE SYSTEMS

8.1: A Classification

Inheritance systems (IHS) have quite a long tradition in Artificial Intelligence. Informally, an IHS is a system in which it is possible to describe hierarchies of objects and classes. The hierarchy is used to pass information associated with general classes to their subclasses (the subclasses 'inherit' the information). The hierarchical organization of knowledge is very economic and natural and arguably corresponds to the way we structure our world knowledge. We will use the term hierarchy in the sense of a directed acyclic graph throughout this chapter.

The interest in these systems rests on two, rather independent, motivations:

(1)   Since the expressiveness of the language of an IHS is usually very restricted it is hoped that quite efficient, yet theoretically well-founded, implementations can be found. Some existing implementations support this expectation.

(2)   The basic idea underlying inheritance, the idea of preferring the most specific information in a case of conflict, is not implicit in most of the nonmonotonic logics (Delgrande's system is an exception). Yet it seems to be a rather general and domain independent principle of commonsense reasoning. Trying to give a precise theoretical foundation of this idea is a necessary step in the formalization of intelligent behavior.

Two different research strategies have been applied within the field: some researchers, like Touretzky, Thomason and Horty, give formal accounts of specificity which are independent of any existing nonmonotonic logic. These approaches, presented in Sections 8.4 and 8.5, define the conclusions sanctioned by an inheritance hierarchy in terms of admissible paths within the hierarchy.

On the other hand, there are researchers who try to model the specialization principle in one of the existing formalisms. Etherington and Reiter's approach to inheritance based on default logic is an example. It is presented in Section 8.3. Others have modelled inheritance in autoepistemic logic (Przymusinska, Gelfond 88) or circumscription (Haugh 88). The formalization of frames described in Section 8.2 which is based on (Brewka 87) belongs also to this category.

Both approaches have their advantages: the path based definitions are usually simpler since they do not need additional explicit axiomatizations of specificity and the machinery of a 'general purpose' nonmonotonic logic. On the other hand, the advantage of formalizing inheritance in one of the existing nonmonotonic logics is that it provides IHS with a model theoretic semantics, which is often missing in the path based approach.

There are two main types of IHS: monotonic inheritance systems do not admit exceptions to inheritance, nonmonotonic inheritance systems, by contrast, do.

Some famous examples of the monotonic type are KL-ONE (Brachman, Schmolze 85) or KRYPTON (Brachman 83). It is not very difficult to describe the semantics of inheritance systems without exceptions in classical first order logic. An inheritance link from class A to class B, for instance, is just interpreted as the universally quantified statement 'All A's are B's'. As an early example of a formalization of monotonic inheritance see (Hayes 79) and (Hayes, Hendrix 81) where frames are interpreted as unary, slots as binary predicates. An exact definition of frames and slots will be given below after some additional terminology has been introduced.

Some researchers have recently criticized this first order view of inheritance without exceptions as too simplistic (Thomason et al. 86). They observe that the behavior of monotonic IHS differs in one important respect from classical logic, namely in the presence of inconsistencies. Inconsistencies in monotonic IHS do not usually lead to the derivability of every formula. Hence, classical logic is insufficient if one is interested in a semantic characterization such that the IHS can be seen as a *sound and complete* logical system. This led the authors to define the semantics of monotonic IHS in terms of a four valued logic (Thomason et al. 86).

Retaining first order logic as the semantics and considering monotonic IHS as sound but incomplete realizations is, however, at least one possible way of looking at monotonic inheritance - particularly since the cases where incompleteness arises can be described precisely.

Our interest in the rest of this chapter will be nonmonotonic IHS exclusively. We shall first introduce some additional terminology, most of which is taken from (Touretzky et al. 87).

Definition 8.1: *An inheritance network is a directed acyclic graph whose nodes represent individuals and classes. The links represent relations between these individuals and classes.*

The most important relations used in IHS are IS-A, written $x \to z$, and NOT-IS-A, written $x \nrightarrow z$. Systems with both positive and negative links are called *bipolar*.

Definition 8.2: *A multiple IHS is a system whose nodes are allowed to have more than one outgoing link.*

Definition 8.3: *A mixed IHS distinguishes between strict (monotonic) links with no exceptions and defeasible (nonmonotonic) links.*

In this chapter we shall be mainly concerned with nonmonotonic bipolar multiple IHS.

Another distinction between types of IHS turns out to be important (see Section 8.6). Assume an inheritance hierarchy contains the sequence of links

$$A_1 \rightarrow A_2 \rightarrow ... \rightarrow A_{n-1} \rightarrow A_n.$$

Some approaches sanction the conclusion 'A_1's are A_n' from this sequence only if 'A_2's are A_n' is also a sanctioned conclusion. These approaches will be called *downward* IHS. Other approaches sanction the same conclusion only if 'A_1's are A_{n-1}' is also sanctioned. Correspondingly, these systems are called *upward* IHS.

As mentioned in the beginning of this section, one of the main motivations for the interest in IHS was the hope that quite efficient inheritance algorithms exist. Unfortunately it has turned out that some of the existing efficient implementations do not produce the theoretically required behaviour. Some early IHS such as FRL (Roberts, Goldstein 77) or NETL (Fahlmann 79) used a shortest path strategy to capture the specialization principle. Touretzky (Touretzky 84) observed that this strategy leads to counterintuitive answers in two cases: firstly when the network contains redundant information and secondly when it is ambiguous. Here is an example of the first case (names in boxes represent instances, names without boxes classes):

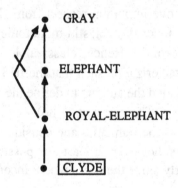

A shortest path reasoner would, as expected, derive CLYDE is not GRAY, since the path

   CLYDE → ROYAL-ELEPHANT ↛ GRAY

is shorter than the path

   CLYDE → ROYAL-ELEPHANT → ELEPHANT → GRAY.

If we add, however, a redundant link from CLYDE to ELEPHANT, then there is a positive path (i.e. a path without negated link) to GRAY not longer than the negative path to GRAY. We certainly do not expect CLYDE to become GRAY just because we added information which was derivable before anyway.

A similar problem arises in the presence of conflicting information. Take the classical Nixon example. Shortest path reasoners would either arbitrarily choose between pacifist and non-pacifist or even yield both conflicting answers.

This shows that the simple algorithms used in the first implementations of IHS fail to produce the intuitively expected results. And it motivates the need for exact formal theories of inheritance.

The Nixon example also illustrates that IHS can be based on different assumptions and intuitions. We can expect, for instance, that our inheritance theory will conclude as much as possible and will create - as known from nonmonotonic logics - multiple extensions to avoid inconsistency. Such a *credulous* reasoner would in the Nixon case produce two extensions, one in which Nixon is a pacifist and one in which he is not. Etherington and Reiter's formalization of inheritance in default logic (Etherington, Reiter 83, see Section 8.3) as well as Touretzky's path-based approach (Touretzky 86, see Section 8.4) follow this line.

On the other hand one can think of a *skeptical* reasoner which will always produce one single extension not containing any conflicting information. In our example the extension would contain neither 'Nixon is a pacifist' nor 'Nixon is not a pacifist'. As we shall see, the results produced by a skeptical reasoner are not necessarily equivalent to the intersection of all extensions of a credulous reasoner. An example is the formalization given in (Horty et al. 87) which is presented in Section 8.5.

First, however, we describe a formalization of (nonmonotonic) *frame systems* based on circumscription. Frame systems are mixed IHS: they consist of a strict superclass hierarchy together with a description of typical properties of class members, the so-called *slots* and *slot values*. What makes their formalization relatively easy is that there are no chains of defeasible inferences and hence specificity is easy to determine. Frame systems are widely used in AI-systems. Almost every commercial AI-tool currently on the market offers some sort of frame system for knowledge representation. Moreover, frames are very often given as examples of non-logical knowledge representation schemes. All this makes a logical formalization interesting enough to be contained in this chapter.

8.2: The Logic of Frames with Exceptions

Frames describe classes of objects by specifying a collection of properties that the elements of the classes, the frame instances, typically possess. In inheritance network terminology frame systems are mixed inheritance systems consisting of

(1)   A strict multiple IS-A hierarchy. The strict IS-A links are divided into instance links denoting the class membership of an object and subclass links representing the subclass relation.

(2)   Named defeasible links (slots) which represent attributes and point from classes (frames) to typical attribute values.

There are no outgoing links from nodes representing attribute values, that is there is no chaining of defeasible links at all. This makes the formalization of frame systems much simpler than that of general nonmonotonic inheritance systems where arbitrary paths of defeasible links are admitted and where it is much more difficult to define specificity.

Frame systems usually do not use a graphical notation. We therefore choose a more familiar language for the definition of frames and instances. It is the frame language used in the expert system tool BABYLON (di Primio, Brewka 85). Similar languages are found in most of the existing expert system tools. The translation into the graphical notation should be obvious.

Frames are defined as follows:

   (defframe FRAME-NAME

          {(supers SUPERFRAME$_1$ ... SUPERFRAME$_L$)}

          {(slots (SLOT$_1$ VALUE$_1$)   ... (SLOT$_K$ VALUE$_K$))}})

{ }-brackets indicate an optional part of a definition. Intuitively, the definition creates a frame FRAME-NAME and specifies its superclasses and slot values. Instances of frames can be defined in the following way:

   (definstance INSTANCE-NAME of FRAME-NAME

          {with SLOT$_1$ = VALUE$_1$ ... SLOT$_H$ = VALUE$_H$})

For the sake of simplicity we do not allow instances to be instances of multiple frames here. This is not a strong restriction, because we can always define an additional frame whose superframes are the multiple frames and instantiate that frame. Moreover, we assume that instances and frames are disjoint.

We further assume that frames must be defined before they can appear in definitions as supers or as frames to be instantiated. Then our language allows us to define directed acyclic graphs with superclass and instance links, but - as just mentioned - at most one instance link may go out from one node.

Here is the simple example from Section 1.1 containing two frame definitions and one instance definition:

   (defframe CAR

          (slots (WHEELS 4) (SEATS 5)))

   (defframe SPORTSCAR

          (supers CAR)

          (slots (SEATS 2) (CYLINDERS 6)))

   (definstance SPEEDY of SPORTSCAR with CYLINDERS = 8)

What is the meaning of these frame and instance definitions? Intuitively, the definitions are intended to allow the derivation of the following slot values for the instance SPEEDY: CYLINDERS 8, SEATS 2, WHEELS 4. To make the intuition precise we define the semantics of frame systems by specifying translation rules from the frame language to logical formulae. The meaning of a set of frame and instance definitions then is the variable circumscription of a certain predicate in the resulting theory, where all predicates are allowed to vary.

A natural idea would be to treat frames as unary and slots as two-place predicates. This is actually the approach followed in (Hayes 79) where frames without exceptions have been formalized. However, we have to represent the specialization principle in our formalization, and so we need to be able to talk about at least one property of frames: we must be able to express the fact that one frame is a specialization of another.

In principle, we could do that in second order logic. We avoid second order logic, however, by 'reifying' predicates, that is by making them elements of the domain of discourse. Instead of writing SPORTSCAR(SPEEDY) to express the fact that SPEEDY is an instance of the frame SPORTSCAR, we introduce a new predicate IS and a constant SPORTSCAR and express the fact as

IS(SPEEDY, SPORTSCAR).

Similarly, if a slot SEATS of SPEEDY has the value 2, then we write

HOLDS(SEATS, SPEEDY, 2)

instead of SEATS(SPEEDY, 2). Thus predicates become objects themselves and the fact that a certain predicate holds for an object, or a pair of objects, is expressed by the new predicates IS and HOLDS. This allows us to remain completely within first order logic.

We now describe how definitions of our frame language are to be translated into a set of first order formulae. We use a three-place AB-predicate. The basic idea is that if frame F has a slot S with value V this will be represented as

$$\forall x. \text{IS}(x,F) \wedge \neg\text{AB}(x,S,F) \supset \text{HOLDS}(S,x,V)$$

Intuitively AB(x,S,F) can be read as 'x does not inherit information about attribute S from frame F'.

Independently of the definitions to be translated our formalization uses four axioms:

(1) $\forall p,q. \text{SPECIALIZES}(p,q) \equiv (\forall x.\text{IS}(x,p) \supset \text{IS}(x,q)) \wedge \neg (\forall x.\text{IS}(x,q) \supset \text{IS}(x,p))$

If a class specializes another class then all members of the class are also members of the other class but not vice versa.

(2) $\forall f,s,v. \text{HAS-SLOT}(f,s,v) \equiv (\forall x. \text{IS}(x,f) \wedge \neg\text{AB}(x,s,f) \supset \text{HOLDS}(s,x,v))$

The first two axioms have been introduced for notational convenience. They make the rest of the translation easier.

(3) $\forall s,x,v_1,v_2.$ HOLDS$(s,x,v_1) \wedge$ HOLDS$(s,x,v_2) \supset v_1 = v_2$

The third axiom forbids slots from having different values. (Of course, we could easily extend our frame language and distinguish between different types of slots, e.g. multi-valued and single-valued slots. In that case the implication would have to be restricted to single-valued slots by introducing an additional condition.)

(4) $\forall x, f_1, f_2, v_1, v_2, s.$

   IS$(x,f_1) \wedge$ HAS-SLOT$(f_1,s,v_1) \wedge$ SPECIALIZES$(f_1,f_2) \wedge$ HAS-SLOT(f_2,s,v_2)

   $\supset$ AB(x,s,f_2)

Intuitively: x is abnormal with respect to a slot of a frame, that is x does not inherit information about the slot from the frame, if x is an instance of a more specific frame for which information concerning the same slot is available. This is the axiom which represents the specialization principle.

Given these formulae we can easily translate frame and instance definitions:
The definition of a frame

   (defframe MY-FRAME

         (supers SUPERFR$_1$ ... SUPERFR$_K$)

         (slots (SLOT$_1$ VALUE$_1$) ... (SLOT$_N$ VALUE$_N$)))

is translated into the following set of formulae:

   SPECIALIZES(MY-FRAME, SUPERFR$_1$),..., SPECIALIZES(MY-FRAME, SUPERFR$_K$),

   HAS-SLOT(MY-FRAME,SLOT$_1$,VALUE$_1$),..., HAS-SLOT(MY-FRAME,SLOT$_N$,VALUE$_N$).

The definition of an instance

   (definstance MY-INSTANCE of MY-FRAME with

         SLOT$_1$ = VALUE$_1$ ... SLOT$_H$ = VALUE$_H$)

yields the following formulae:

   IS(MY-INSTANCE,MY-FRAME),

   HOLDS(SLOT$_1$,MY-INSTANCE,VALUE$_1$), ..., HOLDS(SLOT$_H$,MY-INSTANCE,VALUE$_H$).

Formula (2) guarantees that if MY-FRAME or any of its superframes has a slot with information conflicting with the explicit values given in the instance definition, then the right instance of the AB predicate is monotonically derivable.

The meaning of a set of frame and instance definitions can now be defined as the variable circumscription of AB in the set of formulae described above, assuming uniqueness of names, where all predicates are allowed to vary during the minimization.

Let us see how this works in case of our SPEEDY example. Our definitions were

   (defframe CAR

         (slots (WHEELS 4) (SEATS 5)))

    (defframe SPORTSCAR

       (supers CAR)

       (slots (SEATS 2) (CYLINDERS 6)))

    (definstance SPEEDY of SPORTSCAR with CYLINDERS = 8)

Besides formulae (1) ... (4) as defined above, the translation yields the following formulae:

    HAS-SLOT(CAR,WHEELS,4)   HAS-SLOT(CAR,SEATS,5)

    HAS-SLOT(SPORTSCAR,CYLINDERS,6)   IS(SPEEDY,SPORTSCAR)

    HOLDS(CYLINDERS,SPEEDY,8)

It is not difficult to verify that under the unique names assumption - the usual companion of McCarthy's technique - circumscription of AB in this theory (allowing all predicates to vary) gives us

$$\forall x,y,z.\ AB(x,y,z) \equiv \quad (x = \text{SPEEDY} \wedge y = \text{SEATS} \wedge z = \text{CAR}) \ \vee$$
$$(x = \text{SPEEDY} \wedge y = \text{CYLINDERS} \wedge z = \text{SPORTSCAR})$$

From this definition of AB together with the assumption that different names denote different objects (e.g. that cylinders and seats are not the same) we get exactly the results we expect:

    HOLDS(WHEELS,SPEEDY,4) is derivable since SPEEDY is a CAR and not AB with respect to WHEELS and CAR.

    HOLDS(SEATS,SPEEDY,2) can be derived since SPEEDY is not AB with respect to SEATS and SPORTSCAR. AB(SPEEDY,SEATS,CAR) holds however, and we therefore get no inconsistency.

    HOLDS(CYLINDERS,SPEEDY,8) was asserted directly in the translation; there is no inconsistency since AB(SPEEDY,CYLINDERS,SPORTSCAR) holds.

Thus, the formalization yields exactly the derivations we intuitively expected from our frame system.

As we saw in Chapter 4 circumscription is a realization of minimal entailment. In our formalization ambiguities correspond to different minimal models. Since circumscription only allows us to derive what is true in all minimal models, our semantics requires us to remain agnostic in cases of ambiguity.

Let us reformulate the Nixon example in terms of frames. Assume we have a frame QUAKER with slot POLITICAL-VIEW and value PACIFIST and a frame REPUBLICAN with the same slot and value NON-PACIFIST. Let us also assume that none of the two frames specializes the other. If NIXON is an instance of both frames, we have minimal models where NIXON is AB with respect to POLITICAL-VIEW and QUAKER, but there are also minimal models where he is AB with respect to POLITICAL-VIEW and REPUBLICAN. In the first case Holds(POLITICAL-VIEW, NIXON , NON-PACIFIST) is derivable, in the second Holds(POLITICAL-VIEW, NIXON , PACIFIST). Circumscription allows us to derive the disjunction of both formulae but does not favour one of them.

This corresponds to the view that *only* subclasses should be allowed to override superclasses - the converse of the specialization principle. In the Nixon example if we derive one of the conflicting conclusions, such as the slot value PACIFIST, then information concerning a class, in this case QUAKER, is preferred to information about another class, here REPUBLICAN, but the first class is *not* more specific than the second.

Current implementations of frame systems (at least all implementations the author knows of) do not follow this view, however. In response to ambiguities they favour one inheritance path instead of remaining agnostic. This makes the algorithms much simpler. In terms of our semantics this means that they produce results which are true in a certain subset of all minimal models. The minimal models can be divided into equivalence classes of models which make the same instances of AB true. One such equivalence class is then chosen. The actual choice depends on the order in which superframes are listed in frame definitions. The user is not even informed about the existence of an ambiguity.

This section showed how a semantics for frame systems based on circumscription could be defined. The choice of circumscription instead of another nonmonotonic logic was not of fundamental importance, however. Of course, one could also think of a similar formalization in terms of - say - default logic, which would coincide with our formalization with respect to atomic sentences.

We do not expect our implementations of frame systems to be complete nonmonotonic theorem provers. The queries admitted in such systems usually have atomic sentences as answers. Therefore, such an alternative formalization differing from ours only with respect to complex formulae can provide a semantics for frames as well.

We shall not further analyze such an alternative approach, but turn now to less restricted inheritance systems which do not forbid chains of defeasible links.

8.3: An Approach Based on DL

Etherington and Reiter developed a default logic formalization of mixed inheritance networks (Etherington, Reiter 83) which is also described in (Etherington 87c). Networks are translated to default theories. Names of instance nodes become logical constants and names of class nodes unary predicate symbols. We shall now show the exact translation rules for links. (We do not need to introduce an extra graphical notation for strict links, since they will not play a major role in our discussion).

(1) A is an instance node:

$$A \rightarrow B \quad ==> \quad B(A)$$
$$A \nrightarrow B \quad ==> \quad \neg B(A)$$

(2) A is a class node, links are strict:

$$A \to B \quad ==> \quad \forall x.A(x) \supset B(x)$$
$$A \not\to B \quad ==> \quad \forall x.A(x) \supset \neg B(x)$$

(3) A is a class node, links are defeasible

$$A \to B \quad ==> \quad \frac{A(x): B(x)}{B(x)}$$
$$A \not\to B \quad ==> \quad \frac{A(x): \neg B(x)}{\neg B(x)}$$

Let's see how our Clyde example from the introduction of this chapter is translated. We get the default theory consisting of the following 3 defaults and a single atomic formula:

(1)   ROYAL-EL(CLYDE)

(2) $\dfrac{\text{ROYAL-EL}(x): \neg\text{GRAY}(x)}{\neg\text{GRAY}(x)}$

(3) $\dfrac{\text{ROYAL-EL}(x): \text{ELEPHANT}(x)}{\text{ELEPHANT}(x)}$

(4) $\dfrac{\text{ELEPHANT}(x): \text{GRAY}(x)}{\text{GRAY}(x)}$

This default theory, unfortunately, has two extensions, one containing ¬GRAY(CLYDE), and one containing GRAY(CLYDE). The second extension clearly violates our expectations. The problem with this approach is that it does not capture the specialization principle.

Etherington and Reiter use explicit exception links to handle this problem. Exception links do not combine two nodes, they combine a node with a link. In our example an exception link from ROYAL-EL to the link ELEPHANT→ GRAY would be introduced. This exception link modifies the translation of the link it points to. Default (4) would in this case be replaced by

(4') $\dfrac{\text{ELEPHANT}(x): \neg\text{ROYAL-EL}(x) \wedge \text{GRAY}(x)}{\text{GRAY}(x)}$

which has the intended effect as the unwanted extension no longer exists.

One objection (Touretzky 86) against explicit exception links is that the translation is not modular: links in the network are not translated independently from each other. This could be remedied by the use of naming techniques as described in Section 3.2. For example we could translate ELEPHANT→ GRAY to

(4'') $\dfrac{\text{ELEPHANT}(x): \text{APPL}(R4,x) \wedge \text{GRAY}(x)}{\text{GRAY}(x)}$

The meaning of the exception link then would simply be

$$\forall x.\text{ROYAL-EL}(x) \supset \neg\text{APPL}(R4,x)$$

The main objection held against exception links is that they are very impractical and that they violate the whole idea of inheritance. The effects of the specialization principle have to be coded into the network by hand. What we are looking for is a formalization in which the specialization principle is implicit.

Indeed, formalizations which solve these problems have been proposed, as we shall see in the next sections.

8.4: Touretzky's Credulous System

Touretzky was the first to present a mathematical, path-based theory of credulous inheritance in (Touretzky 86). This theory handles multiple inheritance networks whose links are nonmonotonic. As observed by Sandewall (Sandewall 86) the original version of Touretzky's system sometimes leads to unwanted results. If, for instance, we add the path CLYDE→AFRICAN-ELEPHANT→ELEPHANT to our CLYDE example, then Touretzky's original system again yields two extensions contrary to our expectations. Touretzky and Thomason, therefore, have modified the theory (Touretzky, Thomason 88). We shall discuss their improved version here (and still refer to it as Touretzky's theory).

Touretzky's basic idea is to replace the shortest path strategy to determine sub/superclass relationships by something better, the inferential distance ordering. Inferential distance means that A is taken to be a subclass of B iff there is an inheritance path from A to B. When this is the case properties of A override conflicting properties of B. We shall show after the precise definition of the theory that this criterion is not affected by redundant links.

We first introduce some additional terminology.

Definition 8.4: *A path is a sequence of links. A path is positive iff it contains no NOT-IS-A link at all. A path is negative iff it contains exactly one NOT-IS-A link at the end.*

Sequences of links with negated links in the middle do not express any reasonable relation between the first and the last node. They are therefore not considered as paths in the definition.

Inheritance networks can be interpreted as sets of paths consisting of one link. The inheritance theory describes how a given set of paths may be extended to a larger set which includes all inheritable paths. In the case of a credulous system the definitions must allow for multiple extensions.

Definition 8.5: *A set of paths Φ is perfect iff every one of its elements is inheritable in Φ and no path not in Φ is inheritable in Φ.*

Definition: *A set of paths Φ is an extension of a set of paths Γ if it is a (set inclusion) minimal perfect superset of Γ.*

What remains to be defined is inheritability:

Definition 8.6: *Let Φ be a set of paths. τ, τ_1 and τ_2 denote paths which may be empty, w may equal x_1 or x_{n-1}, respectively. The notion of inheritability in Φ is inductively defined as follows:*

Basis: $x \to y$ is inheritable in Φ iff $x \to y \in \Phi$,
           $x \nrightarrow y$ is inheritable in Φ iff $x \nrightarrow y \in \Phi$.

Induction: Case 1: $x_1 \to \ldots \to x_n$ is inheritable in Φ iff
    (1) $x_1 \to \ldots \to x_{n-1} \in \Phi$,
    (2) $x_2 \to \ldots \to x_n \in \Phi$,
    (3)   (contradiction) there is no path $x_1 \to \tau \nrightarrow x_n \in \Phi$,
    (4)   (preemption) there is no w such that
           $x_1 \to \tau_1 \to w \to \tau_2 \to x_{n-1} \in \Phi$ and $w \nrightarrow x_n \in \Phi$.

    Case 2: $x_1 \to \ldots \nrightarrow x_n$ is inheritable in Φ iff
    (1) $x_1 \to \ldots \to x_{n-1} \in \Phi$,
    (2) $x_2 \to \ldots \nrightarrow x_n \in \Phi$,
    (3)   (contradiction) there is no path $x_1 \to \tau \to x_n \in \Phi$,
    (4)   (preemption) there is no w such that
           $x_1 \to \tau_1 \to w \to \tau_2 \to x_{n-1} \in \Phi$ and $w \to x_n \in \Phi$.

Touretzky and Thomason describe this definition as follows (Touretzky, Thomason 88):

The notions of contradiction and preemption are the heart of the nonmonotonic inheritance definition. Contradiction keeps paths with conflicting conclusions from both being present in the same extension, as in Reiter's classic Nixon/pacifist example. Preemption is what allows subclasses to override the properties they would inherit from superclasses, even in the presence of redundant links.

Let us see how this definition works in our CLYDE example with a redundant link from CLYDE to ELEPHANT. The network Γ consists of the following links:

CLYDE $\to$ ROYAL-EL	ROYAL-EL $\to$ ELEPHANT
ELEPHANT $\to$ GRAY	ROYAL-EL $\nrightarrow$ GRAY
CLYDE $\to$ ELEPHANT	

It is not difficult to verify that these elementary paths together with

CLYDE $\to$ ROYAL-EL $\to$ ELEPHANT

CLYDE $\to$ ROYAL-EL $\nrightarrow$ GRAY

form an extension of Γ. There is no other extension, particularly no extension containing the path CLYDE $\to$ ELEPHANT $\to$ GRAY, since it is preempted by the path CLYDE $\to$ ROYAL-EL $\to$ ELEPHANT which cannot be contradicted and has to be contained in every extension.

For more illustrative examples see (Touretzky 86) (Touretzky et al 87) and also (Sandewall 86).

The theory just described formalizes credulous inheritance. One possible way of defining a skeptical system could be just to take the intersection of all extensions as the set of derivable paths. An alternative approach has been proposed by Horty, Thomason and Touretzky (Horty et al. 87). This is presented in the next section and use an example to illustrate its difference from the extension intersection approach.

8.5: A System for Skeptical Inheritance

The principal idea of skeptical inheritance is that in a case of conflicting information nothing is concluded unless all arguments against believing something are completely ruled out by better, that is more specific, arguments for it. It turns out that there is no need to define different extensions to avoid inconsistencies in the skeptical approach. The inheritability relation '|=', Horty et al. call it the permission relation, which specifies the paths inheritable from a set of direct links, can be defined directly, without resorting to extensions and their intersection.

In (Horty et al. 87) an inductive definition of the inheritance relation is given which is based on a complexity measure on paths.

Definition 8.7: *The degree of a path $\sigma = x_1 \to ... \to x_n$ in a network Γ - written $deg\Gamma(\sigma)$ - is the length of the longest generalized path in Γ from x_1 to x_n, where a generalized path is any sequence of positive or negative links. (The restriction on paths which allows only the last link to be negative is omitted).*

Definition 8.8: *Let Γ be a set of direct links. The inheritability relation $|=$ is inductively defined as follows (σ_1, τ, τ_1, τ_2 denote, possibly empty, paths):*

(I) σ *is a direct link. Then $\Gamma |= \sigma$ iff $\sigma \in \Gamma$.*
        Since all paths with $deg\Gamma(\sigma) = 1$ are direct, this case serves also as the basis for induction.

(II) σ *is a compound path with $deg\Gamma(\sigma) = n$. As an inductive hypothesis, we can suppose it is settled whether $\Gamma |= \sigma'$ whenever $deg\Gamma(\sigma') < n$. There are two subcases to consider:*

        (1) $\sigma = x \to \sigma_1 \to u \to y$ *(positive path). $\Gamma |= \sigma$ iff*
        (a) $\Gamma |= x \to \sigma_1 \to u$,
        (b) $u \to y \in \Gamma$,
        (c) $x \nrightarrow y \notin \Gamma$,
        (d)   *For all v such that $\Gamma |= x \to \tau \to v$ with $v \nrightarrow y \in \Gamma$, there exists $z \neq v$ such that $\Gamma |= x \to \tau_1 \to z \to \tau_2 \to v$ and $z \to y \in \Gamma$.*

        (2) $\sigma = x \to \sigma_1 \to u \nrightarrow y$ *(negative path). $\Gamma |= \sigma$ iff*
        (a) $\Gamma |= x \to \sigma_1 \to u$,
        (b) $u \nrightarrow y \in \Gamma$,
        (c) $x \to y \notin G$,

> *(d)   For all v such that $\Gamma \models x \to \tau \to v$ with $v \to y \in \Gamma$, there exists $z \neq v$ such that $\Gamma \models x \to \tau_1 \to z \to \tau_2 \to v$ and $z \nrightarrow y \in \Gamma$.*

Let us see how this works in the case of the Nixon example. Γ consists of the following paths:

NIXON → REP   REP ↛ PAC

NIXON → QUAK   QUAK → PAC

It is not difficult to see that this is also the set of inheritable paths. NIXON → REP ↛ PAC is not inheritable since requirement 2(d) does not hold: $\Gamma \models$ NIXON → QUAK, and QUAK → PAC , but there is no path from NIXON to QUAK with an intermediate z such that z ↛ PAC . For symmetrical reasons the path NIXON → QUAK → PAC is not inheritable, since 1(d) does not hold.

The next figure shows an example from (Horty et al. 87) where this approach and the intersection of all extensions of a credulous system disagree:

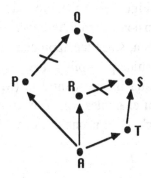

In the credulous approach there is an extension containing A → P ↛ Q as well as an extension containing A → T → S → Q. The approach based on the intersection of extensions therefore remains agnostic with respect to A's being Q. In the directly skeptical approach, however, A → P ↛ Q is inheritable. The ambiguity with respect to A's being S neutralizes the potentially conflicting path A → T → S → Q. This ambiguity is not propagated further in the network to possibly invalidate conflicting arguments. This approach reflects a particular view of what effects an ambiguity within a network should have. In the next section we shall see that this view has been criticized recently.

As our analysis of Etherington and Reiter's approach in Section 8.3 showed, it is not possible to capture the specialization principle when the defaults from the network are directly translated to normal defaults in the default logic. It is, however, possible to reconstruct the path based inheritance theories in default logic when instead of the network defaults the policy of deriving conclusions is represented as a default schema (Brewka 89). This amounts to translating the definition of inheritability to a corresponding schema.

In (Brewka 89) two schemata, one corresponding to the skeptical approach and another to Touretzky's credulous approach are described. With these schemata a modular translation from networks to DL is possible, that is the union of the translations of two sets of links equals the translation of the union of the sets of links. Such a translation to classical logic is obviously, not possible because of the nonmonotonicity of inheritance. It is shown that the ground literals of the IS-A predicate in the generated extension(s) correspond in each case exactly to the inheritable paths in the original approaches. The possibility of the translation tells us that DL is general and expressive enough to model reasoning based on the specialization principle. It does, however, not provide much new insight into the problems of inheritance themselves.

8.6: Further Approaches

As we saw from Horty's example the skeptical inheritance system defined in the last section did not propagate ambiguities, i.e. there may be skeptical conclusions not contained in all credulous extensions of an inheritance hierarchy. It has been questioned whether this is real skepticism, since the approach may result in conclusions being believed, even if there is a genuine possibility that they are wrong. The problem has been discussed in (Stein 89) and independently in (Makinson, Schlechta 90). Both papers also contain a number of examples which severely question the intuitiveness of the ambiguity blocking approach. Here is one of the examples from (Stein 89):

Given this inheritance hierarchy, Horty's approach computes a kind of 'parity' on the number of ambiguities: we establish that A is a C, a G, and a J, but not that A is an E and an I. Moreover, A is a J, D is a J, and H is a J, but we do not obtain B is a J and F is a J. It is difficult to see how such outcomes could be justified.

Another problem has been described in these papers. If the definition of skeptical inheritance is based on the intersection of extensions then it is not sufficient to consider the paths contained in the intersection alone. Assume we have in all extensions either the path $A \rightarrow B_1 \rightarrow C$, or the path $A \rightarrow B_2 \rightarrow C$, but none of these paths is contained in all extensions. Intuitively, the inference 'A is a C' seems justified, even if there is not a single path justifying it in all extensions. The authors of both papers therefore propose distinguishing between paths and inferences sanctioned by paths, and to define 'ideally' skeptical inheritance (the term is due to Stein and includes ambiguity propagation) in terms of inferences sanctioned in all extensions by, possibly different, paths.

Stein presents an interesting approach to computing ideally skeptical inheritance. Firstly, to obtain ambiguity propagation ambiguous nodes are marked as ambiguous but then used further in the inheritance process. Marked nodes cannot be contained in conclusions, but they can play the role of counterarguments and prevent other nodes from being unambiguous. Secondly, to obtain all ideally skeptical inferences, the system keeps track of the conditions under which an inference has support. This book-keeping mechanism is similar to the ATMS-labelling technique (Section 9.3) and also has also some resemblance to the technique used to make default logic cumulative (Section 3.4). Starting from a focus node A the label of each node S in the network describes the conditions under which A is S. The labels themselves are propositional expressions. Nodes labelled TRUE represent ideal skeptical inferences about A.

There is a great number of alternative approaches to inheritance which we describe very briefly without going into any detail.

Touretzky, Thomason and Horty have proposed various refinements and further elaborations of their theories. Touretzky also formalizes inheritable relations (Touretzky 86). Touretzky and Thomason treat generic reflexive statements such as 'Elephants love themselves' (Touretzky, Thomason 88). They give a formalization of credulous inheritance in which that sentence can be derived from, say, 'Elephants are gray' and 'Elephants love gray things'. Horty and Thomason (Horty, Thomason 88) describe a formalization of mixed inheritance which combines the monotonic inheritance theory from (Thomason et al. 86) with the skeptical theory presented above.

Padgham presents a lattice-based approach to inheritance where objects and types are described by sets of characteristics (Padgham 89). Some of the characteristics of a type represent strictly necessary properties, other characteristics represent properties of a typical object of that type. Padgham's main emphasis is on allowing negative conclusions, that is both strict and default conclusions about what an object is not.

Boutilier (Boutilier 89) interprets network links as sentences in the conditional logic E which is an extension of Delgrande's logic N described in Chapter 6. To characterize the nonmonotonic inferences of a set of conditional sentences he introduces, following Shoham's preferential entailment approach, an ordering on the models of these sentences. The resulting skeptical inheritance reasoner is stable in the following sense: if it sanctions the conclusion 'A's are B' then adding the link A → B to the network does not change the derivable conclusions. It is still a matter of debate whether the instability of approaches like that of Touretzky and Horty is really a disadvantage, as claimed by Boutilier.

In (Krishnaprasad, Kifer 89) a way of formalizing inheritance is outlined which combines concepts from logic programming and multi-valued logics. Inheritance networks are specified in a Horn-clause language. Literals in this language are of the form p:t, where p is an atom and t, the priority constant, expresses the type and relative strength of evidence in support of p. A model theory for the language is provided and it is shown that a unique intended model can be associated with every inheritance network.

A probabilistic interpretation of defaults underlies the inheritance reasoner in (Bacchus 89). A defeasible link A $\rightarrow$ B is read as 'most A's are B' or, more precisely, 'at least c $*$ 100% of all A's are B', where c is a fixed constant strictly greater than 0.5 and smaller than 1. This interpretation has of course an important consequence: it does not sanction any chaining of defaults. If we know that at least c $*$ 100% of all A's are B and at least c $*$ 100% of all B's are C, we cannot conclude that at least c $*$ 100% of all A's are C. In this sense the system behaves 'super'-skeptically. The author claims that this limitation does not prevent the system from performing a large amount of useful inheritance reasoning. It is questionable however, whether the simple examples given in the paper are really sufficient to support his claim.

As mentioned in the beginning of Section 8.1, one of the motivations for the interest in inheritance systems was the hope that efficient, yet theoretically well-founded algorithms could be designed. For most of the approaches described in this chapter algorithms have been proposed in the original papers. Touretzky (Touretzky 86), for instance, shows that efficient parallel marker-passing algorithms can be used for his credulous theory when the networks are conditioned properly, i.e. when certain redundant links are added to the network. Or, to mention another example, in (Horty et al. 87) an algorithm is given which is provably correct with respect to their skeptical theory of inheritance.

We shall not discuss any of the existing algorithms in detail but refer the interested reader to the original papers. Instead, we shall describe some general tractability results which have recently been established (Selman, Levesque 89). The authors show that Touretzky's credulous approach to inheritance is NP-hard, even when restricted to unambiguous networks. The same holds for the skeptical approach based on the intersection of Touretzky's extensions. An immediate consequence of this result is that Touretzky's conditioning technique mentioned in the previous paragraph is itself intractable (provided P $\neq$ NP).

Touretzky's system is, in the terminology from Section 8.1, a downward reasoner. Interestingly, the design choice between downward and upward reasoning has a major effect on the complexity of inheritance: upward inheritance, as it is performed in the directly skeptical system (Horty et al. 87), can be performed in polynomial time.

These results imply that the use of general nonmonotonic multiple inheritance systems does not guarantee, by itself, efficient retrieval of information. The systems have to be designed very carefully to allow for tractable implementations.

CHAPTER 9: NONMONOTONIC RULE-BASED SYSTEMS

9.1: Introduction

As we have discussed in Section 1.4 the nonmonotonic logics examined in Chapters 2 to 6, at least in their general form, do not lend themselves to direct implementations. In Chapter 7 we looked at various theorem proving techniques for restricted versions of the logics. Now, in this chapter we turn to a somewhat more pragmatic, implementation-oriented field of research in the area of nonmonotonic reasoning. We discuss an alternative approach to implementing nonmonotonic reasoners based on nonmonotonic rules of the form IF ... THEN ... UNLESS ... .

Research within this field was originally performed quite separately from the more logically oriented research. One of the main purposes of this chapter is therefore to clarify the relation between the techniques developed and the results obtained within the two streams.

Nonmonotonic rules allow inferences to be drawn from a set of formulae not only if some other formulae are *present* (provable) but also if some formulae are *absent*. But what does absent mean here ? At least two different answers can be given to this question.

Nonmonotonic formal systems (NFS) take absent to mean 'absent from the set of all derivable formulae'; see for instance (Reinfrank 85), which is based on (Doyle 83a). This notion of derivability corresponds to the fixed point definitions we know from the logics. In fact, as we show in the next section, nonmonotonic formal systems are a generalization of Reiter's DL. Informally, these systems interpret being absent as *being unprovable*. Unsurprisingly this interpretation makes theoremhood not even semi-decidable.

Therefore another notion of derivability is commonly used in nonmonotonic rule-based systems such as AMORD (de Kleer et al. 77), CAPRI (Freitag 87), PROTEUS (Petrie et al. 86), or WATSON (Goodwin 87). The current problem solving state is taken into account. A formula is taken to be absent if no proof for it has been found in the current problem solving state, that is absence is interpreted as *current un-provenness*. This is an approximation to derivability which avoids the problem of non-semidecidability. We call a system following this approach a nonmonotonic process system (NPS) since it takes the process of making inferences into account. A similar terminology has been used by Goodwin (Goodwin 87) whose logical process theory is the best developed formal description of such systems.

To keep track of what has been proven, that is what is currently believed by the problem solver, nonmonotonic process systems use a truth maintenance system (TMS). The term truth maintenance system is somewhat misleading, and Doyle proposes using the term reason maintenance system (RMS) instead. Nevertheless TMS remained the more popular name and is therefore used here.

The purpose of a TMS is, in short, to record proofs of the problem solver. We shall discuss such systems and their integration into an NPS in Section 9.3. There we also show that a TMS can be seen as a propositional DL-prover allowing us to approximate one extension of the NPS's knowledge base.

In Section 9.4 we point out some theoretical problems with the NPS approach which arise when dependency directed backtracking is used to remove inconsistencies.

9.2: Nonmonotonic Formal Systems: A Generalization of DL

As a short reminder, let us start this section with the standard definitions of a (monotonic) formal system and of derivability in such a system:

Definition 9.1: *A formal system S is a triple (L, A, R) where L is a formal language, A (the set of axioms of S) a recursive subset of L, and R a recursive set of inference rules of the form*

> *IF a_1, ..., a_n THEN q*

where a_1, ..., a_n, and q are members of L.

S specifies an inference relation R_S: $2^L \to 2^L$ which is defined as follows:

Definition 9.2: *Let S = (L, A, R) be a formal system. A formula p is derivable in S from a set of premises P - i.e. $p \in R_S(P)$ - iff there is a sequence q_1, q_2, ... q_n such that*

(1) $q_n = p$

(2)   For all $i \in \{1,...,n\}$:

> *$q_i \in A \cup P$ or*
>
> *there exist $j_1,...,j_k < i$ with (IF q_{j1}, ..., q_{jk} THEN q) $\in R$.*

The notion of a nonmonotonic formal system (NFS) admits a more general form of rules:

Definition 9.3: *A nonmonotonic formal system S is a triple (L, A, R) where L is a formal language, A (the set of axioms of S) a recursive subset of L, and R a recursive set of nonmonotonic inference rules of the form*

$$IF \ a_1, \ ..., \ a_n \ UNLESS \ b_1, \ ..., \ b_m \ THEN \ c$$

where a_1, ..., a_n, b_1,...,b_m, c are elements of L.

a_1, ..., a_n are called IF-conditions, b_1, ..., b_m UNLESS-conditions of the rule. Both may be empty. In this case the strings IF, UNLESS, and THEN, respectively, may be left out. (Thus axioms can be seen as IF- and UNLESS-conditionless rules). The notation used in Definition 9.3 stresses the connection between nonmonotonic and standard inference rules. We also use the alternative notation

$$< a_1, \ ..., \ a_n \ | \ b_1, \ ..., \ b_m \rightarrow c >$$

for nonmonotonic inference rules which is commonly used in the context of TMS.

Derivability in an NFS is defined in terms of extensions. (In the literature they are usually called *admissible* extensions, but since something like an extension which is not admissible is of no interest we feel free to leave out the adjective.) The following definitions are taken from (Reinfrank 85) which in turn is based on (Doyle 83a).

Definition 9.4: *Let S=(L, A, R) be an NFS, P a set of premises. A set of formulae F is closed with respect to P and S iff*

(1)   P and A are subsets of F,
(2)   for every rule (IF a_1, ..., a_n UNLESS b_1, ..., b_m THEN c) ∈ R:
         if a_1, ..., a_n ∈ F and b_1, ..., b_m ∉ F then c ∈ F.

Thus F is closed iff it contains the axioms and premises and if all 'applicable' rules have been applied. Applicability is determined through F itself.

Closure is not sufficient to define a notion of derivability. Closure only guarantees that all applicable rules have been applied, but there may be formulae in a closed set which are in no sense grounded in the premises or axioms; for instance the whole language L is always closed.

We need another condition to define the extensions. We certainly want only those formulae to be derivable which are either axioms or premises or for which a noncircular argument can be constructed. This idea is captured by the following definitions:

Definition 9.5: *Let F be a set of formulae, S = (L, A, R) an NFS. A sequence q_1, q_2, ... q_n is an S-proof for q_n from P valid in F iff for all i ∈ {1,...,n}:*

(1) q_i ∈ F,
(2) q_i ∈ A ∪ P or
         there exist j_1,...,j_k < i with
            (IF q_{j1}, ..., q_{jk} UNLESS r_1,...,r_m THEN q_i) ∈ R
            and r_1, ..., r_m ∉ F.

Definition 9.6: *A set of formulae F is S-grounded in P iff for every formula $p \in F$ there is an S-proof from P valid in F.*

Definition 9.7: *E is an extension of S and P iff E is closed with respect to S and P and S-grounded in P.*

If S is determined by the context we simply speak of extensions of P, and if P is empty we also speak of extensions of S instead of extensions of S and P.

It should not be surprising that NFS may have zero, one, or more than one extensions. Take the following examples:

(1) $S=(\{p\},\{\},\{< \mid p \rightarrow p >\})$

No extension exists.

(2) $S=(\{p,q\},\{\},\{< \mid q \rightarrow p >\})$

The single extension is $\{p\}$.

(3) $S=(\{p,q\},\{\},\{< \mid q \rightarrow p >, < \mid p \rightarrow q >\})$

We get two extensions, namely $\{p\}$ and $\{q\}$.

The reader will certainly have realized that there is a close relation between NFS and DL. Default theories can be seen as a special type of NFS where some of the axioms and rules, namely those guaranteeing first order completeness, are left implicit.

Definition 9.8: *An NFS S=(L, A, R) is first-order complete iff*

(1)   L is a first order language consisting of the standard logical connectives, quantifiers, and generation rules, and

(1)   S is complete with respect to classical logical derivability, i.e. A and R contain a first order complete set of axioms and rules.

The translation of a first-order complete NFS to DL is straightforward.

Definition 9.9: *Let S=(L, A, R) be a first-order complete NFS. The DL-translation of S is the default theory (D, W) with*

(1)   W = A, and

(2)   D is the set of all defaults

$$\frac{a_1 \wedge ... \wedge a_n : \neg b_1, ...}{\neg b_m, c}$$

such that (IF $a_1, ..., a_n$ UNLESS $b_1, ..., b_m$ THEN c) $\in$ R. [1]

Strictly speaking we do not need to represent those rules and axioms in DL which are in the NFS only for guaranteeing first order completeness. They do no harm, however, so for sake of simplicity we assume them all to be translated.

---

[1] If a rule has no IF-conditions the prerequisite of the default consists of the empty conjunction which, as usual, is taken to be equivalent to TRUE.

For rules without UNLESS conditions we get somewhat degenerate defaults of the form

$$\frac{a_1 \wedge...\wedge\ a_n:}{q}$$

Such defaults correspond to standard inference rules. It should be noted that these defaults without justification are not excluded by Reiter's original definitions.[1] Some researchers have argued against their use because, in a sense, they violate the idea of a default allowing derivations which depend on the underivability of some formula(e). They could with some additional technicality be replaced by defaults of the form

$$\frac{a_1 \wedge...\wedge\ a_n:\ \text{TRUE}}{q}$$

The only difference is that defaults of the first form may - as is the case in NFS - lead to inconsistent extensions consisting of the set of all formulae even if the set of facts of the default theory is consistent. For instance the default theory

$$T = (\{\text{TRUE: / A, TRUE: / }\neg A\},\ \{\})$$

has an inconsistent extension. With defaults of the second form this is impossible. Consider the default theory

$$T' = (\{\text{TRUE: TRUE / A, TRUE: TRUE / }\neg A\},\ \{\})$$

for which no extension exists. Admitting defaults without a consistency check is just a matter of convenience and avoids having to mention the special case every time.

The following proposition (Brewka 89) establishes the expected connection between a first order complete NFS and its DL-translation:

Proposition 9.1: *Let S=(L, A, R) be a first order complete NFS, (D,W) the DL-translation of S. E is an extension of S iff E is an extension of (D,W).*

The reverse translation from default theories to NFS is also possible:

Definition 9.10: *Let (D,W) be a default theory. S = (L, A, R) is an NFS translation of (D,W) iff A and R are smallest sets such that*

1) S is first order complete,
2) W ⊆ A, and
3) if (a:b_1,...,b_m/c) ∈ D then (IF a UNLESS ¬b_1, ..., ¬b_m THEN c) ∈ R.

Proposition 9.2: *Let T=(D,W) be a default theory and S an NFS translation of T. Then T and S have exactly the same extensions.*

Both propositions establish the - unsurprising - equivalence between default theories and first order complete NFS.

The NFS that are used in process systems are often not first order complete (note that a first order complete NFS is infinite). Each NFS S with a logical language can

---

[1] He does not seem to have intended them, however, since his corollary 2.2 in (Reiter 80) presupposes at least one justification for each default.

easily be made first order complete, however, simply by adding sets of first order complete rules and axioms to it. We call the resulting system the *logical completion* of S. In some cases systems produce results which are correct with respect to their logical completion. Here are some useful definitions:

Definition 9.11: *Let S, S' be nonmonotonic formal systems. S is correct with respect to S' iff S has at least one extension and every extension of S is the subset of an extension of S'.*

Existence of extensions is required in this definition to avoid an NFS with no extension being correct with respect to all NFS.

Definition 9.12: *Let S be an NFS with a logical language. S is logically correct iff it is correct with respect to its logical completion.*

Logical correctness can be obtained by restricting the language L of S accordingly. In particular, when L consists only of propositional constants then we have the following result (Brewka 89):

Proposition 9.3: *Let S = (L, A, R) be an NFS such that L is a set of propositional constants. Let T = (D, W) be the DL-translation of S. Then each extension E_S of S corresponds exactly to an extension E_T of T and vice versa, in the sense that E_S is exactly the set of propositional constants contained in E_T.*

We shall see in the next section that the TMS used in nonmonotonic process systems are exactly of the form required in Proposition 9.3, i.e. they are logically correct and with respect to atomic formulae even complete propositional default logic provers.

9.3: Nonmonotonic Process Systems: A Pragmatic Approach

In the last section we discussed nonmonotonic formal systems and their relation to nonmonotonic logics. NFS in general are not semi-decidable (more precisely: membership of a formula in an extension is not semi-decidable). This follows directly from the fact that default theories can be seen as NFS, as we showed in the last section. Various systems have been implemented which use a trick to avoid this problem. As mentioned in the introduction to this chapter we call them nonmonotonic process systems since they take the process of problem solving into account.

There is no general way of establishing non-derivability. Therefore NPS follow a very simple pragmatic approach which replaces the concept of 'unprovability' by the concept of 'current unprovenness'. Applicability of a rule thus becomes dependent on the current problem solving state. A rule is applicable not only if it has been established that the UNLESS conditions are unprovable, but also if the UNLESS conditions have not been proven in the current problem solving state.

To record information about this current state, that is about the inferences made so far, or in other words, about what is currently believed and not believed, a TMS is used.

A TMS is a subsystem of a problem solver. Its purpose is to keep track of logical dependencies between facts in a knowledge base. There are three advantages of doing this, of course at the cost of memory:

(1)   Costly recomputations can be avoided.

(2)   Changes in the set of premises the deductions are based on can be supported.

(3)   Sources of inconsistencies can be identified.

The first advantage comes into play when, for instance, the same fact has to be deduced twice or when intermediate results of a proof are needed in other proofs.

The importance of advantage 2 is clear when for example the premises in the knowledge base represent the current state of a time varying world. It is necessary to remove and add premises whenever the modelled world changes. The same is true when unreliable information is represented in the premises and then later on we learn that something in the premises has to be altered. If the reasoner does not keep track of logical dependencies (i.e. of inferences already made) everything has to be recomputed whenever a premise is removed (or added in the case when the underlying reasoning process is nonmonotonic).

Recording sources of inconsistencies is important if we do not want our systems to break down whenever an inconsistency arises. As we shall see the TMS used in nonmonotonic process systems can also include techniques of maintaining consistency.

The need for a TMS is not restricted to cases where the underlying reasoning process is nonmonotonic. Even for the situation when only classical monotonic inferences are made, the three advantages hold. If the reasoning process is nonmonotonic, however, a TMS is needed not only if premises are removed but also if some are added, since in that case also the addition of premises can make deductions invalid. Moreover, the intended distinction between 'unprovability' and 'current unprovenness' would not be possible without recording what has in fact been proven in the current state.

The two most influential types of TMS are Doyle-style TMS (Doyle 79) and assumption based TMS (de Kleer 86 a,b,c), abbreviated ATMS.

De Kleer's ATMS is a system that in its basic form, supports monotonic reasoning from multiple hypothetical premise sets. Assumptions in de Kleer's terminology can be seen as hypothetical premises. The ATMS maintains a network of nodes with which formulae in the language of the problem solver are associated. The main purpose of the ATMS is to compute for each node minimal consistent assumption sets such that the node's associated formula is (monotonically) derivable from the corresponding hypothetical premises. The relevance logic based model of belief revision developed in (Martins, Shapiro 88) can serve as a theoretical foundation of the ATMS.

The ATMS is used for monotonic reasoning in multiple hypothetical contexts. But this does not imply that the ATMS is not relevant to nonmonotonic reasoning. It is not difficult to show that the formulae derivable from maximal consistent assumption sets correspond to DL-extensions if the hypothetical premises are interpreted as normal defaults without prerequisite. The close relation between hypothetical and nonmonotonic reasoning should be clear from our discussion of Poole's approach in Section 5.2.

We are, however, only concerned with Doyle-style truth maintenace systems here. They support nonmonotonic inferences and are therefore commonly used in combination with NPS. The name 'justification based TMS' (JTMS) has sometimes been used for this type of TMS. But since the ATMS is also based on the concept of justification we do not feel it emphasizes the main distinguishing feature. 'Nonmonotonic TMS' is probably a better name. We shall drop the adjective and use the term 'TMS' in the sense of 'Doyle-style TMS' in this chapter unless we explicitly say otherwise.

Examples of such TMS are, besides Doyle's original one, those implemented by Goodwin (Goodwin 87), Reinfrank and colleagues (Reinfrank et al. 86) and the TMS of MCC's expert system tool PROTEUS (Petrie et al. 86).

It should be added however, that there have recently been some very interesting attempts to integrate nonmonotonic and multiple context reasoning within an extended ATMS. Dressler (Dressler 88a) introduced a special class of assumptions, the so-called Out-assumptions, representing the assumption that something is not believed. Together with an additional inference rule the Out-assumptions are used to model nonmonotonic inferences within the monotonic framework of the ATMS. Dressler's approach guarantees that a formula and its corresponding Out-assumption cannot both be contained in a consistent context. In certain cases however, results are possible which do not correspond to those of a TMS.

Junker (Junker 88) has fixed the problem by introducing an additional check. The check has some similarity with the second main step of our modal default prover presented in 3.2.2. In another paper (Dressler 88b) Dressler presents an alternative test for the same purpose. We shall not go into the details here but refer the reader to the original papers.

Our interest here is in TMS and its role within an NPS. A TMS is a system that manipulates a finite network consisting of

(1)   nodes which represent the facts the problem solver might believe, and

(2)   links between the nodes (justifications) which represent dependencies between nodes (strictly speaking between the facts represented by the nodes).

The nodes are treated like propositional constants and the corresponding facts are not used by the TMS.

An NPS consists of a problem solver and a TMS. The problem solver operates on a knowledge base containing facts (premises) and nonmonotonic rules or rule schemata. In other words the knowledge base defines an NFS. The premises are usually interpreted as conditionless rules. The problem solver selects an applicable rule instance, say

$$< f_{i1}, ...,f_{ij} \mid f_{o1}, ..., f_{ok} \rightarrow f >$$

and transforms it to a corresponding justification of the form

$$< n_{i1}, ..., n_{ij} \mid n_{o1}, ..., n_{ok} \rightarrow n >$$

$n_{i1}, ..., n_{ij}$ are called IN-nodes, $n_{o1}, ..., n_{ok}$ OUT-nodes, n is the consequent of the justification. The nodes can be viewed as unique names for the formulae associated with them. The justification can intuitively be read as: if nodes $n_{i1}, ..., n_{ij}$ are believed (IN) and nodes $n_{o1}, ..., n_{ok}$ are not believed (OUT) then node n must be believed (IN). Justifications with no OUT-nodes are called monotonic justifications. If both OUT- and IN-nodes are missing the justification is called premise justification.

The justification is integrated into the network. The most important task of the TMS is to determine what is currently believed by the problem solver. For that purpose the nodes are labelled IN or OUT. The nodes labelled IN represent the problem solver's current beliefs. The labelling must have the following properties:

I.   A node is labelled IN iff there is at least one valid justification for it. A justification is valid iff in a belief state all of its IN-nodes are IN and all of its OUT-nodes OUT.

II.   For each node labelled IN there exists a noncircular argument, i.e. a node cannot justify itself.

More formally this can be described as follows (Reinfrank 87):

Definition 9.13: *Let L be an IN/OUT labelling, i.e. a function from the set of nodes to {IN,OUT}. L is grounded iff every node n with the label IN has a valid support of the form $(n_1,...,n_p)$ where*

(1) $n_p=n$, and

(2)   each n_i either has a premise justification or is the consequent of a justification valid in L whose IN-nodes are contained in $\{n_1,...,n_{i-1}\}$.

Definition 9.14: *An IN/OUT labelling L is closed iff the consequents of all justifications valid in L are labelled IN in L.*

Definition 9.15: *An IN/OUT labelling L is admissible iff it is grounded and closed.*

It is not difficult to see that these definitions are just reformulations of the definition of NFS extensions in Section 9.2. The admissible labellings correspond exactly to extensions of the NFS consisting of the problem solver rules applied so far. A labelling tells us exactly which formulae are contained in the corresponding NFS extension and which are not. A TMS hence is just a finite NFS with a very simple language consisting exclusively of propositional constants. This together with Proposition 9.3 implies that a TMS can be seen as a correct and with respect to propositional constants even complete DL-prover (Brewka 89) or, according to Konolige's equivalence result, as a propositional AEL prover (Reinfrank et al. 89).

Lemma 9.4: *Let J be a set of justifications, T = (D,{}) the default theory consisting of the defaults obtained by translating each justification*

$$< n_{i1}, ..., n_{ij} \mid n_{o1}, ..., n_{ok} \to n >$$
from J to the default
$$\frac{n_{i1} \wedge ... \wedge n_{ij} : \neg n_{o1}, ..., \neg n_{ok}}{n}$$

Then each admissible labelling L of J corresponds exactly to an extension E of T and vice versa, in the sense that the nodes labelled IN in L are exactly the propositional constants contained in E.

This result provides TMS with a semantics defined in terms of a nonmonotonic logic. Before turning to some examples we want to mention at least some alternative, non DL-based attempts to define a semantics for the TMS (and ATMS). The algebraic interpretation in (Brown et al. 87) has the advantage that it captures TMS as well as ATMS. A disadvantage certainly is the lack of a model theory. Ginsberg (Ginsberg 87 a,b,c) formalizes assumption based truth maintenance in terms of multi-valued logics. Brown and Shoham (Brown, Shoham 88) give a semantic account of Doyle-style TMS in Shoham's framework of preferential entailment. Their reconstruction of TMS sheds much light on how difficult it is to integrate the concept of groundedness into this framework. We believe that for Doyle-style TMS the DL-based view is simpler and does not provide less insight than the other proposed interpretations.

The task of the TMS is to determine an admissible labelling, or in other words the set of propositional constants contained in one extension of a certain propositional default theory, efficiently. Some examples may help to clarify these ideas. We use Goodwin's graphical notation for TMS networks (Goodwin 87) where a justification

$$< N_1, ..., N_j \mid N_{j+1}, ..., N_m \to N >$$

is represented as follows;

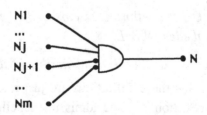

Assume we have a network consisting of the following justifications (suggestive names have been chosen for the nodes; they have, as mentioned before, no meaning for the TMS).

< l → BIRD-TW >

< BIRD-TW l NOT-FLIES-TW → FLIES-TW >

< PENGUIN-TW l → NOT-FLIES-TW >

The graphical representation shows the unique admissible labelling:

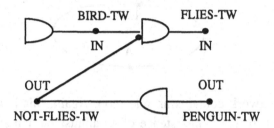

Integration of the premise justification

< l → PENGUIN-TW >

leads to the following modification of the network.

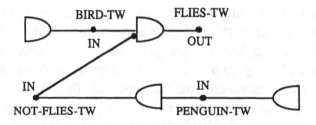

We gave in Section 9.2 an example of an NFS with two and an example with zero extensions. Here are the corresponding networks with their labellings. The simplest network with more than one labelling is the following:

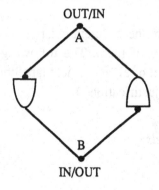

It is interesting to see that the network contains a loop. The number of nonmonotonic links in this loop (that is links with a fat dot at the gate representing the justification) is even. Such loops are therefore called even (nonmonotonic) loops. In fact, it has been shown (Charniak et al. 80) that the existence of an even loop in a network is a necessary (but not sufficient) condition for the existence of multiple admissible labellings.

The following network is the simplest one without any admissible labelling:

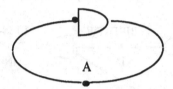

In this case the network contains an odd loop. Again, this is a necessary, but not sufficient, condition for the nonexistence of an admissible labelling (Charniak et al. 80).

We shall now describe the interaction of the problem solver and the TMS within an NPS. The problem solver operates on a knowledge base consisting of premises, that is conditionless rules, and nonmonotonic rules (or rule schemata). The problem solver selects one of the unfired rules according to a specific control strategy. Firing the rule means transforming it into a justification such that the justified node is associated with the rule's conclusion, IN- and OUT-nodes with the rule's IF- and UNLESS-conditions. This new justification is integrated into the TMS network. After the computation of a new labelling the problem solver selects the next rule and so on until the problem solver's termination criterion becomes true. The standard termination criterion is: there is no more rule such that the nodes representing its IF-conditions are IN and the nodes representing its UNLESS-conditions are OUT in the current labelling of the network. As mentioned before, the labelling at each step corresponds exactly to an extension of the rules applied so far. We shall see in the next section that this simple and neat relation between the problem solver's knowledge base and the TMS labelling holds only as long as the techniques for removing inconsistencies are not applied

We do not want to compare the different existing labelling algorithms here, but do want to describe at least one of them. The following recursive algorithm (Junker, Konolige 90) computes the set of all admissible labellings of the network consisting of the finite set of nodes N and justifications J.

Algorithm Ext$_J$ (I, O, U)

(1)   if I $\cap$ O $\neq$ {} then {} else

(2)   if U = {} then {I} else

(3)   if U $\neq$ {} then

   (a)   *if $U \cap apply_{J,I} (I - U) = \{\}$ then $Ext_J (I, O \cup U, \{\})$*

   (b)   *if $\exists q \in U - apply_{J,N - O} (I - U)$ then $Ext_J (I \cup \{q\}, O, U - \{q\})$*

   (c)   *if $\exists q \in U \cap apply_{J,I} (N - O)$ then $Ext_J (I, O \cup \{q\}, U - \{q\})$*

   (d)   *if $\exists q \in U - (I \cup O)$ then $Ext_J (I, O \cup \{q\}, U) \cup Ext_J (I \cup \{q\}, O, U)$*

The apply-operator in the algorithm is defined as follows:

$$apply_{J,Y} (X) := \{c \mid < a_1,..., a_j \mid b_1,..., b_m \rightarrow c > \in J, a_1,..., a_j \in X, b_1,..., b_m \notin Y\}$$

The sets I and O in the algorithm are the nodes which so far have been labelled IN or OUT, respectively. Since some of the chosen labels for nodes are unconfirmed, that is may fail in the presence of odd loops, a third set U is introduced containing all unlabelled and unconfirmed nodes. Rule (b) looks for a justification whose IN-nodes are confirmed and whose OUT-nodes are labelled OUT. If such a justification exists the justified node gets a confirmed IN-label. Rule (c) checks whether a justification for a node $q \in U$ exists which might become valid when some unlabelled nodes get an IN-label. If there is no such justification q gets a confirmed OUT-label. Rule (d) introduces a choice point and treats both labellings as unconfirmed possibilities. Rule (a) adds all remaining nodes to O whenever there is no justification for a node in U whose IN-nodes have a confirmed IN-label. Calling $Ext_J (\{\},\{\}, N)$ produces the set of all admissible labellings of the network.

For implementation issues and an efficiency analysis of one of the other algorithms see (Goodwin 87).

So far we have interpreted the nodes of a dependency network as propositional constants. The associated problem solver formulae were irrelevant for the TMS. This is not the whole story, however. There is a class of nodes, the contradiction-nodes, representing FALSE. If in an admissible labelling a contradiction-node is labelled IN, the TMS interprets that as an inconsistent belief state and tries to remove the inconsistency by adding - depending on the technique used - one or more justifications (and, possibly, a new node, the nogood-node). This process is called dependency directed backtracking (DDB). All of the mentioned semantics for TMS (Brown et al. 87) (Brown, Shoham 88) as well as our DL-based semantics have not captured this important part of the TMS.

9.4: Dependency Directed Backtracking

Assume the TMS labelling algorithm has produced a labelling where a contradiction-node is IN. There are two possibilities. Either there exists an alternative labelling where no contradiction-node is IN, in which case we would certainly expect the system to simply switch to the alternative labelling, or there is no such alternative labelling. In this case the TMS network has to be changed to make a consistent labelling possible. It is the latter case that mainly interests us in this section.

We use a slightly modified version of the example from the last section to illustrate the techniques used to remove inconsistencies in TMS networks. Assume the network consists of the following justifications:

    < I → PENGUIN-TW >

    < I → BIRD-TW >

    < BIRD-TW I NOT-FLIES-TW → FLIES-TW >

    < FLIES-TW, PENG-TW I → FALSE >

FALSE here is the name of a contradiction-node. We get the following labelling:

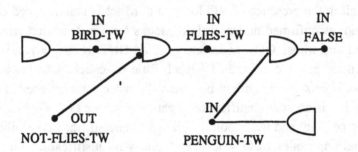

The labelling makes the contradiction-node IN, which signals an inconsistent belief state. In monotonic systems inconsistencies can be removed only by removing premises. Remembering that the justifications correspond to rules of the problem solver's knowledge base and that therefore they represent external knowledge, we certainly do not want to throw justifications away. But since our justifications are nonmonotonic it is sometimes possible to remove an inconsistency by *adding* one or more justifications. This is the case when the OUT-label of a node q contributes to the contradiction-node's IN-label. Forcing q to become IN, by additional justifications, may remove the inconsistency. This is the basic idea of *dependency directed backtracking*.

In our case we could for instance add the justification

    < BIRD-TW, PENG-TW) I → NOT-FLIES-TW >

FALSE would now get the label OUT (justifications created by the backtracker in this and the following figures are painted black):

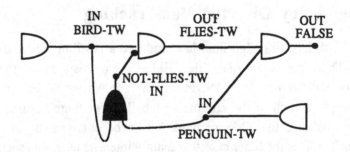

The question that arises is, where does the new justification come from? One possibility is to ask the system using the TMS for help. If this is done and the TMS gets the necessary information on how to resolve the inconsistency from the same source as all the other information, then most of the analysis of the rest of this section is not applicable and becomes obsolete. However, in many systems, such as for example Doyle's (Doyle 79) (Doyle 83a) (Doyle 83b), removing inconsistencies, at least in certain cases, is seen as an additional task of the TMS. We adopt this view here.

The addition of new justifications makes it difficult to describe the exact relation between the TMS network and the problem solver's knowledge base after DDB. The new self-generated justifications are not necessarily instances of problem solver rules. We distinguish from now on between

(1)   K-justifications, which correspond to rules of the knowledge base and represent external knowledge, and

(2)   B-justifications, which are generated by the backtracking algorithm and represent internal information.

Various algorithms for generating the B-justifications have been developed. Doyle's original algorithm (Doyle 79) even generates new nodes, so called nogood-nodes, which contain information accessible for the problem solver. Perhaps the most advanced algorithm is Petrie's (Petrie 87), which in our example would yield the B-justification

< BIRD-TW, PENG-TW) I FALSE → NOT-FLIES-TW >

Petrie regards as an advantage that this justification admits both the contradictory as well as the new consistent labelling.

As in the last section we are again not concerned with a detailed discussion and comparison of the various available algorithms. Rather, we are interested in a logical analysis of DDB. In fact, our analysis in the rest of this section will be independent from any specific DDB- algorithm.

It is a usual requirement that changes performed in a system to restore consistency should be minimal in a reasonable sense. Techniques for resolving inconsistencies with minimal changes have been studied in the field of counterfactual reasoning (Ginsberg 86) and play a central role in the area of theory revision (Gärdenfors 88). Also TMS use techniques to remain as close as possible to the external knowledge base. Provision is made that the B-justifications are valid as rarely as possible. That us the reason why in our example we included BIRD-TW and PENG-TW in the IN-list of the new B-justification. However, as we shall see, there are cases where this technique is insufficient.

Doyle (Doyle 83a) investigates various possible definitions of minimality. In particular, he gives an example where the symmetric difference[3] between the believed nodes of two belief sets is used to characterize the closeness of these sets. Given a

---

[3] The symmetric difference between two sets A and B is the set $(A - B) \cup (B - A)$.

state S and a new piece of information p the state which is closest to S, consistent, and contains p is chosen as successor state. This gives rise to what Doyle calls a 'conservative' reasoner. Doyle also discusses DDB in this context and remarks (Doyle 83b, p. 351):

> *However, I cannot exactly characterize the 'nearness' relation actually realized ... because RMS only uses a heuristic choice based on the structure of arguments which support contradiction-nodes.* [4]

Conservativism certainly is an important principle of rationality. However, we consider the external groundedness of beliefs as more fundamental. The task of the TMS is to compute a belief set based on the external information provided by a problem solver. It therefore seems important that the TMS produces results which are only based on this external information, and that all changes needed to restore consistency are minimal *with respect to the external information*. It will become clear in the rest of this section why we insist here on this seemingly trivial remark.

Unfortunately, as we shall see, even when the changes introduced by DDB are minimal in each step, according to a given minimality criterion, the sequence of minimal changes may lead away from the external information. Situations may arise where the labelling of the network has not much to do with the problem solver's knowledge base and the nice picture presented in the last section: TMS labelling = extension of the rules applied so far, disappears.

Let us now be somewhat more precise about what we mean by minimality. Paul Morris (Morris 88) recently proposed a modified version of AEL with a revised notion of extension. The revisions - at first sight - *'appear to agree well with intuition and to be closely related to those resulting from dependency-directed backtracking in a TMS'* (Morris 88).

His simple modification of AEL guarantees the existence of extensions. If there is no extension for a set of premises then he allows a minimal set of ordinary premises (premises without modal operator) to be added such that an extension exists. (To achieve independence of the premises' syntactical form he defines minimality in terms of set inclusion with respect to the logical closure of the premises.) This captures our ideas about the way in which inconsistencies in the TMS network should be removed very well: we want to modify our networks as little as possible, and we want to add justifications, not remove them. The set inclusion minimality of added premises, in terms of TMS the minimality of nodes which additionally are made IN by B-justifications, seems to be a necessary condition for any reasonable definition of minimal change.

Is this the formalization of TMS with dependency directed backtracking we were looking for? Unfortunately, the result of a closer look at DDB is disappointing. We first apply the ideas underlying the modification of AEL to NFS.

---

[4] As mentioned before Doyle prefers the term RMS instead of TMS.

Definition 9.16: *Let S = (L, A, R) be an NFS. A forced extension of S is an extension of S' = (L, A', R), where A' is a (set inclusion) minimal superset of A such that an extension for S' exists.*

We call A' - A an *augmentation* of S.

It would, of course, be nice to have a relation between TMS labellings and the knowledge base as simple as the one described in the previous section, in which we disregarded DDB. What we would like to have is a result like:

> *Let L be an admissible labelling of the TMS network, A the set of nodes labelled IN in L only by virtue of a valid B-justification. Then the nodes labelled IN in L correspond exactly to a forced extension of the rules applied so far, and A represents the minimal augmentation corresponding to this forced extension.*

But the result does not hold, unfortunately, as a simple counterexample shows. For sake of simplicity we do not distinguish between nodes and their associated formulae in this example. Assume the knowledge base (KB) of the problem solver consists of the rules

(1) $< A, B \mid \to FALSE >$

(2) $< \mid B \to A >$

Remember that the system incrementally approximates an acceptable belief set induced by the KB. If the KB-rules are applied in exactly the order they are written down we get an inconsistency after (1) has been applied. Assume during DDB a justification is created that makes B IN to remove the inconsistency.[5] The exact output of the DDB algorithm is not important here, but any of the algorithms used will make it possible to have B IN whenever A is OUT, so for our purposes it is sufficient to assume the justification is $< \mid A \to B >$. Note that at this time B actually is contained in a minimal augmentation of the rules applied so far.

After application of (2) we get two admissible labellings: one makes A IN and B OUT and corresponds to the only extension of the K-justifications.[6] But there is also another admissible labelling making B IN and A OUT. This labelling does not correspond to any extension, forced or not, of the KB. The unwanted labelling is shown in the following figure:

---

[5] If your favourite DDB-algorithm makes A IN change (2) to $< \mid A \to B >$ and you get the same problem as in our example.

[6] Many systems would not even apply the rule corresponding to the second justification in this case since its precondition (B is OUT) does not hold. As a consequence the right labelling corresponding to the external system's knowledge base would not even be among the possible labellings of the computed network. If we add $< \mid C \to A >$ after (1) and $< \mid \to C >$ after (2) we run into exactly the same problems even when rules without valid preconditions are never applied.

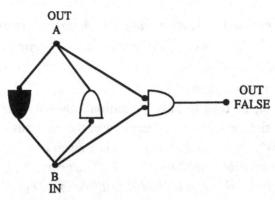

Here we have an example where the knowledge base as a whole is consistent, but has inconsistent subsets. During the stepwise generation of an extension for the knowledge base an inconsistency arised which was resolved by the addition of a justification. The set of nodes additionally made IN, {B}, was a minimal set necessary to obtain a consistent admissible labelling. But the introduction of the justification had the consequence that in later steps of the approximation process a labelling became admissible which was not grounded in the external knowledge.

Let us make precise what the point here is: we are not criticizing the fact that the results produced depend on the order in which information is supplied to the TMS. However, this order should only have a bearing on which extension is actually chosen. Labellings which do not represent a, possibly forced, extension of the external information should not be possible. And this is exactly what happens in our example. Here the external information is even consistent, so the minimal change should certainly be a non-change, and we would expect to get only one possible labelling corresponding to the single extension of the external knowledge.

Is it possible to solve this problem by checking whether the K-justifications alone can be labelled? In our example this is the case; in the final state we can find an admissible labelling for the network without B-justifications. We therefore know that no augmentation at all is needed. But, as shown in (Brewka 89), there are more complex examples in which minimality is violated but no admissible labelling exists for the K-justifications alone. Thus the simple test does not help.

The paper cited contains several examples showing that some other simple modifications of the TMS algorithms also fail to guarantee minimality. In particular, it is not guaranteed that an admissible labelling corresponding to a minimal augmentation, i.e. to a forced extension, is always among the possible labellings. There seems to be no simple way of revising the TMS adequately. One possible way of achieving minimality as required by our semantics is to check *all* subsets of a found augmentation as possible candidates for a smaller augmentation. This is really not a very encouraging result. On the other hand these difficulties do not seem entirely surprising since the revision of beliefs is difficult even for humans.

Note that without the distinction between B- and K-justifications there is no chance at all of ensuring the intended minimality property since then no information about the epistemic status of a justification is available.

All we can say then is that the current nonmonotonic truth maintenance systems produce an admissible labelling corresponding to an extension of a finite set of rules applied so far, together with some additional premises. The additional premises are *not necessarily minimal* for ensuring the existence of an extension. If the backtracking algorithm is adequate they are contained in minimal augmentations of subsets of the rules (that is the reason why a B-justification for them was created in an earlier problem solving state) but nothing ensures that they are needed for guaranteeing the consistency of the whole set of rules at hand.

There is another important difference between minimal augmentation semantics and the current systems; minimal augmentation semantics requires additional premises in the presence of unsatisfiable odd loops in the network, not only in the case when the contradiction-node is labelled IN. It follows that DDB also has to be invoked in this case. Actually, if the contradiction-node is interpreted as representing propositional falsity, then a 'virtual' justification from FALSE to all nodes exists (ex falso quodlibet). The case where a node N labelled OUT contributes to the contradiction-node's being IN, that is the case where DDB is invoked in current systems, is just an unsatisfiable odd loop when the virtual justification $< FALSE \mid \rightarrow N >$ is taken into account. In the DL-based semantics discussed in the last section both cases correspond to incoherent default theories, that is default theories without extension, and not to default theories with inconsistent extension. There seems to be no good reason from a logical point of view to treat the two cases differently.

In this section we asked whether a proposal of Paul Morris can provide us with a formal semantics of nonmonotonic TMS with dependency directed backtracking. Our analysis showed that this is not the case. Systems in use today produce in certain cases results which cannot be justified with this minimal augmentation semantics. As a special case we may even end up with an extension of an augmented KB when the KB itself is consistent.

On the other hand it has emerged that the changes necessary to avoid this behaviour are extremely expensive - so expensive that the whole idea of consistency maintenance in a TMS might become impractical. The dilemma we face is that we have to choose between one system that in certain cases unnecessarily adds premises, and another that is logically more satisfying but highly inefficient.

CHAPTER 10: NONMONOTONIC REASONING - WHERE DO WE STAND?

10.1: What has been Achieved?

Nonmonotonic reasoning has been a very active area of research in the last decade and is still in a state of rapid development. The study of nonmonotonicity is a widely recognized challenge within Artificial Intelligence and other, related fields. The motivation is not an interest in exotic formalisms, but rather the need for a formal theory of everyday reasoning.

We have presented in this book what we consider the most promising approaches and the most important results established so far in nonmonotonic reasoning. A number of alternative formalizations have been proposed. In this account of these formalizations, we have tried not to present one approach as superior to the others. Rather we wanted to give a fair picture of what has been done. It is probably still too early for final judgements. However, it comes as no surprise to learn that I have some personal, subjective, and perhaps biased preferences towards the preferred subtheory framework. The advantages have been mentioned: it needs no special formulae, priorities between defaults can be easily expressed, the approach is close to classical logic, and it seems possible to integrate other forms of commonsense reasoning. However, this does not mean that I think other logics have no use. Approaches like DL or circumscription are more general, though it is still open for evaluation how much of their additional expressiveness is really needed to capture the nonmonotonic phenomena of commonsense reasoning.

The sometimes irritating disconformity and fragmentation within the field has been increased by the fact that research has been performed by relatively independent subcommunities: the logicians defined and analyzed their logics, inheritance specialists defined their own theories without relating them to the existing logics, and the more implementation oriented researchers wrote programs based on nonmonotonic inference rules and truth maintenance systems. One of the goals of this book was to provide at least some of the missing links between these different research activities.

After the development of the first nonmonotonic formalisms their mathematical properties were studied intensively. The main focus was - not surprisingly, given the large variety of different approaches - the relationship between them. As we saw, interesting and sometimes astonishing results have been established. In the beginning it seemed that everybody tried to find out whether his favourite formalism was as strong and expressive as the others. ('Anything you can do I can do better').

Meanwhile some abstract criteria for comparison have been established; in particular Gabbay proposed focussing on general properties of the inference relation defined by a logic (Gabbay 85). Following this suggestion Makinson has investigated a large number of desirable properties of nonmonotonic inference relations (Makinson 89) (Makinson 90). An example is the property of cumulativity discussed in Chapter 3. The lack of cumulativity of Reiter's default logic led to the definition of a new version, CDL. Many other interesting properties of nonmonotonic inference relations are defined in (Makinson 90). Makinson's paper contains a classification of several important nonmonotonic formalisms based on the properties they satisfy. The investigation of these properties has, for instance, led to the definition of special cases of preferential entailment which behave in a very regular manner. We cannot go into further detail here but highly recommend Makinson's original papers.

All these research activities have substantially improved our understanding of nonmonotonicity and the problems involved in trying to formalize it.

The implementation of theoretically founded but nevertheless efficient nonmonotonic systems is a difficult task. We have explored several ways of achieving this goal. Various promising results in the area of nonmonotonic theorem proving were described in Chapter 7. We also saw that some inheritance systems can quite efficiently treat certain important subcases of nonmonotonic reasoning. The activities in the area of nonmonotonic rule based systems and truth maintenance systems can be seen as alternative ways to achieve the same goal. We tried to give a logical analysis of rule based systems, an analysis which also demonstrated some discrepancy between the system behavior which is theoretically required and that which is actually obtained.

In any case, some theoretically well-founded systems exist and can be used for building nonmonotonic applications.

A final but nevertheless important achievement we should mention is the large number of test cases to be found in the literature which can be used for checking the properties of formalisms. A collection of important examples has been compiled by Lifschitz in the Appendix of the Proceedings of the Second International Workshop on Nonmonotonic Reasoning (Reinfrank et al 89).

There are at least two additional important research topics closely related to nonmonotonic reasoning where interesting results have been established, but which are not explicitly discussed in the book. The first is the formalization of logic programming. We saw in Section 7.2 that under certain conditions logic programs can be used to compute circumscription. It has turned out that nonmonotonic logics can be used to give precise formal foundations to logic programming. In the general case however, it is necessary to shift to a three valued version of either circumscription or default logic (Przymusinski 89) to capture the case where a logic programming interpreter returns no answer at all.

The other research area that has almost been excluded and surely deserves more attention than was given to it in the book is called theory revision. We touched on theory revision very briefly in Section 9.4 in the context of dependency directed backtracking, and in Section 5.5. We saw there that in most approaches to default reasoning only those beliefs which are conclusions of defaults are revised automatically given new contradictory information. Revisions are handled only when possible inconsistencies have been anticipated. (Preferred subtheories constitute an exception, as demonstrated in Section 5.5.) In theory revision no such anticipation is necessary. The basic question investigated in this field is the following. Given a belief state S, usually defined in terms of a deductively closed set of logical formulae, what are the rational principles guiding the change of S when either new information is added or old information is removed? A detailed description of the achievements in this field with further references can be found in (Gärdenfors 88).

After this list of positive achievements in the field we must turn to the open problems. As shown by the various proposals to refine the logics, including the redefinitions of DL and the generalization of Poole's approach given here, there are reasons to doubt that the best possible formalizations have already been found.

Meanwhile the most famous example which demonstrates that the logics do not produce the expected results in all cases is the Yale shooting problem (Hanks, McDermott 87). This example is examined in the next section.

10.2: The Yale Shooting Problem

In Chapter 1 we discussed the frame problem, i.e. the problem of finding an adequate representation of what does not change when an event occurs, as one of the main challenges which has motivated research in the whole field. The idea was to solve this problem by the introduction of a frame axiom which roughly says that if a fact holds in a situation then this fact typically still holds after an event has occurred.

It was commonly believed that the nonmonotonic logics which had been developed could be used to formalize this axiom in a straightforward manner and would produce the intended results. Nobody seems to have actually tried to do it, however, until Hanks and McDermott (Hanks, McDermott 86) came up with a simple example, now known as the Yale shooting problem. In a certain situation S_0 an object (some say it was a turkey, some say it was Fred) is alive. A gun is loaded, nothing happens for a short period (a waiting action occurs) and then somebody shoots at the object. The question is: is the object still alive or not? In the normal course of events we certainly expect the object to be dead. Let us see what a straightforward formalization produces. Assume we base our axiomatization on circumscription. Axioms similar to the following ones are used in (Hanks, McDermott 87):

(1) $S_1 = \text{RESULT}(\text{LOAD},S_0)$

(2) $S_2 = \text{RESULT}(\text{WAIT},S_1)$

(3) $S_3 = \text{RESULT}(\text{SHOOT},S_2)$

(4) $\text{HOLDS}(\text{ALIVE},S_0)$

(5) $\forall s.\text{HOLDS}(\text{LOADED},\text{RESULT}(\text{LOAD},s))$

(6) $\forall s.\text{HOLDS}(\text{LOADED},s) \supset$

   $\text{AB}(\text{ALIVE},\text{SHOOT},s) \wedge$

   $\text{HOLDS}(\text{DEAD},\text{RESULT}(\text{SHOOT},s))$

(7) $\forall f,e,s.\text{HOLDS}(f,s) \wedge \neg\text{AB}(f,e,s) \supset \text{HOLDS}(f,\text{RESULT}(e,s))$

(7) is the representation of the frame axiom. As usual we minimize AB. The predicate HOLDS is allowed to vary. What you get is what you see in the next figure which is taken from (Hanks, McDermott 87). The boxes contain the true facts in the corresponding situation:

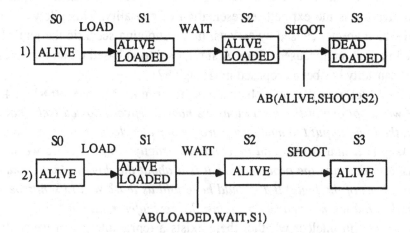

(1) represents a model of the axioms which corresponds to our intuition: the load action makes LOADED true, waiting changes nothing, and shooting has the expected effect. The model is minimal; it makes exactly one instance of AB true, namely $\text{AB}(\text{ALIVE},\text{SHOOT},S_2)$. (For those who are astonished that the gun is still loaded after firing: it is a six-shooter).

But unfortunately (2) also represents a minimal model. Here LOADED is abnormal with respect to waiting in S_1, in the sense that it ceases to persist. And if the gun is no longer loaded, nothing is abnormal with being alive after a shooting action. However, it seems to be curious that waiting magically unloads the gun.

The problem is not restricted to the particular circumscriptive approach. If a similar DL or AEL formalization instead of circumscription is chosen the same problem arises. Two extensions are produced corresponding to the two minimal models described above.

It is interesting to see that the intended model in our scenario is the one in which the abnormality appears later. Shoham has argued (Shoham 86) that this is actually what is required for temporal reasoning: *chronologically minimal* models are those models in which normality is assumed in chronological order and where abnormality occurs as late as possible. They seem in many cases to produce the expected results in temporal reasoning.

Hanks and McDermott's paper prompted a large number of researchers to look for solutions. It was unbelievable that nobody had been aware of the problem for years (nearly as unbelievable as magically unloaded guns). Meanwhile the Yale shooting example is one of the standard benchmarks for every approach. We can merely indicate the most important solutions which have been proposed very briefly here. For a critical discussion of these and other approaches see (Hanks, McDermott 87).

Lifschitz (Lifschitz 87) presented a reformulation of the axioms which does not lead to the unwanted minimal model. His approach is based on a shift in ontology. The main innovation is the explicit representation of causality. This allows effects to be avoided which are not caused by actions. In the shooting scenario the gun's becoming unloaded is such an uncaused effect. A similar solution based on an explicit representation of causality has been proposed in (Haugh 87).

Hanks and McDermott's main objection is that (Hanks, McDermott 87, p. 404f):

> *if we adopt one of these solutions we have in effect allowed technical problems in the logic to put too much pressure on our knowledge representation. ...*
>
> *Why is it that causes and precond[1] are exactly the predicates we should have used to describe the problem? What is it about the domain (not about technical problems of the logic) that should have told us that? Will Lifschitz be around to bail us out when we come up against the next inferential bug?*

In fact, it is still unclear whether there exists a representation of causality suitable for all problems of temporal reasoning, or whether it is possible at all to list all causal connections explicitly. See (Baker, Ginsberg 89b) for a critical example.

Another proposal is to modify circumscription in such a way that the chronological minimality criterion can be expressed directly in the circumscription axiom (Lifschitz 86b) (Kautz 85). It can be shown that both modifications produce exactly the desired theorems, true in all chronologically minimal models.

Shoham (Shoham 86) proposes a third alternative. We have already described his framework for defining preferential logics in Section 4.5. Shoham defines for temporal reasoning a specific preference relation on models which captures the idea of

---

[1] causes and precond are predicates used in Lifschitz's formalization.

chronological minimality. What is interesting about his approach is that he does not go on to define a new circumscription axiom or any other syntactical characterization of the corresponding notion of preferential entailment. Instead he directly describes an efficient algorithm which produces for certain classes of theories, so-called causal theories, exactly the atomic sentences which are true in all preferred models.

This purely semantic approach to nonmonotonic reasoning is also advocated by McDermott (McDermott 86). He characterizes circumscription as an 'epiphenomenon' which can only be used to verify answers which are known in advance. According to McDermott we have to know the results before we can find the right instantiations of the circumscription axiom. His conclusion is that the syntactical characterization of minimal entailment in terms of second order logic is useless without a major break-through in higher order theorem proving.

This comment certainly has to be taken seriously. If we can show that a program produces semantically justified results, why care about a syntactical characterization of entailment at all? One answer may be that sometimes it is easier to think in syntactical terms. This seems to be the case, for instance, in DL. It is questionable however whether a circumscription axiom is conceptually simpler than the corresponding semantic notion of preferred models.

On the other hand a syntactical characterization can guide the development of theorem proving techniques even when no proof techniques exist for the general case. The discussion of circumscriptive theorem proving in Section 7.2 is a good example. It then seems to be a pragmatic question whether - given a certain semantics - one uses a complete and correct, but generally unimplementable, syntactical definition or not.

The idea of chronological minimality can quite easily be modelled in prioritized default logic (PDL) as defined at the end of Section 3.2. All we have to do is to put 'earlier' instances of the frame axiom into sets of defaults with higher priority. As in the circumscription formalization we need

(1) $S_1 = \text{RESULT}(\text{LOAD}, S_0)$

(2) $S_2 = \text{RESULT}(\text{WAIT}, S_1)$

(3) $S_3 = \text{RESULT}(\text{SHOOT}, S_2)$

(4) $\text{HOLDS}(\text{ALIVE}, S_0)$

(5) $\forall s.\text{HOLDS}(\text{LOADED}, \text{RESULT}(\text{LOAD}, s))$

The next formula has been simplified somewhat since we need no ab predicate:

(6') $\forall s.\text{HOLDS}(\text{LOADED}, s) \supset \text{HOLDS}(\text{DEAD}, \text{RESULT}(\text{SHOOT}, s))$

We explicitly state that dead is equivalent to not alive:

(7') $\forall s.\text{HOLDS}(\text{DEAD}, s) \equiv \neg\text{HOLDS}(\text{ALIVE}, s)$

The main innovation is that we have to split the instances of the frame axiom into partitions accordingly. Our default theory is $T = (D_0, D_1, D_2, W)$. W is the above set of formulae. Each D_i (i=0,1,2) consists of the single open normal default:

$$\frac{\text{HOLDS}(f,S_i): \text{HOLDS}(f,\text{RESULT}(e,S_i))}{\text{HOLDS}(f,\text{RESULT}(e,S_i))}$$

This explicitly represents the chronological minimality criterion in PDL.[2] Let us see how it handles the example. We first apply the frame axiom instances for S_0. This gives ALIVE in S_1, together with LOADED from (5). The frame axiom in D_1 guarantees the persistence of ALIVE and LOADED in S_2. In S_3 we get, as intended, LOADED from the frame axiom in D_2 and DEAD from (6').

The next figure shows the ground instances of HOLDS obtained by this kind of reasoning forwards in time together with the instances of the frame axiom from D_i applied in each situation.

HOLDS(ALIVE,S0)   Axiom

$$\frac{\text{HOLDS(ALIVE,S0): HOLDS(ALIVE,RESULT(LOAD,S0))}}{\text{HOLDS(ALIVE,RESULT(LOAD,S0))}} \quad \text{F1}$$

HOLDS(ALIVE,S1)   F1
HOLDS(LOADED,S1)   (5)

$$\frac{\text{HOLDS(ALIVE,S1): HOLDS(ALIVE,RESULT(WAIT,S1))}}{\text{HOLDS(ALIVE,RESULT(WAIT,S1))}} \quad \text{F2}$$

$$\frac{\text{HOLDS(LOADED,S1): HOLDS(LOADED,RESULT(WAIT,S1))}}{\text{HOLDS(LOADED,RESULT(WAIT,S1))}} \quad \text{F3}$$

HOLDS(ALIVE,S2)   F2
HOLDS(LOADED,S2)   F3

$$\frac{\text{HOLDS(LOADED,S2): HOLDS(LOADED,RESULT(SHOOT,S2))}}{\text{HOLDS(LOADED,RESULT(SHOOT,S2))}} \quad \text{F4}$$

HOLDS(DEAD,S3)   (6')
HOLDS(LOADED,S3)   F4

---

[2] Our intention here is to illustrate chronological minimality. We do not claim to have solved the frame problem.

If, on the other hand, additionally

(8)   HOLDS(ALIVE,S$_3$)

is known (i.e. contained in W) then we can monotonically derive

$\neg$HOLDS(LOADED,S$_2$)

from (7') and (6'). This blocks the application of the frame axiom instance

$$\frac{\text{HOLDS(LOADED,S}_1): \text{HOLDS(LOADED,RESULT(WAIT,S}_1))}{\text{HOLDS(LOADED,RESULT(WAIT,S}_1))}$$

This time, there is a mixture of reasoning forwards and backwards in time. Again we can illustrate the results graphically:

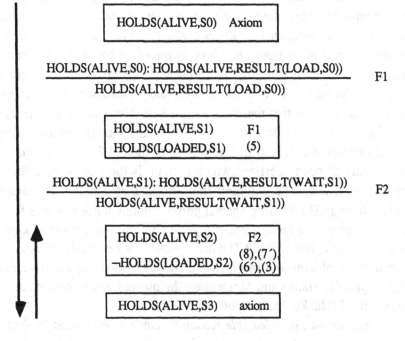

Hence we get exactly what we expect in both cases.

There has also been criticism of the chronological minimality principle (Kautz 86). It seems to be adequate only for reasoning forwards in time. In examples involving reasoning backwards in time, for instance when we look for an explanation of a known fact, counterintuitive results may be obtained. Assume for instance, you left your car in the parking lot and returning hours later you find it has been stolen. Chronological minimality forces you to believe that it was stolen immediately before you arrived back, i.e. as late as possible, given it is abnormal for a car to disappear.

An interesting new approach which avoids the problems has been described in (Baker Ginsberg 89b). The authors introduce vectors representing the current state. State vectors are related to situations they describe via a new predicate DESCRIBES. Two types of abnormality are introduced: abnormality of state vectors and abnormality of situations. Only the first type is minimized while all other predicates are allow-ed to vary. This simple representation solves the Yale shooting problem. In addition the authors discuss a rather more complex example taken from the blocks world which can also be handled adequately.

10.3: What Next?

One of the conclusions to be drawn from the Yale shooting scenario and the solutions proposed is that the formalizations examined in this book do not themselves solve the problems of reasoning about action and time. This certainly also holds for other possible applications. Partly this is due to the fact that the formalizations are not yet in a final commonly accepted state. Our modifications of some of them have tried to overcome some of the deficiencies, others certainly remain, and some still have to be detected. Moreover, it is far from clear how to represent commonsense knowledge in the formalisms. Methodologies for using each particular nonmonotonic logic are lacking. Given a formalism F, what is the adequate representation of a commonsense default in F? It is not clear that there is a simple one to one translation from a comm-onsense default to a single default in F. For instance, in (Konolige, Myers 89) a translation of one 'natural' default to a collection of three AEL schemata is proposed.

There are plenty of open questions which remain. Is there (or should there be) *one* formalization, or at least one common framework, that captures all forms of non-monotonic reasoning? Do we need special purpose nonmonotonic logics for, say tem-poral reasoning, diagnosis etc.? What is a good compromise between expressiveness and tractability in implementations? The list of questions can easily be extended.

The unresolved problems and in particular the Yale shooting example made some researchers, especially Hanks and McDermott themselves, rather pessimistic about the role of logic for AI (Hanks, McDermott 85):

> *... a significant part of defeasible reasoning can't be expressed by default logics, and if in the cases where the logics fail we have no better way of describing the reasoning process than by a direct procedural characterization ..., then logic as an AI representation language begins to look less and less attractive.*

The philosophical remarks about the role of logic in their paper has given rise to a number of highly critical reactions. Much of this interesting discussion is contained in a special issue of Computational Intelligence (1988). We do not want to add or repeat arguments against the views they held, particularly since the authors themselves gave up their extreme position in a later paper (Hanks, McDermott 87, p.411):

> *... while the conclusion about the role of logic in theory development was admittedly overstated, our second conclusion, about the acceptable uses of non-monotonic logics, was not. One thing that our result, and even the responses, makes clear is that the relationship between these logics and human reasoning is*

not well understood. We can no longer engage in the logical 'wishful thinking' that led us to claim that circumscription solves the frame problem, or that 'consistent' is to be understood in the normal way it is construed in nonmonotonic logic.

We agree absolutely with these last remarks. And the best way to stop the 'wishful thinking' is to write programs which actually perform logical inferences from commonsense knowledge bases. We have to represent parts of the knowledge of realistic domains using the available formalisms, and we have to test whether systems based on these representations work as expected.

It could be objected that focussing on computational aspects is not appropriate in a situation where it is far from clear whether the right formalization has been found yet. Why not look for 'the' nonmonotonic logic first and delay the problems of computation until we have found it?

The answer is simple. There will probably not be much progress in the development of formalizations, nor an increase in the trust in the existing ones, without programs which handle more realistic examples than those which have been studied so far. Tweety and Clyde will not be of much further help in developing our logics. Three-default examples will not be able to avoid hidden surprises as unpleasant as the Yale shooting scenario in the future. It is time to build systems which solve real life problems. This is one of the lessons the Yale shooting problem and many other examples have taught us.

Much remains to be done. But there is no reason for pessimism. What are the ten, fifteen years of research in the area of nonmonotonic reasoning described in this book compared with the ambitions of our goal, to formalize human commonsense reasoning in all its different varieties? Even now we can look back over a lot of interesting ideas, high quality mathematical work, and, what is more, there are already some interesting programs available fit to use for building applications.

LOGICAL SYNTAX

First Order Logic

Let F be a recursive set of function symbols, arity$_F$ a function from F to the natural numbers.

Let P be a recursive set of predicate symbols, arity$_P$ a function from P to the natural numbers.

Let V be a recursive set of variable symbols. F, P and V are disjoint. We define *terms* and *formulae* as the smallest sets such that:

(T1) every $v \in V$ is a term,

(T2) if $f \in F$, arity$_F$(f) = n and t_1, ..., t_n are terms then $f(t_1,...,t_n)$ is a term,

(F1) if $p \in P$, arity$_P$(p) = n and t_1, ..., t_n are terms then $p(t_1,...,t_n)$ is an (atomic) formula,

(F2) if q and r are formulae and x is a variable then

$(\neg q)$, $(q \wedge r)$, $(q \vee r)$, $(q \supset r)$, $(q \equiv r)$, $(\forall x.q)$, $(\exists x.q)$ are formulae.

A formula p is called a *literal* if it is atomic or of the form $\neg q$ where q is atomic. A literal is *ground* if it does not contain variables. A *clause* is a finite set of literals interpreted as the disjunction of the literals.

A variable y is *free* in a formula p if one of the following conditions hold:

(1)   p is atomic and contains y, or

(2)   p is of the form $(\neg q)$ and y is free in q, or

(3)   p is of the form $(q \wedge r)$, $(q \vee r)$, $(q \supset r)$ or $(q \equiv r)$ and y is free in q or in r, or

(4)   p is of the form $(\forall x.q)$ or $(\exists x.q)$, y is free in q and $y \neq x$.

A formula is called a *sentence* if it contains no free variable.

A *schema* is a representation of the set of formulae obtained by replacing parameters in the schema by terms or formulae, respectively.

When no ambiguity arises brackets are omitted from formulae using the standard binding rules where the strength of binding decreases in the order $\neg, \wedge, \vee, \supset, \equiv, \forall, \exists$, that is $\forall x.P(x) \wedge Q(x) \vee R(x) \supset S(x)$ reads as $(\forall x.([(P(x) \wedge Q(x)) \vee R(x)] \supset S(x)))$.

NML
additional generation rule for formulae:

(F3) if q is a formula then Mq is a formula.

AEL
additional generation rule for formulae:

(F3) if q is a sentence then Lq is a formula.

DL
Default theories are pairs (D,W) where W is a set of first order formulae and D a set
of defaults of the form

$$\frac{A(x): B_1(x), \ldots, B_n(x)}{C(x)}$$

where $A(x)$, $B1(x)$, ..., $Bn(x)$, and $C(x)$ are classical formulae whose free variables
are contained in $x = x_1, \ldots, x_m$.

Alternative notation for defaults: $A(x): B_1(x), \ldots, B_n(x) / C(x)$.

Circumscription
Finite sets of first order formulae plus an additional first order schema or a second
order formula.

Preferred Subtheories
Default Theories are possibly inconsistent sets of first order formulae with an additional structure used to handle inconsistencies.

Examples:

Poole's system	two sets of formulae, premises and hypotheses.
Reliability levels	premises P split into different sets P1,...,Pn with different reliability.

Delgrande's Approach
The language of the logic N for reasoning about defaults has the additional generation
rule for formulae:

(F3) if q and r are formulae not containing => then (q => r) is a formula.

A default theory is a pair (D,C) where D is a set of formulae of N and C is a consistent set of first order formulae.

Nonmonotonic Logics at a Glance

	AEL	DL	Circumscription	Conditionals (Delgrande)	Preferred Subtheories
syntactical basis	modal operator fixed points	non-standard inference rules fixed points	additional (2nd order) axiom	conditional logic for defaults	handling of inconsistencies
semantics	1) autoepist. models 2) possible worlds	relation on sets of models	relation on models	possible worlds	models of maximal consistent subsets
attitude towards conflicting defaults	credulous	credulous	skeptical	skeptical	credulous
relation to other approaches	"equivalent" to DL	"equivalent" to AEL	variable circumscript. expressible in extension of AEL (with quantifying in)	differs from other approaches (see next line)	without constraints: Poole's system equiv. to subset of DL reliability levels equiv. to subset of PDL
prefers most specific information	no	no	no	yes	no
problems with contraposition	no (if right defaults are used)	no	can (partly) be handled by fixed predicates	no	are handled by constraints
expressiveness	very general	very general	very general, but no minimization of equality	possible to reason about defaults adequately	adequate for default reasoning purposes
priorities between defaults	1) can be coded into defaults 2) are possible, but also necessary in HAEL	1) can be coded into defaults 2) are possible in PDL	prioritized circumscription	built in priority of most specific default	yes in generalized version
additional remarks	formalizes ideal introspective agent, general enough to capture many non-monotonic systems, e.g. TMS, inheritance	general enough to capture many non-monotonic systems, some unintuitive results avoided in CDL	reduction of nonmonotonicity to classical higher order reasoning makes it possible to apply many classical results	intuitive advantages, probably difficult to implement	no non-classical components in language, problem of handling inconsistencies solved

REFERENCES

(Appelt, Konolige 89) Appelt, Douglas E., Konolige, Kurt: A Non-Monotonic Logic for Reasoning about Speech Acts and Belief Revision, *Proc. 2nd Int. Workshop on Nonmonotonic Reasoning*, Springer, LNCS 346, 1989

(Asher 84) Asher, Nicholas: Linguistic Understanding and Non-Monotonic Reasoning, *Proc. 1. Int. Workshop on Nonmonotonic Reasoning*, New Paltz, 1984

(Asher, Morreau 90) Asher, Nicholas, Morreau, Michael: A Modal Semantics for Default Reasoning and Generics, in: Brewka, Gerhard, Freitag, Hartmut (eds.): *Proceedings Workshop on Nonmonotonic Reasoning, Sankt Augustin, Dec. 1989*, Arbeitspapiere der GMD Nr. 401, 1990

(Bacchus 89) Bacchus, Fahiem: A Modest, but Semantically Well Founded, Inheritance Reasoner, *Proc. IJCAI 89*, 1989

(Baker, Ginsberg 89a) Baker, Andrew B., Ginsberg, Matthew L.: A Theorem Prover for Prioritized Circumscription, *Proc. IJCAI 89*, 1989

(Baker, Ginsberg 89b) Baker, Andrew B., Ginsberg, Matthew L.: Temporal Projection and Explanation, *Proc. IJCAI 89*, 1989

(Benthem, Doets 83) Benthem, Johan van, Doets, Kees: Higher-Order Logic, in: Gabbay, D., Guenthner, F.: *Handbook of Philosophical Logic*, Vol. I, Reidel Publ., Dordrecht, 1983

(Besnard 89) Besnard, Philippe: *An Introduction to Default Logic*, Springer, Symbolic Computation Series, 1989

(Besnard et al. 89) Besnard, Philippe, Moinard, Yves, Mercer, Robert E.: The Importance of Open and Recursive Circumscription, *Artificial Intelligence* 39, 1989

(Bibel 84) Bibel, Wolfgang: Knowledge Representation from a Deductive Point of View, *Proc. IFAC Symposium Artificial Intelligence*, Pergamon Press, Oxford 1984

(Bibel 85) Bibel, Wolfgang: Methods of Automated Reasoning, in: Bibel, Wolfgang, Jorrand, Ph. (eds): *Fundamentals of Artificial Intelligence*, Springer, Lecture Notes in Computer Science 232, 1985

(Bibel 86) Bibel, Wolfgang: A Deductive Solution for Plan Generation, *New Generation Computing* 4, 1986

(Bossu, Siegel 85) Bossu, G., Siegel, P.: Saturation, Nonmonotonic Reasoning and the Closed World Assumption, *Artificial Intelligence* 25 (1), 1985

(Boutilier 89) Boutilier, Craig: A Semantical Approach to Stable Inheritance Reasoning, *Proc. IJCAI 89*, 1989

(Brachman 83) Brachman, R.J.: KRYPTON: Integrating Terminology and Assertion, *Proc. AAAI 83*, 1983

(Brewka 86) Brewka, Gerhard: Tweety - Still Flying: Some Remarks on Abnormal Birds, Applicable Rules and a Default Prover, *Proc. AAAI-86*, 1986

(Brewka 87) Brewka, Gerhard: The Logic of Inheritance in Frame Systems, *Proc. IJCAI 87*, 1987

(Brewka 89) Brewka, Gerhard: *Nonmonotonic Reasoning - From Theoretical Foundation Towards Efficient Computation*, Ph. D. thesis, University of Hamburg, 1989

(Brewka 90a) Brewka, Gerhard: Cumulative Default Logic - In Defense of Nonmonotonic Inference Rules, submitted for publication

(Brewka 90b) Brewka, Gerhard: Belief Revision in a Framework for Default Reasoning, *Proc. Workshop on the Logic of Theory Change*, Konstanz, Oct. 89, Springer, 1990

(Brewka, Wittur 84) Brewka, Gerhard, Wittur, Karl: *Nichtmonotone Logiken*, Universität Bonn, Informatik Berichte 40, 1984

(Brown et al. 87) Brown, A. L. Jr., Gaucas, D.E., Benanav, D.: An Algebraic Foundation for Truth Maintenance, *Proc. IJCAI 87*, 1987

(Brown, Shoham 88) Brown, A. L. Jr., Shoham, Y.: New Results on Semantical Nonmonotonic Reasoning, *Proc. 2nd Int. Workshop on Nonmonotonic Reasoning*, Springer, LNCS 346, 1988

(Chang, Lee 73) Chang, C., Lee, R.: *Symbolic Logic and Mechanical Theorem Proving*, Academic Press, New York, San Francisco, London, 1973

(Charniak et al. 80) Charniak, E., Riesbeck, C., McDermott, D.: *Artificial Intelligence Programming*, Lawrence Earlbaum Ass., New Jersey, 1980

(de Kleer 86) de Kleer, Johan: An Assumption Based Truth Maintenance System, *Artificial Intelligence* 28, 1986

(de Kleer et al. 77) de Kleer, Johan, Doyle, J., Steele, G.L., Sussman, G.J.: *Explicit Control of Reasoning*, MIT AI Lab, Memo 427, 1977

(de Kleer, Konolige 89) de Kleer, Johan, Konolige, Kurt: Eliminating the Fixed Predicates from a Circumscription, *Artificial Intelligence* 39, 1989

(Delgrande 87) Delgrande, James P.: A First-Order Logic for Prototypical Properties, *Artificial Intelligence* 33, 1987

(Delgrande 88) Delgrande, James P.: An Approach to Default Reasoning Based on a First-Order Conditional Logic: Revised Report, *Artificial Intelligence* 36, 1988

(Di Primio, Brewka 85) Di Primio, F., Brewka, G.: Babylon - Kernel System of an Integrated Environment for Expert System Development and Operation, *Proc. Int. Workshop Expert Systems and their Applications*, Avignon, 1985

(Doyle 79) Doyle, J.: A Truth Maintenance System, *Artificial Intelligence* 12, 1979

(Doyle 83a) Doyle, J.: *Some Theories of Reasoned Assumptions: An Essay in Rational Psychology*, Carnegie Mellon University, CMU CS-83-125, 1983

(Doyle 83b) Doyle, J.: The Ins and Outs of Reason Maintenance, *Proc. IJCAI 83*, 1983

(Dressler 88a) Dressler, Oskar: Extending the ATMS, *Proc. ECAI 88*, 1988

(Dressler 89) Dressler, Oskar: An Extended Basic ATMS, *Proc. 2nd Int. Workshop on Nonmonotonic Reasoning*, Springer, LNCS 346, 1989

(Doyle 79) Doyle, Jon: A Truth Maintenance System, *Artificial Intelligence* 12, 1979

(Etherington 86) Etherington, David W.: *Reasoning With Incomplete Information*, University of British Columbia, Vancouver, Dep. of Computer Science, Technical Report 86-14, 1986

(Etherington 87a) Etherington, David W.: A Semantics for Default Logic, *Proc. IJCAI 87*, 1987

(Etherington 87b) Etherington, David W.: Relating Default Logic and Circumscription, *Proc. IJCAI 87*, 1987

(Etherington 87c) Etherington, David W.: Formalizing Nonmonotonic Reasoning Systems, *Artificial Intelligence* 31, 1987

(Etherington et al. 84) Etherington, David W., Mercer, Robert, Reiter, Raymond: On the Adequacy of Predicate Circumscription for Closed-World-Reasoning, *Proc. 1. Int. Workshop on Nonmonotonic Reasoning*, New Paltz, 1984

(Etherington, Reiter 83) Etherington, D.W., Reiter, R.: On Inheritance Hierarchies with Exceptions, *Proc. AAAI 83*, 1983

(Fahlman 79) Fahlman, S.E.: *NETL: A System for Representing and Using Real-World Knowledge*, MIT Press, Cambridge, 1979

(Freitag 87) Freitag, H.: *An Admissible Extension Theory-Based Non-Monotonic Reasoning System*, Siemens, Report INF2 ARM-2-87, München, 1987

(Gabbay 85) Gabbay, Dov: Theoretical Foundations for Non-Monotonic Reasoning in Expert Systems, in: K.R. Apt (ed.): *Logics and Models of Concurrent Systems*, Springer, 1985

(Gärdenfors 88) Gärdenfors, Peter: *Knowledge in Flux*, MIT Press, Cambridge, MA, 1988

(Gärdenfors, Makinson 88) Gärdenfors, Peter; Makinson, David: Revisions of Knowledge Systems Using Epistemic Entrenchment. In: Vardi, M. (ed): *Proceedings of the Second Conference on Theoretical Aspects of Reasoning about Knowledge*, Morgan Kaufmann, Los Altos, 1988

(Geffner, Pearl 88) Geffner, Hector; Pearl, Judea: *A Framework for Reasoning With Defaults*, UCLA Cognitive Systems Lab., TR 870058, 1988

(Gelfond, Lifschitz 89) Gelfond, Michael; Lifschitz, Vladimir: Compiling Circumscriptive Theories into Logic Programs, *Proc. 2nd Int. Workshop on Nonmonotonic Reasoning*, Springer, LNCS 346, 1989

(Genesereth, Nilsson 87) Genesereth, Michael R., Nilsson, Nils J.: *Logical Foundations of Artificial Intelligence*, Morgan Kaufmann, Los Altos, 1987

(Ginsberg 86) Ginsberg, Matthew L.: Counterfactuals, *Artificial Intelligence* 30, 1986

(Ginsberg 87a) Ginsberg, Matthew L.: *Multi-valued Logics I: Formal Description*, Technical Report 87-4, Logic Group, Stanford University, 1987

(Ginsberg 87b) Ginsberg, Matthew L.: *Multi-valued Logics II: Inference*, Technical Report 87-5, Logic Group, Stanford University, 1987

(Ginsberg 87c) Ginsberg, Matthew L.: *Multi-valued Logics III: Applications*, Technical Report 87-6, Logic Group, Stanford University, 1987

(Ginsberg 89) Ginsberg, Matthew L.: A Circumscriptive Theorem Prover, *Artificial Intelligence* 39 , 1989

(Goodwin 87) Goodwin, James W.: *A Theory and System for Non-Monotonic Reasoning*, Linköping University, Computer and Information Science Dep., Dissertation No. 165, 1987

(Gordon 87) Gordon, Thomas F.: Oblog-2: A Hybrid Knowledge Representation System for Defeasible Reasoning, *Proc. 1st. Intl.Conference on Artificial Intelligence and Law*, Boston, ACM Press, 1987

(Halpern, Moses 84) Halpern, J., Moses, Y.: *Towards a Theory of Knowledge and Ignorance: Preliminary Report*, IBM Research Laboratory, San Jose, RJ 4448 48136, 1984

(Hanks, McDermott 85) Hanks, Steven; McDermott, Drew: *Temporal Reasoning and Default Logics*, Computer Science Res. Rep. 430, Yale University, New Haven, 1985

(Hanks, McDermott 87) Hanks, Steven; McDermott, Drew: Nonmonotonic Logic and Temporal Projection, *Artificial Intelligence* 33, 1987

(Haugh 87) Haugh, Brian A.: Simple Causal Minimizations for Temporal Persistence and Projection, *Proc. AAAI 87*, 1987

(Haugh 88) Haugh, Brian A.: Tractable Theories of Multiple Defeasible Inheritance In Ordinary Nonmonotonic Logics, *Proc. AAAI 88*, 1988

(Hayes 77) Hayes, Patrick: In Defense of Logic, *Proc. IJCAI 77*, 1977

(Hayes 79) Hayes, Patrick: The Logic of Frames, in: Metzing, D.: *Frame Conceptions and Text Understanding*, de Gruyter and Co., Berlin, 1979

(Hayes, Hendrix 81) Hayes, Patrick; Hendrix, G.G.: A Logical View of Types, *SIGART Newsletter* No. 74, 1981

(Hayes, McCarthy 69) Hayes, Patrick; McCarthy, John: Some Philosophical Problems from the Standpoint of AI, *Machine Intelligence* 4, 1969

(Hewitt 72) Hewitt, C.E.: *Description and Theoretical Analysis (Using Schemata) of PLANNER: a Language for Proving Theorems and Manipulating Models in a Robot,* MIT AI Lab., TR-258, 1972

(Horty, Thomason 88) Horty, J.F., Thomason, R.H.: Mixing Strict and Defeasible Inheritance, *Proc. AAAI 88,* 1988

(Horty et al 87) Horty, J.F., Thomason, R.H., Touretzky, D.S.: A Skeptikal Theory of Inheritance in Nonmonotonic Semantic Nets, *Proc. AAAI 87,* 1987

(Hughes, Cresswell 68) Hughes, G.E., Cresswell, M.J.: *An Introduction to Modal Logic,* Methuen, London, 1968

(Imielinski 85) Imielinski, T.: Results on Translating Defaults to Circumscription, *Proc. IJCAI 85,* 1985

(Junker 88) Junker, U.: *Reasoning in Multiple Contexts,* GMD Arbeitpapiere Nr. 334, Sankt Augustin, Fed. Rep. of Germany, 1988

(Junker 89) Junker, Ulrich: A Correct Nonmonotonic ATMS, *Proc. IJCAI 89,* 1989

(Junker, Konolige 90) Junker, Ulrich, Konolige, Kurt: Computing the Extensions of Autoepistemic and Default Logic with a TMS, *Proc. AAAI 90,* 1990

(Kautz 85) Kautz, H.: The Logic of Persistence, *Proc. IJCAI 85,* 1985

(Konolige 88a) Konolige, Kurt: On the Relation Between Default and Autoepistemic Logic, *Arftificial Intelligence* 35 (3), 1988

(Konolige 88b) Konolige, Kurt: Hierarchic Autoepistemic Theories for Nonmonotonic Reasoning, *Proc. AAAI 88,* 1988

(Konolige 89) Konolige, Kurt: On the Relation Between Autoepistemic Logic and Circumscription - Preliminary Report, *Proc. IJCAI 89,* 1989

(Konolige, Myers 89) Konolige, Kurt; Myers, Karen: Representing Defaults with Epistemic Concepts, *Computational Intelligence,* Vol. 5, Nr. 1, 1989

(Krishnaprasad, Kifer 89) Krishnaprasad, T., Kifer, Michael: An Evidence-Based Framework for a Theory of Inheritance, *Proc. IJCAI-89,* 1989

(Lewis 73) Lewis, D.: *Counterfactuals,* Harvard University Press, Cambridge, 1973

(Lifschitz 84) Lifschitz, Vladimir: Some Results on Circumscription, *Proc. 1. Int. Workshop on Nonmonotonic Reasoning,* 1984

(Lifschitz 85a) Lifschitz, Vladimir: Closed-World Databases and Circumscription, *Artificial Intelligence* 27, 1985

(Lifschitz 85b) Lifschitz, Vladimir: Computing Circumscription, *Proc. IJCAI 85,* 1985

(Lifschitz 86a) Lifschitz, Vladimir: On the Satisfiability of Circumscription, *Artificial Intelligence* 28, 1986

(Lifschitz 86b) Lifschitz, Vladimir: Pointwise Circumscription, *Proc. AAAI 86,* 1986

(Lifschitz 87) Lifschitz, Vladimir: Formal Theories of Action, in: F.Brown (ed), *The Frame Problem in Artificial Intelligence,* Proceedings of the AAAI-Workshop, Morgan Kaufman, 1987

(Lifschitz 89a) Lifschitz, Vladimir: Circumscriptive Theories: A Logic Based Framework for Knowledge Representation, In: Thomason, R. H. (ed.): *Philosophical Logic and Artificial Intelligence*, Kluwer Academic Publishers, Dordrecht, 1989

(Lifschitz 89b) Lifschitz, Vladimir: Between Circumscription and Autoepistemic Logic, *Proc. 1. Intl. Conference on Principles of Knowledge Representation and Reasoning*, Toronto, 1989

(Lukaszewicz 85) Lukaszewicz, W.: Two Results on Default Logic, *Proc. IJCAI 85*, 1985.

(Lukaszewicz 88) Lukaszewicz, W.: Considerations on Default Logic, *Computational Intelligence* 4, 1-16, 1988

(Makinson 89) Makinson, David: General Theory of Cumulative Inference, *Proc. 2nd Int. Workshop on Nonmonotonic Reasoning*, Springer, LNCS 346, 1989

(Makinson 90) Makinson, David: General Patterns in Nonmonotonic Reasoning, to appear

(Makinson, Schlechta 90) Makinson, David; Schlechta, Karl: On Some Difficulties in the Theory of Defeasible Inheritance Nets, to appear

(Marek, Truszczynski 89) Marek, Wiktor; Truszczynski, Miroslaw: Relating Autoepistemic and Default Logics, *Proc. 1. Intl. Conference on Principles of Knowledge Representation and Reasoning*, Toronto, 1989

(Martins, Shapiro 88) Martins, Joao; Shapiro, Stuart C.: A Model for Belief Revision, *Artificial Intelligence* 35, 1988

(McCarthy 80) McCarthy, John: Circumscription - A Form of Nonmonotonic Reasoning, *Artificial Intelligence* 13, 1980

(McCarthy 84) McCarthy, John: Applications of Circumscription to Formalizing Common Sense Knowledge, *Proc. 1. Int. Workshop on Nonmonotonic Reasoning*, New Paltz, 1984 (also in *Artificial Intelligence* 28, 1986)

(McDermott 82) McDermott, Drew: Nonmonotonic Logic II: Nonmonotonic Modal Theories, *JACM* 29(1), 1982

(McDermott 86) McDermott, Drew: *A Critique of Pure Reason*, Yale University, Computer Science Dep., Research Report 480, 1986

(McDermott 87) McDermott, Drew: AI, Logic and the Frame Problem, in: F.Brown (ed), *The Frame Problem in Artificial Intelligence*, Proceedings of the AAAI-Workshop, Morgan Kaufman, 1987

(McDermott, Doyle 80) McDermott, Drew, Doyle, Jon: Nonmonotonic Logic I, *Artificial Intelligence* 13, 1980

(Moore 82) Moore, Robert, C.: The Role of Logic in Knowledge Representation and Commonsense Reasoning, *Proc. AAAI 82*, 1982

(Moore 84) Moore, Robert C.: Possible-World Semantics for Autoepistemic Logic, *Proc. 1. Int. Workshop on Nonmonotonic Reasoning*, New Paltz, 1984

(Moore 85) Moore, Robert C.: Semantical Considerations on Nonmonotonic Logic, *Artificial Intelligence* 25, 1985 (short Version in *Proc. IJCAI 83*)

(Moore 88) Moore, Robert C.: Autoepistemic Logic, in: Smets, P., Mamdani, E. H., Dubois, D., Prade, H.(eds): *Non-Standard Logics for Automated Reasoning*, Academic Press, 1988

(Morris 88) Morris, P.: Stable Closures, Defeasible Logic and Contradiction Tolerant Reasoning, *Proc. AAAI 88*, 1988

(Mott 87) Mott, Peter L.: A Theorem on the Consistency of Circumscription, *Artificial Intelligence* 31, 1987

(Minker, Perlis 84) Minker, Jack; Perlis, Donald: Protected Circumscription, *Proc. 1. Int. Workshop on Nonmonotonic Reasoning*, New Paltz, 1984

(Nute 84) Nute, D.: Conditional Logic, in: Gabbay, D., Guenthner, F. (Hrsg.): *Handbook of Philosophical Logic*, Vol. II, Reidel Publ., Dordrecht, 1984

(Nutter 87) Nutter, T.: Reasoning, Default, in: Shapiro, S.C. (ed): *Encyclopedia of Artificial Intelligence*, Wiley & Sons, 1987

(Padgham 89) Padgham, Lin: Negative Reasoning Using Inheritance, *Proc. IJCAI 89*, 1989

(Pearl 89) Pearl, Judea: Probabilistic Semantics for Nonmonotonic Reasoning: A Survey, *Proc. 1. Intl. Conference on Principles of Knowledge Representation and Reasoning*, Toronto, 1989

(Perlis 87) Perlis, Donald: Circumscribing with Sets, *Artificial Intelligence* 31, 1987

(Perlis 88) Perlis, Donald: Autocircumscription, *Artificial Intelligence* 36, 1988

(Perlis, Minker 86) Perlis, Donald, Minker, Jack: Completeness Results for Circumscription, *Artificial Intelligence* 28, 1986

(Perrault 87) Perrault, Raymond C.: *An Application of Default Logic to Speech Act Theory*, Research Report CSLI 87-90, 1987

(Petrie 87) Petrie, C.J.: Revised Dependency-Directed Backtracking for Default Reasoning, *Proc. AAAI 87*, 1987

(Petrie et al. 86) Petrie, C.J., Russinoff, D.M.,Steiner, D.D.: *PROTEUS: A Default Reasoning Perspective*, MCC TR AI-352-86, Austin, 1986

(Poole 88) Poole, David: A Logical Framework for Default Reasoning, *Artificial Intelligence* 36, 1988

(Poole 89a) Poole, David: What the Lottery Paradox Tells Us About Default Reasoning, *Proc. First Intl. Conf. Priciples of Knowledge Representation and Reasoning*, Toronto 89, 1989

(Poole 89b) Poole, David: Normality and Faults in Logic-Based Diagnosis, *Proc. IJCAI 89*, 1989

(Poole et al. 86) Poole, D., Goebel, R., Aleliunas, R.: *A Logical Reasoning System for Defaults and Diagnosis*, University of Waterloo, Dep. of Computer Science, Research Rep. CS-86-06, 1986

(Przymusinska, Gelfond 88) Przymusinska, Halina; Gelfond, Michael: *Inheritance Hierarchies and Autoepistemic Logic*, Technical Report, Computer Science Department, University of Texas at El Paso, 1988

(Przymusinski 86) Przymusinski, T.: Query Answering in Circumscriptive and Closed-World Theories, *Proc. AAAI 86*, 1986

(Przymusinski 89a) Przymusinski, T.: An Algorithm to Compute Circumscription. *Artificial Intelligence 38*, 1989

(Przymusinski 89b) Przymusinski, T.: Three-Valued Formalizations of Non-Monotonic Reasoning and Logic Programming, *Proc. 1. Intl. Conference on Principles of Knowledge Representation and Reasoning*, Toronto, 1989

(Rathmann, Winslett 89) Rathmann, Peter K.; Winslett, Marianne: Circumscribing Equality, *Proc. IJCAI 89*, 1989

(Reinfrank 85), Reinfrank, Michael: *An Introduction to Non-Monotonic Reasoning*, Universität Kaiserslautern, Memo SEKI-85-02, 1985

(Reinfrank 87) Reinfrank, Michael: Reason Maintenance Systems, in: H. Stoyan (ed.): *Proc. Workshop on Truth Maintenance Systems*, Berlin 86, Springer, 1987

(Reinfrank et al. 89) Reinfrank, Michael; de Kleer, Johan, Ginsberg, Matthew L., Sandewall, Erik (eds.): *Proceedings 2nd Int. Workshop on Nonmonotonic Reasoning*, Springer, LNCS 346, 1989

(Reiter 80) Reiter, Raymond: A Logic for Default Reasoning, *Artificial Intelligence 13*, 1980

(Reiter 87a) Reiter, Raymond: A Theory of Diagnosis from First Principles, *Artificial Intelligence 32*, 1987

(Reiter 87b) Reiter, Raymond: Nonmonotonic Reasoning, *Ann. Rev. Comput. Sci.*, 2, 1987

(Reiter, Criscuolo 81) Reiter, Raymond; Criscuolo G.: On Interacting Defaults, *Proc. IJCAI 81*, 1981

(Reiter, de Kleer 87) Reiter, Raymond; de Kleer, Johan: Foundations of Assumption-Based Truth Maintenance Systems: Preliminary Report, *Proc. AAAI 87*, 1987

(Rescher 64) Rescher, Nicholas: *Hypothetical Reasoning*, North-Holland Publ., Amsterdam. 1964

(Roberts, Goldstein 77) Roberts, R.B., Goldstein, I.P.: *The FRL Manual*, MIT AI Memo No. 409, Cambridge, 1977

(Sandewall 86) Sandewall, E.: Nonmonotonic Inference Rules for Multiple Inheritance with Exceptions, *Proc. IEEE*, Vol. 74, No. 10, 1986

(Selman, Levesque 89) Selman, Bart; Levesque, Hector J.: The Tractability of Path-Based Inheritance, *Proc. IJCAI 89*, 1989

(Shoham 86) Shoham, Yoav: *Reasoning About Change: Time and Causation from the Standpoint of Artificial Intelligence*, Ph.D. Thesis, Yale University, 1986

(Stein 89) Stein, Lynn Andrea: Skeptical Inheritance: Computing the Intersection of Credulous Extensions, *Proc. IJCAI 89*, 1989

(Thomason, Horty 88) Thomason, R.H., Horty, J.F.: Logics for Inheritance Theory, *Proc. 2nd Int. Workshop on Nonmonotonic Reasoning*, Springer, LNCS 346, 1988

(Thomason et al. 86) Thomason, R.H., Horty, J.F., Touretzky, D.S.: *A Calculus for Inheritance in Monotonic Semantic Nets*, Carnegie Mellon University, Research Note CMU-CS-86-138, 1986

(Touretzky 84) Touretzky, D.S.: Implicit Ordering of Defaults in Inheritance Systems, *Proc. AAAI 84*, 1984

(Touretzky 86) Touretzky, D.S.: *The Mathematics of Inheritance*, Pitman Research Notes in Artificial Intelligence, London, 1986

(Touretzky et al. 87) Touretzky, D.S., Horty, J.F., Thomason, R.H.: A Clash of Intuitions: The Current State of Nonmonotonic Multiple Inheritance Systems, *Proc. IJCAI 87*, 1987

(Touretzky, Thomason 88) Touretzky, D.S., Thomason, R.H.: Nonmonotonic Inheritance and Generic Reflexives, *Proc. AAAI 88*, 1988

(Veltmann 75) Veltman, Frank: *Logics for Conditionals*, dissertation, Univ. of Amsterdam, 1975

INDEX

Printed in the United States
By Bookmasters